Terrorism in Western Europe

Terrorism in Western Europe

Explaining the Trends since 1950

Jan Oskar Engene

Associate Professor, Department of Comparative Politics, University of Bergen, Norway

Edward Elgar

Cheltenham, UK • Northampton, MA, USA

Published by
Edward Elgar Publishing Limited
Glensanda House
Montpellier Parade
Cheltenham
Glos GL50 1UA
UK

Edward Elgar Publishing, Inc.
136 West Street
Suite 202
Northampton
Massachusetts 01060
USA

A catalogue record for this book
is available from the British Library

Library of Congress Cataloguing in Publication Data

Engene, Jan Oskar, 1966–
    Terrorism in Western Europe: explaining the trends since 1950/
Jan Oskar Engene.
        p. cm.
    Based on the author's thesis (doctoral)—University of Bergen, Norway.
    Includes bibliographical references and index.
    1. Terrorism—Europe, Western. 2. Offenses against public safety—Europe,
Western. 3. Legitimacy of governments—Europe, Western. I. Title.
HV6433.E85E543   2004
303.6'25'09409045—dc22

                                                                    2004050638

ISBN 1 84376 582 9

Printed and bound in Great Britain by MPG Books Ltd, Bodmin, Cornwall

Contents

Acknowledgements

The present work has developed through a number of stages from dissertation to book. It is based on the main parts of the author's doctoral dissertation, submitted to the University of Bergen, for which the Research Council of Norway generously provided the doctoral scholarship. In the long and cumbersome process that produced this book a number of people have offered valuable comments and helpful suggestions. Thus, I would like to thank Frank Aarebrot, Daniel Heradstveit and Ole-Johan Eikeland, who were of particular help in the earliest stages, and also Ulf Lindström and Stein Kuhnle who added more valuable advice later on. In the very final stage, the publisher's reviewer, Professor Rosemary H.T. O'Kane, offered constructive criticism and helpful suggestions on how to turn the manuscript into a book. Naturally, all errors and shortcomings remain solely the responsibility of the author.

Introduction

Almost every day we are presented with news reports of bomb attacks and other atrocities committed by terrorists. Looking closer at news reports on terrorism, one may discern certain patterns: it seems some regions and countries are more seriously affected by acts of terrorism than others. Though Western Europe today seems relatively peaceful, looking at it historically the fact is that countries in the region have been exposed to relatively high levels of terrorism for decades. Moreover the threat has not only been from international terrorists moving into Europe from the Middle East and elsewhere to commit their acts of terrorism in West European countries. The countries in the region have themselves experienced conflicts that have resulted in terrorist campaigns, producing significant levels of internal terrorism with relatively large losses of life. This book undertakes to map the trends in internal terrorism in Western Europe since 1995 and to explain these trends. Why is it that some countries have been harder hit by internal terrorism than other countries in the same region?

Western Europe may be seen as a bastion of freedom and democracy in the world. It is something of a puzzle that terrorism appears in countries enjoying such privileges. The countries in Western Europe are modern, wealthy and provide social well-being for their citizens. Moreover in these countries political rights are guaranteed and respected. Citizens enjoy the right to organize freely and express their opinions. Compared with other regions of the world, West European countries are models of responsible government. Yet in the period following the Second World War, Western Europe has been hit by significant levels of terrorist violence, not only by acts of terrorism imported into the region by external actors, but also by groups and actors originating in the West European countries themselves. This might make one wonder why anyone would want to create difficulties for the model democracies through the use of violence. Is there a reason terrorism appears in the otherwise stable and advanced democracies of Western Europe?

When following the reporting on terrorism over the decades, one is immediately struck by an impression that the acts of terrorist violence occur more frequently in some countries, and that other countries are more peaceful. For instance we only sporadically hear of acts of terrorism in Norway or this country's Nordic neighbour countries. True, occasional acts of terrorism reach the news, but at first sight these acts appear to be rather rare compared with the steady stream of reports of bombs and armed attacks in countries such as Spain or the United Kingdom. Thus we are left with an impression that terrorism strikes unevenly. Some countries appear to be hard hit by the problem while others seem to be able to avoid it almost altogether. Is there a reason for such differences?

The overarching research question of the present investigation is to find the reasons why some West European countries have been more severely hit by terrorism than other countries in the region. In other words, the aim is to describe and explain differences between the West European countries in terms of the terrorism these countries have been faced with since the Second World War. Do some of the West European countries have characteristics that may help explain why they are subject to more terrorism than their neighbouring countries?

To answer these questions, the investigation into the patterns of terrorism in Western Europe since 1995 will proceed first along theoretical lines, and then move on into the empirical. When discussing terrorism, the question of definitions quickly appears: what is terrorism? who is a terrorist? Some see the term as simply an instrument of propaganda and manipulation, making a disagreement into a conceptual dispute concerning the normative implications of definitions. The discussion in this book is more concerned with the definitional debates, on the description of the phenomenon in question, in other words a discussion about the central characteristics of terrorism. In Chapter 1 a definition of terrorism that views it as a form of political communication is introduced and placed into a theoretical context that may serve as a starting point for investigating patterns of terrorism and variations between countries.

In Chapter 2 we extend the definition discussed in Chapter 1 into a theoretical perspective that associates terrorism with the state through legitimacy. The aim is to develop a theoretical perspective that can explain the variations in terrorism in modern European states, or more specifically Western Europe after the Second World War. Diverging opinions on the sources or roots of terrorism, such as socio-economic versus structural and political factors, are dealt with in Chapter 2. In this chapter it is argued that problems of legitimacy originating in the political history and characteristics of the political system are important to the understanding of the development of organized terrorist campaigns.

Any investigation into trends and patterns of terrorism will need some sort of empirical evidence, some statistical basis, for exploring the variations over time and between countries. Chapter 3 discusses the source of data on terrorism that was used for the present investigation, the data set called Terrorism in Western Europe: Event Data (TWEED). This data set, based on recording acts of terrorism, offers data for West European countries throughout the period from 1950 to 1995, and Chapter 3 examines its strengths and weaknesses.

The remaining chapters are devoted to describing and explaining patterns of terrorism in Western Europe in the post-Second World War period. This is done stepwise from the general to the specific in three successive chapters. Chapter 4 gives an overview of political terrorism in Western Europe as a region, in order to present some important background information for the subsequent two chapters. It first focuses on the occurrence of terrorism over time. Here attention is also directed to terrorism originating from outside the West European region, so that it might be determined which kind of terrorism dominates in Western Europe: that of internal (domestic) or of international terrorism. Following this we take a closer look at other important patterns of domestic terrorism. This includes the intensity of terrorist violence and the ideological tendencies of the terrorists, as well as characteristics of the organized challenge presented by terrorism in Western Europe.

In Chapter 5 patterns of terrorism in West European countries are analysed on the macro level. Drawing on the theoretical discussion in Chapter 2, the analysis investigates possible systematic relationships between variations in terrorism in the West European countries and the factors that were theoretically expected to influence the occurrence of terrorism. The chapter first analyses and discusses the importance of democracy and freedom in stimulating terrorism. Then attention is given to socio-economic explanatory factors. Finally in Chapter 5, the relationship between terrorism and the problems of legitimacy discussed in Chapter 4 is analysed.

The third and last of the chapters describing and explaining patterns of terrorism in post-war Western Europe, Chapter 6, goes into detail and examines terrorism in each of the countries under scrutiny. The problems of legitimacy facing each country are identified and we will compare the levels of terrorism in the countries studied. The subsequent analysis charts how the problems of legitimacy facing a particular country may be related to the occurrence and extent of terrorism in that country. Particular emphasis is placed on organized terrorism, that is the groups that have been able to launch particularly significant challenges to the states they operate within.

1. Defining Terrorism: A Communications Perspective

Terrorism, Robert A. Friedlander wrote, is 'abominable means used by political fanatics for contemptible ends' (Quoted in Byrne 1987, p. xv). This frequently quoted definition of terrorism is a reminder of the emotional and normative perspective often laid on the term. As no study of terrorism can avoid discussing definitions, this chapter will start by discussing problems related to definitions, after which the definition on which the theoretical and empirical investigation developed in subsequent chapters will be presented.

WHAT IS TERRORISM?

Despite Wilkinson's observation that 'in recent years ... a surprisingly broad consensus has emerged in the academic usage of the term in liberal democratic societies' (Wilkinson 1987, p. xi), it is still not uncommon to open a study on terrorism with comments on definitions and conceptual difficulties. Indeed, the two articles following the foreword where the comment was made, both take a less encouraging position vis-à-vis agreement on definitions. Thackrah (1987, p. 24) starts by emphasizing the emotive and moral dimension of the concept, while Crelinsten (1987a, p. 5) includes conceptual fuzziness in his list of things that are wrong in terrorism research. In fact, the controversies over the meaning of the term have been so great that there have also emerged works devoted to the study of the discipline itself, with concept formation and the formation of meaning as a central focus of their study (Hoffman 1984; Schmid 1984, pp. 5–158; Schmid et al. 1988, pp. 1–38; Crenshaw 1992; Silke 1996). Critics point to the ideological purposes the term 'terrorism' often serves (Chomsky and Herman 1979, p. 85ff; Herman and O'Sullivan 1989; Perdue 1989; Chomsky 1991, p. 13f; Herman and O'Sullivan 1991, p. 39ff; George 1991, p. 76ff). These controversies may explain why Wilkinson found the emerging consensus so surprising.

Conceptual difficulties, such as the ones mentioned here, together with the ensuing problem of collecting data, are seen as the fundamental reason for the lack of theoretical progress Schmid et al. (1988, p. xiv). Crenshaw (1992, pp. 1–3) makes comments to the same effect, pointing out the 'theoretically impoverished' character of the field. Schmid et al. (1988, p. 3) contend that: 'Without some solution to the definitional problem, without isolating terrorism from other forms of (political) violence, there can be no uniform data collection and no responsible theory building on terrorism.'

Let us look at a few definitions, to get an idea of the differences involved as well as some of the issues that have been debated. The definitions presented here show the span in definitions of one single term, but the list is only illustrative and could certainly have been made longer. An early example of a definition of the term is found in the 1949 edition of the *Encyclopaedia of the Social Sciences*, where Hardman (1949, p. 575) explained that:

> Terrorism is a term used to describe the method or the theory behind the method whereby an organized group or party seeks to achieve its avowed aims chiefly through the systematic use of violence. Terroristic acts are directed against persons who as individuals, agents or representatives of authority interfere with the consummation of the objectives of such a group.

This definition is very general, a trait it shares with many definitions of terrorism, but in the subsequent discussion Hardman is almost exclusively preoccupied with non-state actors, though the definition itself does not preclude state actors from being engaged in terrorism. This highlights one of the issues that have come to dominate the discussions over the term: should violent actions perpetrated by states be included or should it only cover opposition, that is non-state, acts? (Crenshaw 1992, p. 2).

Another much-quoted author, Martha Crenshaw Hutchinson (1978, p. 21), points out four crucial characteristics of terrorism:

> The essential components of a definition of revolutionary terrorism may be summarized as follows:
> 1. Terrorism is a systematic and purposeful method used by a revolutionary organization to seize political power from the incumbent government of a state.
> 2. Terrorism is manifested in a series of individual acts of extraordinary and intolerable violence.
> 3. Terrorism involves a consistent pattern of symbolic or representative selection of its physical victims or objects.
> 4. Terrorism is deliberately intended to create a psychological effect on specific groups of people (with the nature of the effect varying according to the identity of the group) in order to change political behavior and attitudes in a manner consonant with the achievement of revolutionary objectives.

In this definition, serving a study of study of the FLN in Algeria, that is what many would call a national liberation movement with a socialist ideology, the emphasis is on revolutionary terrorism. Thus according to the definition terrorism is identified as opposition terrorism with a specific ideological and political background. Crenshaw Hutchinson's definition also points out that terrorism involves 'extraordinary and intolerable violence'. This has also been much discussed in debates over definitions. How extraordinary are acts of terrorism and how arbitrary are they in the selection of human targets? Finally it is worth noting that the definition includes normative elements, partly because of the characterization of the means as extraordinary, but also because of the inclusion of the word 'intolerable' in the same point. Terrorism, according to this view, breaks the norms for civilized behaviour.

Ronald D. Crelinsten (1987a, pp. 6–7) offers a different perspective with a distinct emphasis. In his perspective:

> [T]errorism is conceived as a form of political communication. More specifically, it is the deliberate use of violence and threat of violence to evoke a state of fear (or terror) in a particular victim or audience. The terror evoked is the vehicle by which allegiance or compliance is maintained or weakened. Usually, the use and threat of violence are directed at one group of targets (victims), while the demands for compliance are directed towards a separate group of targets.

Crelinsten's definition does not specifically include or exclude any particular group or actor. Instead the definition offers a perspective in which violence is seen as serving communicative purposes. This definition is offered as the cornerstone of the perspective Crelinsten develops, where emphasis is put on the dynamic relationship between violence from the state and violence from non-state actors. It is in this perspective that terrorist violence is seen as being exercised for communicative purposes.

VIOLENCE AS COMMUNICATION: DEFINING TERRORISM

An extensive definition of terrorism, also emphasizing the communicative, has been presented by Schmid et al., and their definition will be used as a basis for this investigation. Schmid et al. (1988, p. 28) define terrorism in this way:

> Terrorism is an anxiety-inspiring method of repeated violent action, employed by (semi-) clandestine individual, group, or state actors, for idiosyncratic, criminal, or political reasons, whereby --in contrast to assassination-- the direct targets of violence are not the main targets. The immediate human victims of violence are generally chosen randomly (targets of opportunity) or selectively (representative

or symbolic targets) from a target population, and serve as message generators. Threat and violence-based communication processes between terrorist (organization), (imperiled) victims, and main targets are used to manipulate the main target (audience(s)), turning it into a target of terror, a target of demands, or a target of attention, depending on whether intimidation, coercion, or propaganda is primarily sought.

We immediately observe that the definition consists of two main parts. Firstly, it points to the effect of terrorist violence and defines the kinds of actors that can potentially be involved in violence of this kind. The definition also, in its first part, points to the motivation actors might have. Secondly, the definition focuses on characteristics of the victims of the violence and the different kinds of targets terrorists might have for the political demands or messages they want to convey. Thus terrorism is defined as a form of communication based on the use of violence.

If we look closer at the definition presented by Schmid et al., we see six important definitional elements. We will discuss these in detail, because they will delineate terrorism against other forms of violence and because the elements together form a definition that opens interesting perspectives.

Fear: the Key Element in Terrorism?

Fear is the conceptual core of terrorism as defined above. Terrorism is regarded as a fear-inducing method of repeated violent actions. This is an element that Schmid et al.'s definition shares with several others, and which expresses the etymological origins of the term. Terror comes from the Latin *terrere*, which means 'to frighten'. In definitions based on the conception of terrorism as fear-inducing violence, the principal characteristic of terrorism is, as Thornton points out, the subjective state of fear that is provoked. This means a state of anxiety in a group or an individual (Thornton 1964, p. 71). Based on this we can describe the behaviour used to induce this state of fear. In Thornton's terminology, this is objective terror, or terrorism. We are then able to distinguish between actors and acts, so that the following labels can be applied: the actor instigating violence is the terrorist, the act is the terrorist attack sometimes also labelled terrorism, while the effect is terror – the state of fear. Somewhat surprisingly though, Schmid et al. (1988, p. 5) found the definitional element of 'fear' present in just over half of the definitions surveyed. This indicates that the element might play a less important, or more problematic, role than appears at first sight. Two lines of criticism can be levelled against the emphasis put on fear.

Firstly, terror is difficult to measure. From a psychiatrist's point of view, it has been pointed out that 'terror is an extreme form of anxiety, often accompanied by aggression, denial, constricted affect, and followed by frightening imagery and intrusive, repetitive recollection' (F. Ochberg quoted in Schmid et al. 1988, p. 19). Non-state actors rarely have the capacity to create a massive state of fear in a population (or even a segment of the population) parallelling this description. What is typically called terrorist violence is usually too small-scale to be able to put the entire population in a serious state of fear. It might not even frighten a section of the public. This launches the question whether we are justified to speak of terrorism without terror (see the heading in Schmid et al. 1988, p. 19). That is to say, whether we are dealing with terrorism in cases when the instigation of a grave state of anxiety or fear is intended, but not achieved. According to Guelke, actual use of the term departs from its etymological origins precisely because terrorism is frequently identified in actions that does not create a grave state of fear (Guelke 1995, pp. 4–6). He also points out that creating fear does not advance political causes.

Secondly, how are we to determine that terrorists have succeeded in putting the whole or sections of the public in a state of fear? What is fear? How overwhelming must fear be to create terror? How can fear induced by violent acts be distinguished from fear created by other factors, such as natural disasters or accidents? How many people would have to experience massive fear before we can say violence created an effect of fear? In short, fear is difficult to measure.

Despite these difficulties, Schmid et al. do not want to give up fear as a central definitional element, for the reason that this would imply deserting the core element of the concept. They argue that terrorism must still be considered as use of violence to instigate a state of fear that those who commit the violence can attempt to exploit. This is what distinguishes terrorists from other violent activities where the goal is achieved when the victim of violence is killed. Violence of this kind is directed against specific people. Thus we are speaking of murder, or if there is a political motivation, of assassination. The tyrant murder would be one classical instance of violent intentions achieved with the killing of one person. If the intention is to eliminate all people sharing certain ethnic or religious traits, we are dealing with genocide (Gurr 1986, p. 47; Harff 1986). Assassination, genocide and terrorism, are all instances of the political use of violence. However only terrorism aims at exploiting the effect violence has on people other than those directly hit by it.

Terrorist Violence and Terrorism as a Method of Struggle

Instrumental in creating a state of fear is the threat that violent acts will be repeated. Schmid et al. see this as a key element (Schmid et al. 1988, p. 19), and include an element to this effect in their definition. Two important distinctions may be developed as a consequence of this definitional element.

First of all, focusing on the inducement of fear through the threat of repeated violent acts, enables us to draw a distinction between individual acts of terrorism, or terrorist violence, and sustained organized terrorist campaigns (Bjørgo 1989, p. 13). In both individual acts of terrorist violence and in extended campaigns, the state of fear induced by acts of violence is the core of the concept. However, following the definition, it is the prolonged series of terrorist attacks that are properly labelled terrorism.

Secondly, it follows from the focus on terrorism as a way of creating fear through repeated violence, that terrorism is a method of struggle, not an ideology. Terrorism is frequently identified exclusively with revolutionary ideologies, and only to a lesser degree with reactionary ideologies. Drake (1996) on the other hand, in a study on loyalist terrorism in Northern Ireland, discusses terrorism used by conservative groups and even points out that 'there is no absolute inconsistency between a group professing liberal ideology and using terrorism in the context of an oppressive government' (Drake 1996, p. 30).

Saying that terrorism is a method of struggle, or even a method of combat, implies the existence of contending parties, like the contending parties of a war. However, terrorism has no specific battlefield. The struggle is not over the control of territory. Despite this, terrorism can be employed by the military, or warring parties, or in situations of war. Though some would disagree, distinguishing between terrorism and war seems necessary, especially guerrilla war.[1]

Terrorism may be distinguished from guerrilla war because the strategy behind the two methods of struggle are different (Laqueur 1987, p. 147). The guerrilla strategy aims at establishing *foci*, that is liberated areas where the guerrilla movement may establish their own alternative political and administrative system. Guerrillas seek control over a territory by expanding from established *foci*. In doing so, they are engaged in more or less regular warfare with the enemy, that is the armed forces of the state. Ideally, violent targets of guerrilla operations are military, and violent means employed are discriminate. The guerrillas should ideally operate in uniformed formations. The same applies to the forces of the government. In guerrilla war, as in regular warfare, there are certain rules limiting legitimate targets and regulating what means may be employed to destroy legitimate targets. Only combatants – that is uniformed personnel – and military installations and equipment, are legitimate targets. The means used to destroy military targets have to be discriminate; only as much violence can be employed as necessary to eliminate the target. That is, one is required to avoid hitting non-combatants (civilians) or limit possible damage that might be inflicted on third parties. In cases of terrorism, as pointed out by Sederberg, these rules are deliberately broken by the perpetrators (Sederberg 1989, p. 31). By breaking the rules of war, terrorist actors create fear by violating the rules defining targets and means. In Silke's view (Silke 1996, pp. 16–20), these rules were agreed on by (mainly) European powers as they encountered what they viewed as irregular war waged against them by non-Europeans (in Asia and Africa). The rules, based on a code of chivalry developed in medieval times, limits war to 'open, pitched and directed warfare' (Silke 1996, p. 15) in which an important line is being drawn between combatants and non-combatants, that is between legitimate and non-legitimate targets. Silke further points out that with the ways and means war is fought today, there is no longer a question of adhering to such rules, and that 'the real difference between terrorist and other forms of warfare is that terrorists do not hide their crimes. On the contrary, it would seem they wish to publicise them to as many as possible' (Silke 1996, p. 19). Terrorism should instead, in Silke's view, be defined as a form of warfare, more specifically as guerrilla warfare (Silke 1996, pp. 29–30).

At the heart of Silke's plea for a new turn in the definition of terrorism lies a concern that the response to terrorism today may be traced to the definition of terrorism. Terrorism is seen as a crime, which conceptually frames both the problem and the response. Terrorist offences are dealt with by the police and the courts, just as any other criminal activity would be. When terrorism is defined as warfare, new response possibilities emerge, responses that may or may not be bound by the legal approach recommended by Silke. Silke's preference is for treating terrorists as war criminals. One tougher line of response is the perspective offered by Carr (1996). He considers terrorists to be highly sophisticated, well-equipped and well-trained warriors that have the capability of striking against major international targets (Carr 1996, p. 2). In such a situation, police, intelligence services and courts have limited powers to strike back effectively. It will come as no surprise that this perspective has the USA on the top of the terrorist target list. Fundamentalist Islam is the number one threat. This illustrates how easily, though not necessarily as Silke's contribution demonstrates, the 'terrorism as warfare' perspective regresses to the top priority that used to frame terrorism to the Western public: that of US foreign policy. Shifting definitional emphasis in the direction suggested by Silke and Carr does not automatically solve the difficulties encountered by non-policy perspectives, such as ours. In fact, we risk turning the clock back 15 or 20 years. In the case of the arguments of Carr, instead of opening the perspective, they actually close it because the warfare response fits so badly to many of today's conflicts in which terrorism is a reality.[2] This is especially the case of terrorist threats in democratic states themselves, that is internal conflict with home-grown terrorism. In such cases, deploying military forces will be of limited practical use. In the best case, it will contribute only symbolically to eliminating the threat (soldiers on the streets may have a calming effect on the public); in the worst case using military forces against the citizens of one's own country may only contribute to raising questions about the legitimacy of the people and institutions that order such measures (which we may suppose is not what the proponents of this perspective wanted).

As pointed out by Silke, experience from situations of war suggests that the rules of war are not always obeyed. Civilian and military targets are not easily distinguished (civilian installations may have military significance), and military measures invariably kill civilians.[3] Frequently, a main goal of war is also to demoralize the enemy, to weaken the motivation of enemy soldiers and undermine civilian confidence in the military and political leadership of the enemy. Terrorism is thus a means that can be employed in wars. The problem of distinguishing terrorism from guerrilla wars is increased by the fact that, frequently, guerrilla movements employ terrorist tactics at some point in their life (Laqueur 1987, p. 148). In many of today's conflicts, battles that may be situated somewhere in between regular warfare and civil wars, irregular measures of a terrorist nature, seem to be more the rule than the exception.[4]

Actors: Who are the Terrorists?

It should now be clear that terrorism has to do with the means employed, not the identity of the actor. Schmid et al.'s definition emphasizes that the terrorist kind of violence can be employed by a wide range of actors: individual, private (that is non-state) groups or states (governments). Herman and O'Sullivan have criticized terrorism research for favouring the established. According to them, research has a bias in favour of government (state) actors to the effect that states are portrayed as victims of terrorism (Herman and O'Sullivan, 1991). Thus definitions contribute to hiding the violence of states, and ignoring human rights violations and state terrorism. The definition by Schmid et al. does not single out particular types of actors. It explicitly mentions the range of actors that may employ terrorist methods, and the state is among them.

The Motivation of Terrorists

Just as the definition does not single out particular actors as terrorists, nor does it define specific motivations as inherently terrorist. What is significant is the means employed. Thus motives for employing violence of a terrorist nature may vary. Usually we think of political motives when an act is labelled terrorism. However as the definition points out, motivation may also be of a personal or idiosyncratic nature. Finally, the definition points out that motivation may be criminal. At this point the definition seems to be operating with an implicit distinction between crime and political terrorism. We must remember however that acts of terrorism – as acts of violence directed against people or material targets – would be criminal regardless of political or idiosyncratic motivation in most societies. They simply break the laws of the land. What is intended in the definition is that acts of terrorism may be committed for economic gain, without political considerations being present. As we will see in the next chapter, by using the violent means labelled terrorism in the definition, actors define themselves in relation to the state. Thus both criminal and idiosyncratic motives are by implication political. It must be emphasized however that terrorism is not in itself an ideology, but can be put to use by actors professing the most diverse ideological convictions. In fact the use of terrorism is not even limited to those belonging to extreme ideologies of revolution or reaction. Given the right circumstances, terrorism may be used even by conservatives or liberals.[5] Further, terrorism is the use of violence to achieve certain goals the actors in question have. Nevertheless, violence is not a goal in itself even if some actors may attach a certain value to violence in itself.

Targets of Violence in Terrorism

What makes Schmid et al.'s definition stand out from others, is the definitional element distinguishing between targets of violence, and the wider targets and audiences. This distinction is also the factor that infuses the definition with the potential for application for purposes not intended by its originators.

Schmid et al. point out that what is special about terrorism, is that the immediate target of the violence is not the main target. This is what distinguishes terrorism from violent acts aiming at physically eliminating certain people, in which case the aim is reached when these people are eliminated. In terrorism, those inflicted with violence are selected for different reasons. This consideration is the function of the targets of violence as messengers.

There are two main ways terrorists pick the targets they inflict violence upon (Schmid et al. 1988, pp. 7–10). The first is random or arbitrary targeting, by aiming terrorist actions at whoever is present when the attack is launched. The typical example is the bomb in a crowded city centre, an airport or railway station. In such cases, terrorists are seeking to take advantage of the effect created by the infliction of death and injury upon a random selection of people. An effect is created by the fact that people not present at the scene of violence can easily put themselves in the position of the victims. Fear may be stirred up by the possibility that the next attack could hit oneself. This is the calculated effect. Secondly, targets of violence may be selected for their symbolic or representative value. Terrorists are then directing violence against people they consider representatives of the enemy they want to take on. In such cases of terrorism, violence will approach liquidation, but the victims of violence are nevertheless chosen mainly for their symbolic value. It is important to stress that the targets of violence selected in this way may have only a peripheral role in the struggle against the terrorists. They represent the enemy because of their political or social status, because of their positions in politics, business or the state apparatus, or membership in a social or cultural group. Victims are not chosen so selectively that those actually hit by violence could not have been substituted with other members of the same category of people. Targets are selected for their ability to carry a message. Regardless of how the targets of violence are chosen, there are two main clusters of targets: the immediate victims of violence and the wider targets or audiences the terrorists wish to influence.

Wider Targets and Audiences

The direct victims of violence are used instrumentally by terrorists, for three main purposes according to the definition presented by Schmid et al. First, it may be that terrorists want to put the wider group of targets in a state of fear. In this case we are talking about targets of terror. Second, terrorists may want to use violence against a group of targets to direct claims and demands at a third party, the targets of demands. At first thought, such demands apparently must be political, that is related to a state of affairs the terrorists want to change. However, demands may be practical or economic, related to the ongoing operation of the terrorist group – in the immediate situation or in the future maintenance of the organization. Third, terrorists use victims of violence to communicate a political message, in which case we speak about targets of propaganda. People are targeted with terrorist violence so that the terrorists may generate attention for their cause, opinions or demands. We can see that the main message of Schmid et al.'s definition is that terrorism is defined by the means used: the violent means function as generators of a message. The definition has no room for specific social causes of terrorism, neither does it single out certain political motives or ideologies as integral to a definition of terrorism.

These were the six elements of the definition. We must now ask where to go from here. It may be argued that the definition points the way to two main paths, the first based on media studies and the second – which will be developed here – seeing terrorism as fundamentally connected with the core concepts of legitimacy and the state. Both directions are based on an understanding of terrorism as a form of communication, and they thus follow one another some way down the road. In the following we will first discuss the views common to the perspective that sees terrorism as a way of communicating. Then we will briefly sketch some directions and questions posed by media studies of terrorism. Finally, in the next chapter we will employ the definition and the communicative approach to terrorism for an alternative perspective that is more based in political science, by focusing on the political aspects of the definition as far as they connect to power relationships and legitimacy.

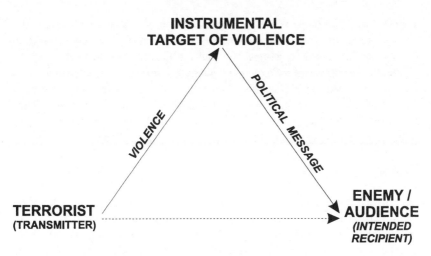

Figure 1.1   A general model of communication in terrorism (adapted from Bjørgo and Heradstveit 1987, p. 123)

A COMMUNICATION MODEL OF TERRORISM

The common denominator of all perspectives seeing terrorism as a form of violence for communication purposes is the distinction made between three groups of actors: (1) the terrorists, those who employ violence, (2) the victims, those who are inflicted by violence, and (3) the targets, those not directly hit by the violence but influenced by observing or learning about it. This makes room for a different terminology, borrowed from studies of communications, where the first group is denoted as the transmitter, the second group becomes the medium communicating a message by being directly inflicted with violence, while the third group is the recipients of that message.

Conceiving terrorism in this way implies that there is a triangular relationship between the terrorists, the victims they inflict violence upon and the audience(s) they want to communicate a message to. The relationship may be summed up in a model of communication as in Figure 1.1 (Bjørgo and Heradtsveit 1987, pp. 122–3; Karber 1971, p. 528).[6] In the figure, the general model of communication for terrorism operates with a common category for the different kinds of targets introduced by Schmid et al. The model does not distinguish between the three main target groups: the targets of terror, targets of demand and targets of attention. All these groups are included under the heading 'enemy/audience'. In the model, terrorists are the transmitters of a message delivered in the form of a violent act. The targets of violence are acting as a medium, while the wider targets are defined as the audience. Usually models of communication distinguish between two parties, the transmitter and the intended recipient, where the transmitter is trying to send a message directly to the recipient with the help of a medium.[7] In terrorism this direct way of conveying a message is complicated by the introduction of a third party, the targets of violence. Thus the targets of violence are used as instruments. Violence is employed because of its strong effects on others than those directly hurt or killed.

Communication without Control

Terrorism is thus seen as a triangular communicative process, in which the victims of violence are an instrument terrorists as transmitters use to communicate a political message. However this is a complicated way of communicating seen from the perspective of the transmitter, the terrorists. If we focus on the axis going between the instrumental victims of violence and the enemy/audience pole, three comments may be made regarding such difficulties.

First, the instrumental victims of violence are seldom themselves capable of communicating directly with the wider audiences. The political message (contents) the terrorist may have wanted the targets of violence to generate, is dependent on yet another party to be communicated to the audiences at the receiver end. The political message the transmitters may want to disseminate is heavily dependent on yet another party external to the model to reach the enemy and/or audience groups. This party is the mass media (Figure 1.2). It is the media that will have to report what has happened and connect the violence to those responsible for it. More importantly, the terrorists depend on the media to convey the political message they had hoped to focus on by employing violence.

Second, this is a very delicate way of communicating, and the possibility for distortion of the message, as seen from the point of view of the terrorists, is significant. Terrorists do not have control over the political message generated by their actions (Schmid and de Graaf 1982, pp. 175–6). The role of the mass media complicates the communication process seen from the perspective of the terrorists. The media may report what happens, conveying to audiences more or less factual information concerning what has happened. However, the media may also act as filters of events and interpreters of terrorist acts.[8] This filter and interpretation function makes terrorism a difficult and uncertain way of communicating for the terrorists. The terrorists themselves are in a weak position to control what is being reported and in what way it is interpreted. Generally speaking they are at the mercy of the media. The effect of this is that frequently, the violent expression of the terrorists gets more attention than the political

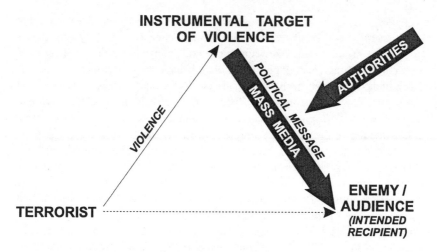

Figure 1.2   Acts of terrorism: influence of authorities on the political message conveyed by the mass media

message they want to transmit simultaneously.[9]

Third, the political message – the content of terrorist actions – is easily determined not by the terrorists themselves but by other parties. Reporters and commentators of newspapers and broadcasting have already been mentioned. Moreover, political parties and politicians, and in particular the government and law enforcement officers, have the opportunity of influencing the message even to the extent of making the terrorist attack generate a message contrary to what the terrorists wanted (Figure 1.2). Terrorists are actually competing with other actors over the meaning and interpretation of their own acts. In sum, terrorism is a difficult form of communication for the terrorists, due to their lack of control over the communication process after the action has been initiated.

Media Studies of Terrorism and Beyond

The approach framing terrorism as a form of political communication in which a political message is attached to violent acts directed at various audiences, lends itself to studies of how news media treats this kind of behaviour. Media studies of terrorism were initiated by Schmid and de Graaf (1982), though there were important studies before theirs (Karber 1971). Media studies of terrorism tend to focus on the role the press and broadcasting play in relation to terrorist actors and also the public and the authorities. Some studies study structural aspects as determinants of coverage of terrorism, whereas others devote attention to editorial values and attitudes concerning the reporting of terrorism.

Particularly interesting from a political science perspective are the studies that examine the role played by news media in causing terrorism by acting as a contagious agent. Terms like 'contagion' and 'contagiousness' are here used metaphorically, associating political violent behaviour with illness and disease. Nevertheless the hypothesis is old and goes as far back as to Gabriel Tarde at the beginning of this century. He observed that sensational coverage of violent crimes seemed to inspire more similar acts, and noted that 'Epidemics of crime follow the line of the telegraph' (quoted in Brosius and Weimann 1991, p. 63).

Adapted to the analysis of the causes of terrorism, the contagion hypothesis argues that coverage of terrorism in the news media publicizes violent means as solutions for social or political conflicts. News coverage of terrorist actions sets examples for others. Political actors will then evaluate these examples and find them attractive by the attention and publicity the acts create for a cause. Thus coverage of violent political actions such as terrorism stimulates new attacks (Holden 1986, pp. 876–7). The contagion hypothesis therefore establishes that the rate of terrorist attacks will increase when attacks have been given broad coverage in the news media (as opposed to attacks without much coverage). Holden investigated hijacks of aeroplanes, and found a contagion effect following successful hijacks in the USA. However he was unable to establish the connection between media coverage and contagion statistically (Holden 1986, pp. 894, 900–901. A later study by Brosius and Weimann (1991, p. 72) however found some support for the contagion hypothesis. The problem is to connect the coverage of a terrorist attack at one point to the motivation of actors instigating attacks at some point later. Picard argues that a causal link between news coverage and increase in terrorist attacks is not established, and that the contagion approach is characterized by broad generalizations and assumptions that are not supported by evidence (Picard 1986, pp. 387, 393).[10]

Media studies as related to terrorism includes at first sight little of what we generally see as political science. When there is such content it is focused on the role of the state in regulating or controlling news media coverage of terrorism. Such control may be imposed in a number of different ways. The strictest way is of course outright censorship and controls imposed on the flow of information. Governments are also known to impose regulations and restrictions concerning coverage.[11] In crisis situations restrictions on coverage may be introduced in agreement with news organizations for instance in handling hostage crises. In such situations newspapers and broadcasting stations are asked to refrain from reporting facts known to them because this would endanger the hostages or reduce the possibility of solving the crisis without loss of life.

With the definition's strong focus on communication, studies focusing on the connection between terrorism and the media come natural. However, it does not seem that this perspective is the best choice when the aim is to describe and explain differences in the levels of terrorism between countries. We are looking for characteristics of the states that might be relevant in explaining the outbreak of terrorism, or the opposite, that is the ability of countries to avoid the problem of terrorism. Our next challenge will be to relate terrorism to two central terms for the theoretical understanding of terrorism put forward in this work. These are the concepts of the state and legitimacy.

NOTES

1. Silke (1996) strongly opposes defining terrorism as something different than guerrilla warfare. According to him, terrorism is best viewed as a form of warfare – a sub-species of guerrilla tactics. Silke is of the opinion that the difficulties encountered in the study of terrorism result from unwillingness to define terrorism as warfare.
2. Note for instance that the military approach is argued in response to state-sponsored, fundamentalist and anti-American terrorism, not against religious fundamentalists (such as anti-abortion terrorists) or extreme right-wing federal-government haters in the USA.
3. Silke (1996, p. 13), quotes Robert Taber to the effect that compared to the savagery of modern war, terrorism is much more selective and thus is actually one of the most humane ways to wage war. Silke refers to Taber's *The War of the Flea*, London: Paladin, 1969.
4. See Benard (1994) for a discussion of rape as an instrument of terror in the case of the war in Bosnia and Herzegovina. Benard points to six functions of mass rape: (1) the function of increasing the incentive to flee, (2) the function of demoralizing the opponents, (3)the function of signalling an intention to break up society, (4) the function of inflicting trauma to achieve social disintegration, (5) the function of providing psychological benefits to the perpetrators (including increased group cohesion), (6) the function of striking symbolically and collectively at the opponent group, by targeting a group with high symbolic value (Benard, 1994, pp. 35–9). As we can see, several of these functions correspond to ingredients in the definition of terrorism.
5. See Drake (1996) for a discussion of terrorism committed by ideological conservatives. He also briefly discusses terrorism and liberal ideology, finding no inconsistency (Drake 1996, p. 30).
6. Also see Karber (1971, p. 528). A similar, but more complicated and far less intuitively understandable model is presented in Schmid and de Graaf (1982, p. 176). In Schmid and de Graaf's model, the mass media are also introduced into the model.
7. For simplicity, we can think of a medium acting as a loudspeaker. Though of course too simplistic, the medium is thought of as more or less conveying the message sent by the originator. Communication is direct, in that the medium is tuned to the audience.
8. See Picard (1991a) for a discussion of the various roles journalists may take in reporting acts of terrorism. Picard distinguishes between four rhetorical traditions used by terrorists. The two roles discussed here, are called the *informative tradition* and the *didactic tradition*. In addition he makes a distinction between the *sensationalist tradition* (focusing on emotions) and the *feature story tradition* (focusing on individuals).

9. Terrorists may attempt to overcome this difficulty by a conscious press relations policy – or by taking advantage of new kinds of media. For a discussion of the press relations techniques used by terrorists, and an investigation into different press relation strategies of terrorist groups, see Picard (1989).

10. Note that Picard published his study in the same year as Holden and five years before the article by Brosius and Weimann. Nevertheless Picard's conclusions were not revised for the 1991 reprint of the article (Picard 1991b). Note also that Picard points out a line of thought that suggests wide coverage of grievances as a way of reducing the threat of terrorist attacks by removing the need to commit such acts to gain attention (Picard 1986, pp. 393–4).

11. The most famous example is perhaps the ban on broadcasting the voices of the Sinn Fein leadership by the United Kingdom government, because Sinn Fein was seen as closely connected to the Provisional IRA. The restrictions were introduced in October 1988 and lifted in September 1994.

2. Explaining Terrorism: Focusing on Legitimacy

This chapter proceeds by developing the perspective tying terrorism to the state through legitimacy into a theoretical perspective that can explain the variations in terrorism in modern European states, that is in Western Europe after the Second World War. This alternative approach conceives terrorism as violence employed for communication, and focuses on the political message attached to violence, the wish to communicate something to various groups in society and in particular the wish to influence bonds of loyalty and allegiance between groups in society.

TERRORISM, COMMUNICATION AND THE STATE

The communications perspective on terrorism has been developed further by Ronald D. Crelinsten, who in response to a questionnaire pointed out:

> The purpose of terrorism can be more succinctly stated in terms of various *allegiances* among the various targets ... Rather than the phrase 'indirect method of combat,' I would say *the double victimization method* (target of violence/threat and target of demands) *is designed to affect allegiances between targets of terror and targets of attention, and targets of attention and the terrorists themselves.* (Cited in Schmid et al. 1988, p. 23, emphasis added).

The fear that is stirred up is then a means to maintain or undermine relationships of loyalty and subordination between different groups in society. Crelinsten operates with different target groups where the general model of communication for terrorism operates with one general category (enemy/audience). Moreover he introduces terms for the political relationships between the groups: loyalty and subordination. In this perspective it is possible to speak about a triangular relationship between the terrorist and two groups of wider targets. Threats of violence are directed against one group, while political claims of loyalty or subordination are directed against the other (Crelinsten 1987a, pp. 6–7). The terrorists are attempting to establish a relationship of allegiance towards this

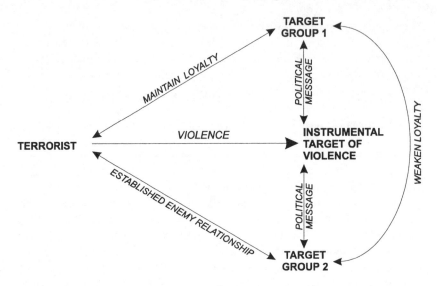

Figure 2.1   Terrorism as communication: political relationships between groups

latter group, while trying to weaken the former group which they see as the enemy. By extending the general model of communication for terrorism, this can be illustrated as in Figure 2.1 (see also Engene 1994, pp. 31–2).

Connecting Terrorism and the State

Acts of terrorism, then, aim at different target groups – friends or foes (or both) of the acting group that it wants to influence. Who these groups are, their precise identity, will vary with the circumstances, and is influenced by the aims and ideology of the terrorists, the political situation at the time of the attack, and so on. There is one notable exception: the state will always be a target group to the terrorists – explicitly or implicitly. But the state does not have to be an enemy target group in all instances. As explained below, terrorists may also be friendly to the state, whether this is reciprocal or not. Nevertheless no matter what the circumstances are, the state will always be affected by terrorist attacks. This is because terrorism strikes at the very core of what the state is about. Weber defined the state as 'a human community which (successfully) lays claim to the *monopoly of legitimate physical violence* within a certain territory.' (Weber 1994, pp. 310–11). These three characteristics – territoriality, monopoly of use of violence, legitimacy – are all directly connected to terrorism.

The state monopoly on the use of violence implies that it is the state that has the right to regulate the use of force and violence in society. This implies two things. First, the state is responsible for regulating its own use of force. The monopoly of violence is bounded. It is defined and regulated by law. The state's use of force must be based in law, or else it is a use of violence which may even fall in the category of state terrorism. Second, the state is responsible for regulating the use of force and violence between other groups and individuals. The state may authorize others to use force, or prohibit the use of violence. The overall aim is to secure order and achieve stability internally (and to protect the territory externally). This is the ultimate responsibility of the state. Terrorism, in relation to this point, is a clear breach of the state's sole right to use violence. It is more than an ordinary violent crime however, because it challenges the state's right to be the sole dispenser and regulator of violence.

Modern states exist within a clearly defined geographical area over which the state exercises authority. This, again, implies two things. First, the state is – ideally – without rivals within the state territory. No other group or actor has rights on equal terms with the state: the state is sovereign and it claims – ideally, successfully – to be the sole and supreme power in the territory. Its laws and regulations apply to everyone within its borders. This model of the state draws heavily upon the European historical experience. In other parts of the world, states have been formed by a different path of action, decolonization, whereby a former dependent territory is declared independent and receives recognition of this from other states (including the former colonial power).[1] Formally however, the key trait of the state is still territorial autonomy, whereby the state claims sovereignty within a certain territory. Nevertheless, the decolonization way of state formation serves as a reminder that states exist within a state system: a set of formally equal sovereign states.

Terrorism threatens the integrity of the state territory. This may occur in three different ways. First, terrorism may explicitly aim at detaching a part of the state's territory, to set up an independent state. Second, irredentist terrorism may threaten to split a piece of a state's territory in order to attach it to another (bordering) state. In both the former and the latter case, a threat to the integrity of the state territory is dependent on the ideological inclination of the terrorists. However, and this is the third point, despite the ideological strains of the perpetrators, terrorism is a sign of internal instability and weakness. Thus terrorism threatens a state's territorial integrity by weakening it in relation to other states, even when no territorial split is intended by terrorists. Terrorism is thus a potential threat to external security and increases the vulnerability of attack from other states or, equally importantly, threatens intrusions into the internal affairs by other states.

By the third point, legitimacy, Weber claims that the state is regarded as the rightful source of law and order in the territory. Further, the means of force the state commands and uses to enforce its decisions are also regarded as reasonable and lawful. This is legitimacy, that is the fact that actions, orders and regulations are regarded as rightful or reasonable by the ones these actions, orders or regulations are to be directed at. As Weber defines it, the state is the executer of rightful authority and force. In this sense, the state is an institution supported by those the state exercises authority over. There is a reciprocal relationship between the government and those governed.

In the modern state, legitimacy is grounded in legality, or in other words, in legal-rational authority, or 'rule by virtue of belief in the validity of legal *statute* and the appropriate ... juridical "competence" founded on rationally devised rules' (Weber 1994, p. 312). In Bendix's terms, there is a distinction between legal order and legal domination (Bendix 1962, pp. 390, 419). Legal order consists of the state's apparatus for the exercise and implementation of force. The apparatus consists of administrative institutions, police and military structures, and the like. In other words, the state possesses personnel, organized in various institutions, to implement its decisions and orders, with force if necessary. This is a relationship in which the state is the dominant part: through its monopoly of violence and the administrative apparatus at its hands, the state has control over and directs its population. Through the legal order the state exercises territorial penetration, by establishing a political and administrative apparatus for exercising authority over a territory and a population.

Legal dominance on the other hand is more of a reciprocal relationship between the state and the population over which the state exercises authority. The relationship implies that the state's decisions and rules are regarded as legal and rightful, or in other words legitimate, by the population. In the eyes of the population the state has the right to command, and the population considers it has a duty to obey. Both the right to command and the duty to obey are derived from the fact that commands are made in accordance with the fundamental and constituting rules of the political system. In other words, laws are legitimate if enacted through prescribed procedures, and a decision is legitimate if made in accordance with the laws regulating how decisions are to be made.

Based on the distinction between legal order and legal dominance, Bendix wants to extend Weber's defining characteristics of the state. His definition is well suited for our purpose. According to Bendix's explanation of Weber:

> . . . a modern state exists where a political community possesses the following characteristics: (1) an administrative and legal order that is subject to change by legislation; (2) an administrative apparatus that conducts official business in accordance with legislative resolution; (3) binding authority over all persons – who usually obtain their citizenship by birth – and over most actions taking place in the area of its jurisdiction; (4) the legitimation to use force within this area if coercion is either permitted or prescribed by the legally constituted government, i.e., if it is in accordance with enacted statutes. (Bendix 1962, pp. 417–18).

The power of the state is grounded, in other words, in legal dominance, in legitimacy. However, Bendix demonstrates that the legal dominance on which the state is founded is not static. He is of the opinion that:

> Any system of domination undergoes change when the beliefs in its legitimacy and the practices of its administrative organization are modified. Such changes occur in and through the struggle for power, which in the modern state may lead to changes of control over the bureaucratic apparatus but not to its destruction. (Bendix 1962, p. 431).

Consequently, legitimacy is not exclusively a trait of stable states and established state orders. The established order may be opposed by a counter-order supported by counter-legitimacy. This implies that citizens in society may direct their loyalties to, and feel committed to, groups that are not state actors. Even challenger groups may experience legitimacy in relation to the population or parts of it. While the modern state bases its authority in legality, the fact that constitutional rules give it the right to exercise power, other groups may be regarded as rightful exercisers of power on the basis of other normative criteria such as ideology, morality, or religion.

While terrorism directly challenges the state by violating its monopoly of force, and threatens its territorial integrity, these two threats also challenge the legitimacy of the state. For the state, it is more serious to be in a situation where its legitimacy is challenged, than to be involved in a struggle limited to the exercise of violence or control over territory. No one can hope to rule a territory with violence over time. A reciprocal relationship between those who govern and those who are governed are needed to establish a stable state order. Power must be rightful. It must be legitimate. The state must control its inhabitants, not only its territory.

As we have here defined terrorism and state, the relationship of loyalty between groups is central to both concepts. Terrorism is the use of violence to influence bonds of loyalty and allegiance between groups in society. The modern state is characterized by an established, reciprocal, relationship of loyalty between those who govern and those governed. As we can see, the two concepts are fundamentally about the same thing: bonds of loyalty. We may therefore regard terrorism as an attempt to influence the relationships of loyalty between the state, the terrorist actor, and various groups in society. This relationship may take different forms. While the first thing that springs to mind is that terrorism is an attempt to weaken the bonds of loyalty to the state, it is perfectly possible that the opposite is the case. Terrorism may also attempt to strengthen the bonds of loyalty to the state.

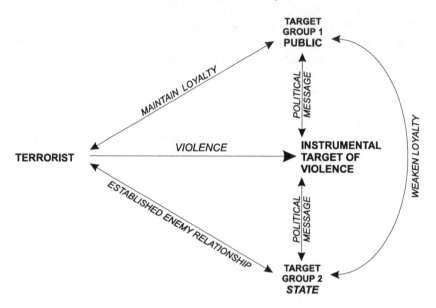

Figure 2.2   Terrorism as an attempt to weaken the state

Terrorism as an Attempt to Weaken Bonds of Loyalty to the State

Terrorism may be regarded as an attempt to break the citizens' trust in the state as the rightful source of laws, regulations and commands, while at the same time attempting to create – or, if already in place, maintain – bonds of loyalty between groups of citizens and the terrorists themselves. Drawing upon the set of figures developed earlier, this may be illustrated as in Figure 2.2 (cf. Figure 2.1). In Figure 2.2 a distinction is made – in addition to the targets of violence – between two main target groups: the state and the public (citizens). In principle, the latter target group may be broken down into several sub-groups of targets with varying attitudes to the state, to the use of violence and to terrorist actors, and which those using terrorist means may want to influence in different ways. The figure illustrates a situation in which terrorists try to weaken the bonds of loyalty between the public and the state, while attempting to establish or maintain bonds of loyalty between themselves and this group. The relationship between terrorists and the state is indicated as that of an enemy relationship.

By breaking the state monopoly on violence, terrorism interrupts and disrupts the order of everyday life. It is the state that is the keeper and maintainer of this everyday order, based on its status as the supreme regulator of the use of violence. Terrorism has a detrimental effect on the rules regulating the use of violence (Sederberg 1989, pp. 6–7). By this, the state is challenged in two ways.

First, it is demonstrated that the state is unable to enforce its monopoly of violence. It becomes clear that challengers exist who possess the ability to put force behind their demands. Second, it demonstrates that the state is no longer able to secure law and order, which is the service the inhabitants get in return for supporting the state. At worst, both effects may contribute to a development in which people's allegiances drifts away from the state and are redirected towards challenger groups representing a new societal or state order.

The potentially disruptive effect on legitimacy is one reason for deciding on the use of terrorism. As we have seen, legitimacy is a central part of the foundation of modern states. By challenging this, terrorists may hope to provoke the state into overreacting. That is, to make the state act beyond what its own rules allow, thereby challenging the principles of legality and infringing the rights of inhabitants. From the perspective of terrorists, this may contribute to a further weakening of the legitimacy of the state, which in turn may lay the foundation for a change of allegiances and loyalties between groups in society.

So far, terrorism has been discussed as if the sole purpose of using terrorist violence is for the terrorist actor to challenge the existing order and replace the incumbent elite with its own personnel. As there are demands and objectives involved concerning the organization of state and society, this is, rightly or wrongly, what is usually understood by 'political terrorism'. However, the definition and perspective developed in this chapter maintain that it is the means employed that are the defining characteristics of terrorism. Thus, also what is known as 'criminal terrorism' must be considered. The overriding consideration for those involved in criminal terrorism is to promote or protect profit making. Regardless of motive, political or economic, terrorism will concern the bonds of allegiance and loyalty in society. Moreover the state will always be involved. Indeed criminals may use terrorism to protect their activities against the laws and regulations of the state. By using violence they may demonstrate their power, establish alliances towards parts of the population, and thereby achieve a certain legitimacy. If politics is about controlling and regulating action, and the state is the institution responsible for regulating the use of violence, then terrorism will affect these matters regardless of motivation. Terrorism is political because the means employed are such that they concern the state as an institution by challenging the state's monopoly of violence and affecting its relationship to other groups in society (legitimacy).

Terrorism as an Attempt to Strengthen the State

The use of terrorist means may also aim at strengthening the state, as illustrated in Figure 2.3 (cf. Figures 2.1 and 2.2). In such cases the terrorist wishes to weaken the bonds of allegiance and loyalty between the state and a group of citizens, while at the same time attempting to strengthen the relationship

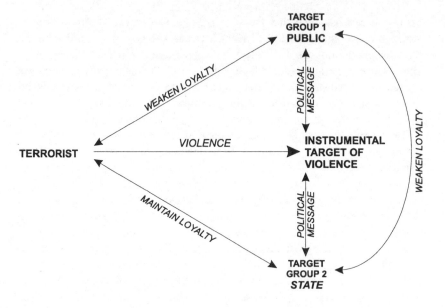

Figure 2.3   Terrorism as an attempt to strengthen the state

between the state and themselves. Actors seeking to strengthen the state through the use of terrorism will first and foremost attempt to create relationships of subordination to the state. This implies that terrorism is used as a means to change state legitimacy away from legality, participation and support. The alternative would be to see the state as just in itself and that it as such should not be bound by legal rules and be under the control of the public. The state has by nature certain interests which give it certain rights. Terrorism attempts to uncover, or provoke, the true nature of the state. In this respect terrorists attempting to strengthen the state are no different from those attempting to weaken it, only whereas the latter have a negative view of the state that implies it should be transformed, the former views the authoritarian nature of the state positively. Terrorism is used in an attempt to free the state of the bindings put on it by rules of law and popular participation in the government.[2] In cases where the state is grounded on legality and the rule of law, terrorism intended to strengthen the state is hardly an easy position, as it immediately conflicts with the rules of the state.

Violence easily overshadows the political message. It is sometimes said that terrorism is counter-productive, and that terrorists get more attention than sympathy, support or understanding (Schmid and de Graaf 1982, pp. 109–12). One aspect in this regard is that the strengthening effect terrorism has on the state may be unintended and undesirable from the point of view of terrorists. This is because instances of terrorism give the parties of established relationships of allegiance and loyalty the opportunity to demonstrate unity and support of each other, thereby closing ranks against common enemies. When this occurs terrorism is counter-productive. Instead of challenging a relationship of loyalty, it ends up reinforcing it.

APPROACHES TO EXPLAINING TERRORISM

In the remaining sections of this chapter, the state-centred perspective developed so far will be extended into an effort to explain the occurrence and distribution of terrorism between modern European states, whether this is state-loyal or state-challenging terrorism. Explanations of terrorism are ultimately guided by notions about pertinent research questions. Different levels of analysis produce diverging opinions about what are the most central questions research on terrorism must answer. We can distinguish between the individual level of analysis, the group level of analysis and the societal level of analysis.

On the level of analysis of the individual, the dominant research approach is psychological. It is asked why some people become terrorists and if these people have particular personality traits that might contribute to explain why these individuals chose terrorism. Questions like these have been important in terrorism research (for an overview, consult Schmid et al. 1988). It is an important assumption that non-violent behaviour is the norm, and that violent behaviour is deviant and must be explained. Social psychology attempts to connect psychological explanations to the societal level. Research at the individual level of analysis may also be guided by presuppositions about rationality and the rational behaviour of individuals. In such cases, terrorism is explained as choices made in the self-interest of individuals. In this view, even terrorism is seen as rooted in an evaluation of costs and benefits of different alternative ways of acting.

The group level of analysis is a second important research approach. Here, research questions revolve around the internal processes of the terrorist group. It is deemed important to understand how goals are defined, how leadership works and how group cohesion functions. A central question is to ask how terrorist groups survive. Researchers are interested in the characteristics and developments of small, isolated groups that are under strong pressure (internally and externally).[3] This analytical angle gets its concepts and methods from organizational psychology (Crenshaw 1988, pp. 19–26; Post 1987). Another approach, still at the group level of analysis, focuses on the terrorist group as a coherent rational actor. Members of the terrorist group are presumed to act together to achieve common goals. In this view, terrorism is a conscious choice and is seen by terrorists as instrumental in achieving their goals (Crenshaw 1988, pp. 13–15).

On the societal level of analysis terrorism is seen as a phenomenon that occurs in a much wider context than is the case at the individual and group level of analysis. In the words of Crenshaw, the main concern for terrorism research at the societal level of analysis may be formulated like this: 'A comprehensive explanation, however, must also take into account the environment in which terrorism occurs and address the question of whether broad political, social, and economic conditions make terrorism more likely in some contexts than in others.' (Crenshaw 1981, p. 380). In other words, uncovering the social and political factors that are influencing the likelihood of terrorism occurring is the main goal at the societal level of analysis in terrorism research. The political or social system with its characteristics is central to the analysis, not the particular individual terrorist group. As will be gathered, the problematique in this work is at the societal level of analysis, as the goal here is to investigate whether there are certain characteristics of political systems that contribute towards explaining variations in terrorism in a set of countries.

Several societal level theories of terrorism have been put forward. Crenshaw (1981) for instance takes as her point of departure is that there are some social and political conditions that make terrorism more likely. There are some 'permissive causes' of terrorism, that is conditions which make terrorism a possible way of action (Crenshaw 1981, p. 381f). These are very general conditions, specifically modernization, industrialization and urbanization. Through the ever-expanding complexity, society has grown increasingly vulnerable and offers more possible targets than before. Improved means of communication and transportation makes it easier to carry out acts of terrorism. At the same time the opportunities for attention through the mass media have increased. Technological developments in the arms and explosives sectors have offered terrorists new possibilities. Urbanization creates an environment in which terrorists may find anonymity, while simultaneously offering a concentrated but wide range of possible targets. No doubt such factors make it easier for people to commit acts of terrorism. Nevertheless terrorism is not a phenomenon of the industrial age. Crenshaw's conclusion is that terrorism has a multitude of causes, but that these usually work only on a minority or elite in society. As far as one can see, there is no attempt to explain at which times these factors have been decisive, or in what countries they have played a part in explaining the rise of terrorism. While explaining that terrorism is a possibility in modern society, Crenshaw's permissive causes are not able to explain why terrorists exploit the possibilities offered by modernization or why actors in some political systems seem to take more advantage of these opportunities than actors in other political systems.

Another researcher, Paul Wilkinson, has specified 11 sources of discontent leading to terrorism. According to him:

It is possible . . . to identify some of the most frequent contributory causes of internal political violence, constantly recurring in the recorded history of political conflict and challenging both our attention and our powers of explanation and analysis: (i) ethnic conflicts, hatreds, discrimination and oppression; (ii) religious and ideological conflicts, hatreds, discrimination and oppression; (iii) socio-economic relative deprivation; (iv) stresses and strains of rapid modernisation tending to accentuate; (v) perceived political inequalities, infringements of rights, injustice or oppression; (vi) lack of adequate channels for peaceful communication of protests, grievances and demands (e.g. denial of franchise or other rights of participation, representation or access to media); (vii) existence of a tradition of violence, disaffection and popular turbulence; (viii) the availability of a revolutionary leadership equipped with a potentially attractive ideology; (ix) weakness and ineptness of the government, police and judicial organs (e.g. under-reaction, over-reaction); (x) erosion of confidence in the régime, its values and institutions afflicting all levels of the population including the government; (xi) deep divisions within governing elites and leadership groups. (Wilkinson 1986, p. 37, footnotes omitted).

The factors on this checklist are collected from a variety of research disciplines in the social sciences. Most of them originate in political science traditions such as state and nation-building studies (factors i, ii and vii), studies of political participation (vi and vii), development or modernization studies (iv), studies of revolutions (viii), the study of the origin of fascism and the establishment of authoritarian regimes (ix, x and xi), and social psychology (iii and v). The broad theoretical range involved here contributes to the difficulties in applying the checklist. The factors are kept on a low level of precision and there is no attempt to discuss or describe the internal relationships (if any) between the factors. Wilkinson points to some factors which are called 'problems of legitimacy' in this work (especially factors i, ii and v). No doubt the factors capture some of the reality, perhaps even too much of it, which makes the line of argument in Wilkinson's work inconsistent. Factor vi on Wilkinson's list points in effect to the lack of democracy as a source of terrorism. This seems to contradict what is said elsewhere in his work about the facilitating effect of democracy, with its freedoms and openness, on terrorism (Wilkinson 1986, pp. 103–9).

Yet another societal theory of terrorism has been forwarded by Harry Targ. His work also represents one of the few attempts to test a theory of terrorism (Targ 1988). Targ developed a hypothesis about the likelihood of terrorism within different socio-structural contexts, in practice the pre-industrial, industrial and post-industrial types of society. The theory is that terrorism is a type of political action occurring when socio-structural conditions are not conducive for systems change through the mobilization of mass movements. Terrorism will not occur if other means for promoting and achieving change are available. Consequently, pre- and post-industrial societies will experience a high level of terrorism because class consciousness, together with party organizations, is weak, and because there is a low degree of mobilization. On the other hand, in industrial society strong class consciousness, party organizations and extensive mass mobilization make terrorism unnecessary as a political means to further social and political change. Targ's theory is tested on a data set covering political assassinations in 35 countries over three years, and Targ is of the opinion that the test supports his hypothesis. However, the test does not confront the theory with the development within countries over time. Rather, countries are grouped according to their type of society.

FOCUSING ON LEGITIMACY

In some ways, explanations at the societal level of analysis run into more difficulties than explanations at the two other levels of analysis, in which one may point to triggering events and specific motivations for selected groups or individuals. At the societal level of analysis, explanations generally tend to rest with structural traits of the political system, and it must be substantiated how such structural characteristics can be related to the actions of terrorist groups. This relates to the difficulty of combining structure and action, the macro and micro levels, the classical challenge in political science. Where then should we look for explanations that may explain the patterns of terrorism experienced in the West European countries since 1950?

    In the previous sections it has been argued that terrorism should be understood in the context of the state and legitimacy. Could it be then that variations in levels of terrorism in the different West European countries may be sought in the challenges to legitimacy that these states have experienced? Such an explanation of terrorism will take the history of political systems as its point of departure, and terrorism is seen as influenced by the very same political issues and cleavages which are found at the basis for politics in general in a political system. Contrary to what some may claim, terrorism is not detached from society and politics in general. It is the contention here that terrorism draws on the same historical and structural sources of conflict as, for instance, party politics. However, terrorism revolves around issues of a fundamental character, that is polarized issues over which parties are not likely to enter into negotiations and arrive at compromises because the actors involved have maximalist goals. In such cases terrorism constitutes offensive means employed by one or more groups of political actors to win and settle the dispute at the expense of the adversaries. That is, to win all or nothing. The situation may also be of such a character that one involved party sees the issues as so fundamental that negotiations and compromises are ruled out, while other parties are willing to negotiate and reach compromises. Terrorism is then easily a defensive course of action one party resorts to in order to keep the remaining parties from agreeing on a settlement. In any case, the issues that incite terrorism are polarized, particularly those involving the nature and legitimacy of the state.

What then might be the sources of fundamental challenges to the legitimacy of states? It may be argued that in modern European states, there are three main sources. These are problems of ethnicity, involving demands for group rights based on shared language, religious difference or attachment to territory; problems of continuity in a country's development towards democracy involving disruptions which may create deep-rooted and lasting cleavages between opposing groups and lead to a debate over the true nature and legitimacy of the state; and, problems of integration, concerning groups at the fringes of the political system and the question of their loyalty to the state. The proposition put forward here, and elaborated in the following sections, is that variations in the presence of these three factors may contribute to explaining differences in the distribution of terrorism. The proposition will be further discussed, first, by looking at the relationship between the state, democracy and terrorism, then by looking closer at the three proposed sources of terrorism in modern European states, namely problems of ethnicity, problems of continuity and problems of legitimacy.

Terrorism and Democracy

Earlier an attempt was made to demonstrate how important legitimacy is for the relationship between the state and terrorism. Historically violence has been an inseparable part of European politics. Power, that is the capability of using violence to force ones objectives through, has given legitimacy.[4]

Rokkan described how European countries grew out of the tradition of violence and into a system that at the same time maintains the state formations and provides for the exclusion of violence in the everyday running of state affairs. This happened through a gradual limitation of violence and an increasingly reciprocal regulation of the relationship between those governing and those governed. The use of violence in politics was gradually replaced by various forms of mass participation (Rokkan 1987, p. 372; Flora 1983, pp. 16, 21–4; Kaase 1990, p. 4). However Rokkan is short in his treatment of the relationship between mass politics and political violence. He is primarily interested in the countries that experience violence in the final stages of the development of mass politics. He has less to say about the conditions for political violence once mass politics is established. The proposition presented here is that democracy as the legitimation of modern democratic European states is by no means a simple or straightforward affair. By this it is claimed that the democratic principles exalted by modern European states, and which constitute their basic foundation of legitimation, in practice hold a number of challenges that democracy has had difficulties in solving. These challenges may have contributed to the growth and distribution of terrorism.

Wilkinson has discussed terrorism and democracy more closely (Wilkinson 1986, pp. 16–17, 103–9). A central tenet, which in character is quite similar to Crenshaw's permissive causes, is that the openness of democracy makes it easier for terrorists to commit their violent acts. In particular, three traits of democracy make terrorism attractive. First, democracies rank freedom higher than order. The state's right to use force to maintain law and order is defined and limited, which implies that law and order cannot be secured at any price. Second, the principles of the rule of law, with independent courts and equality before the law, secures protection from the state. This also includes terrorists. Third, democracy is based on voluntariness and freedom. Citizens are allowed to express their opinions and organize themselves in the ways they see fit. This includes the right for dissidents and enemies of democracy to put their opinions forward and even (within some limits) to organize freely. Other writers have discussed the relationship between the freedom of the press and terrorism (Schmid and de Graaf 1982, Crelinsten 1987b, Schlesinger 1991). Terrorists gain from the fact that attention is afforded them by the independent mass media. In democracies it is admitted that the political system is composed of groups holding diverging views and interests, and it tolerates them. This is, as Wilkinson sums up, the fundamental principle of liberal democracy. In the perspective of Aron, the systems in question are constitutional-pluralistic, in contrast to the monopolistic systems (Ionescu 1976, pp. 198–9). The existence of political minorities and marginal groups is recognized and their right to express their views is accepted. Moreover this pluralism is made into a constitutional principle.

Summing up, we may say that European states have experienced a process of democratization through which the legitimacy of the state has come to rest in the final instance on the participation of citizens in elections, representativeness and the exercise of control over state affairs. Through mass participation, modern European states have developed into something distinctly different from the state formations of earlier times, dominated by military or civilian autocracies or totalitarian systems.[5] The existence and efficiency of democratic arrangements is a central part of the legitimation of modern European states. Let us now turn to the three circumstances that are closely related to the state and democracy, but which may also contribute towards explaining the existence and levels of terrorism in modern European states.

Problems of Ethnicity: Democracy and the Delineation of the People

The analysis covers 18 West European countries (Austria, Belgium, Denmark, Finland, France, the Federal Republic of Germany, Greece, Iceland, the Republic of Ireland, Italy, Luxembourg, the Netherlands, Norway, Portugal, Spain, Sweden, Switzerland and the United Kingdom.[6] Out of these 18 countries, 11 introduced universal suffrage before the Second World War. Of the remaining seven, four gave women the vote in the years immediately after the war. One country waited until the early 1970s, while in two countries universal suffrage had to wait until after the downfall of dictatorships (Lane et al. 1997, p. 118). The right to vote is one of the individual rights granted by liberal democracies to their citizens and is indicative of the reciprocal relationship between the government and those it rules. This relationship is based on individual rights and duties. It is far more difficult for democracy to relate to group rights, which in effect discriminates for some citizens over others and may indicate that loyalty to other groups than the state is important. The latter is especially important in case of ethnic identities and group rights.

The ideology of the nation-state asserts that one nation, that is members of the same ethnic group, should constitute the people in a political sense (*demos*). This idea can be traced back to the times of the French Revolution, when the revolutionary republic refused to recognize any other loyalty than that which the citizens were required to give the state. Men were equal because they were free citizens of the state. This hostility towards competing loyalties was particularly strong in the case of feudal, regional and religious bonds. The idea of the cultural, especially linguistic, foundation of the people was the idea of German romanticism. Thus the ideology of the nation-state is that the boundaries of the nation (people) and the state must coincide.

However, state and nation boundaries only rarely coincide. Most states in Europe are not ethnically or linguistically homogeneous. The population of most countries is split into different groups expressing conflicting identities or loyalties based on communities founded on common language, but also rooted in religious differences or in conflicting conceptions of the territorial arrangements of groups and states. In heterogenous states like this, a fundamental question appears: who constitutes the people? Ordinary rules of majority decisions will not work when applied to the question of delimiting the people (*demos*). By claiming loyalties and rights on a group basis, minority ethnic loyalties threaten both the universalism that is the principle that rights are equally distributed and apply to all citizens – and the individualism that is the principle of granting rights to individuals not groups – of liberal democracy. Loyalty to ethnic minority groups is a potential threat to the legitimacy of the state, by challenging the state's definition of the constituting people. Additionally, minority ethnic groups are a potential threat to the integrity of state territory.

Ethnicity then is based on distinctions between groups of people in terms of common ancestry or history, or shared linguistic, religious or even racial characteristics, or 'markers' as these are often called. The significance of an ethnic characteristic varies with the social and political context. In one case, the distinction between religious denominations (such as Catholic versus Protestant) may be significant, while in another setting the same distinction is not important. Ethnic identities are created by mobilization that makes such distinctions socially and politically significant. We may say that an ethnic group exist in cases when members of a group themselves think that they are distinct from other groups and when others treat them as a distinct group. Thus ethnicity is always a distinction made in relation to other groups. It is important to note that an ethnic group is not necessarily a minority group. The ethnic group may be the majority in a country, and may even cover more than one country.[7]

In Crenshaw's discussion of the direct causes of terrorism, general factors are emphasized. In particular, discontent and perceptions of injustice in an identifiable sub-group of the population (especially among elite groups), combined with closed channels of political participation, will contribute towards causing terrorism. Such factors may of course play a part, but Crenshaw only touches the source of discontent and injustice. The example given is ethnic discrimination (Crenshaw 1981, pp. 383–4), the one emphasized here. As already mentioned, Wilkinson also mentions ethnic (and religious) discrimination in his list of possible causes of terrorism (Wilkinson 1986, p. 37). In the perspective offered here, it does not however have to be discrimination that causes terrorism, as the ethnic factor can by itself be a latent source of conflicts over legitimacy.

The question is whether it is possible to deduce more specific hypotheses about the relationship between the existence of ethnic minorities in a state and the occurrence of terrorism. One hypothesis would be that there is a linear relationship between ethnic mobilization, that is the fact that ethnic conflicts actually manifest themselves in the political system, and the presence of terrorism. Terrorism would then not occur in cases where ethnic conflicts are not the issue of mobilization. Nevertheless it may also be that the relationship is not that clear, and that terrorism may occur both in political systems with strong ethnic mobilization and in political systems with low ethnic mobilization. The question is more what makes latent ethnic conflicts manifest themselves in the political system. It is important to describe the circumstances in which we may expect ethnic diversity to give rise to terrorism.

One factor to consider is the self-image of the group, regarding how it defines itself in relation to the European tradition of state formation. In the European tradition the aim of the political work of groups has always been directed towards the state. This may have been through forming and building states, or through conquering or overturning states. Within states ethnic relations have been emphasized through attempts at cultural or linguistic standardization, also known as nation-building (or, to use the vantage point of those being standardized, nation-destroying). Ethnic groups may define themselves within this tradition, or reject it.

Ethnic groups that accept the European state tradition aspire to attaining equal status among the state-building peoples. They want to play the same role as other ethnic groups. Consequently their position is potentially offensive with respect to their own political situation. The state-building consciousness inspires defence of the ethnic group, its characteristics and interests, while holding the realization of the group as a state-building agent as the overall aim. Terrorism may be a suitable political means, as terrorism deals with the bonds of loyalty between groups in society.

On the other hand, ethnic groups may emphasize their difference and peculiarities in such a way that they define themselves as not part of the state-building tradition. Such a view would be more defensive, attempting to realize an ideal society based on tradition and the 'original' state of affairs. Terrorism would be less likely in such cases, because using terrorist violence implies accepting a part of the state-building process.

Among ethnic groups that define themselves as part of the state-building tradition, we may distinguish between two different aims concerning what to do with the existing state. On the one hand, ethnic groups may aspire to forming a state of their own, that is they have separatism as their goal. On the other hand, they may seek to join their part of the territory to another state where the ethnic group is the state-forming group. In such cases of irredentism, terrorism may expect more sources of support as mobilization may spring both internally from the ethnic minority itself and externally from the state with which the group wants to join. This is a peculiarity to irredentist conflicts, and may contribute to making them more intense and irreconcilable, thus making them more liable to terrorism. However it may also be the case that irredentist conflicts are easier to solve by compromise, because the interests of two states are at stake. Where effective bilateral agreements on minority protection exist, terrorism is then not to be expected. In cases where such agreements have not been reached, and the relationship between the two states is tense, terrorism will be more likely.

The position of ethnic groups and minorities within states may also influence the decision of an ethnic group to take up terrorism. In cases where ethnic groups have been granted protection, ranging from legal protection of language to institutional arrangements amounting to self-rule or autonomy, it is to be expected that terrorism is less likely. On the other hand, in cases where the state does not accept minority ethnic groups and refuses to recognize them through legal or institutional protection, terrorism is a much more likely element of politics. This will especially be the case where the state has been conducting strong centralist and standardization policies, without succeeding in eradicating ethnic identities.

The starting point of this discussion was that the existence of ethnic groups within a state in itself poses a problem to the legitimacy of the state, simply because questions may be raised over how to define the people, the source of legitimacy. Ethnic diversity is a latent source of conflict for many states. We expect terrorism to be more likely in cases where the ethnic group defines itself as a part of the European state-building tradition, but where the ethnic group is in an unsolved irredentist conflict, or does not enjoy cultural rights or political autonomy.

Democracy and Problems of Continuity

A country's political past is important for its political present because the issues of the past may be politicized for purposes in the present. This happens in three main ways (Fentress and Wickham 1992, pp. ix–xi, 25–6, 87–9; Rousso 1991, pp. 80–82). First, the past is common heritage, shared among all members of society and shaping identities in the present. This implies the existence of latent conflicts, based on deep, old wounds. Such latent conflicts may surface and become manifest. Second, the past may be the source of nostalgia, in which case it is made into something heroic and grand in contrast to the present detrimental state of affairs. Third, the past may be constructed more or less as fiction, a reservoir from which enemy pictures may be drawn and projected into the present. In the case of a ruptured democratic development process, both the nostalgic and the fiction element may contribute to the construction of challenges against state legitimacy. The element of nostalgia may manifest itself in inheritor organizations and parties, while the fiction element may be used to pose questions about how compatible the democratic self-image of the present is with the non-democratic past. Questions may be raised about how decisive the break with the past is, drawing on real continuities in institutions or personnel.

History may in this way be decisive for how members of a political system regard the state at a later point in time. The past may be the source of both legitimacy and illegitimacy. If there are elements of non-democratic periods in the near past, this may contribute to the raising of questions about the true character and legitimacy of the state in the present. This means that agonizing political events such as civil wars, revolutions or revolution attempts, dictatorships and the like may constitute a challenge to the legitimacy of states even in democracies. The argument is that terrorism is more likely to appear in countries with problems of continuity in their democratic development. Thus though some of these experiences, revolutions in particular, are historically rare events, the political history of countries needs to be examined for the occurrence of potential disruptive experiences like the ones mentioned.

Among Crenshaw's permissive causes we find traditions and acceptance of the use of violence for political purposes, the spread of revolutionary ideologies, together with the authorities' lack of ability or will to strike against terrorism. The first of these factors has something in common with what have been called problems of continuity, but as discussed above these problems are closely connected with democracy and do not have to imply that violence in politics is accepted. As we have seen earlier, terrorism does not have to have a revolutionary aim, even if the agents of the state are the main targets. Lastly, it should be remembered that what appears to be weakness in the face of terrorist assaults may in fact be caused by the fact that the legitimate uses of force from the state is subject to rules and regulations.

Democracy and Problems of Integration

States that have an exclusivist political system will more likely face terrorism than political systems characterized by inclusiveness. Democracies must give real opportunities for the expression of opposition, and not systematically suppress certain views or convictions. If this is the case, difficulties as to the loyalty of fringe groups to the political system and the state may appear. Therefore such problems of integration may increase the likelihood of terrorism.

Problems of integration may appear in several forms. It may be the case that certain attitudes or organizations are viewed as irreconcilable with the basic values of the state and by that are denied participation in politics altogether. It may also be that the basis of the exclusion is the difficulties involved in integrating one or more of the parties from an undemocratic past into the politics of the present. Further, problems of integration may be expressed by the fact that the ideology or democratic conviction of a group or party is doubted, and that they consequently are kept out of the processes of political cooperation and bargaining that other parties take part in (including government formation). Certain ideologies – communism, fascism, Nazism – may also lead to the rejection of the existing social and political system by the parties and groups themselves. This may not only lead to these parties or groups being distrusted or rejected by other political actors, but may in effect also create a situation in which such parties or groups, spurred by their ideology, exclude themselves from full or conventional political participation. Finally, problems of integration may be expressed through the monopolization of power, to the effect of excluding others.

Problems of integration facilitate further alienation from the political system, and may contribute to a crisis of legitimacy between the state and those excluded from real participation. If this problem of integration is nevertheless solved, problems of legitimacy may arise with respect to groups regarding the integration as an unacceptable form of co-option because the integrated group had to accept the values of the political system to achieve full recognition as an equal actor. This means that the apparent solution to a long-standing problem of integration may in fact cause divisions within the group subject to integration attempts. Such divisions may also stimulate terrorism.

Both Crenshaw and Wilkinson mention the possibility that terrorism may be caused by the absence of channels of expression. However the theory that terrorism is caused by exclusion has been most pertinently formulated by Luigi Bonante (1979, pp. 204–6). His theory states that terrorism appears in blocked societies, that is societies that are so solid and unyielding that they have approached a self-preserving phase characterized by immobility and the lack of ability to answer demands for change. In such societies there are no channels other than terrorism to express discontent or to advance political demands.

This theory has a certain resemblance to what have here been called problems of integration. However, such problems may lead to terrorism even when legal means of expression are not blocked. Modes of expression and participation may be open and effective. Nevertheless they are not chosen. This may be because it is the means and procedures of participation and expression themselves that are regarded as illegitimate in the present state of affairs, rather than that these ways of participation are blocked. Bonante's argument is that immobility and blocking may lead to terrorism. Here it is argued that difficulties in integrating opinions and groups into the political process may contribute to challenges against the legitimacy of the state. These challenges may again serve as the starting point for terrorism.

EXPECTED PATTERNS IN WEST EUROPEAN TERRORISM

The theoretical approach that sees terrorism as a struggle over legitimacy with the state is at the societal level of analysis. No claim is made to explain the individual motivation behind the choice of using terrorism. The theoretical approach developed above only claims that terrorism is more likely in some historical and political circumstances. Summing up then, we may ask what patterns of terrorism to expect when we view terrorism in the way we have done in this chapter. Which states are most likely to experience terrorism? First, as we have seen, it has been suggested that democracy and freedom facilitates terrorism. Thus we will expect countries that are the most advanced in terms of freedom and democracy to experience higher levels of terrorism compared to countries that are less advanced in these fields. On the other hand, we have also seen that socio-economic factors have been launched as explanatory factors for the appearance of terrorism. Based on this line of reasoning, we will expect terrorism to appear more frequently in those countries that have undergone a rapid process of economic growth (modernization). We will also expect terrorism to appear in those countries in which social injustices are more prevalent and that countries with greater social equality will tend to avoid the problem of terrorism. Finally, drawing on the discussion of the relationship between terrorism and the post-industrial society, we will expect terrorism to be present in higher levels in those countries that have advanced the farthest towards the post-industrial society.

Based on the theoretical perspective developed in this chapter, in which terrorism is closely related to the potential problems of legitimacy that may affect a state, terrorism is expected to be more of a problem in those countries in which one or more such problem of legitimacy may be identified. Thus terrorism is to be expected in states that have ethnic conflicts. Multi-ethnic states will experience greater difficulties in defining *demos* than homogeneous states. Therefore terrorism is more likely in heterogeneous states. In heterogeneous states terrorism is more likely in those states where ethnic mobilization for group rights has been unsuccessful or has been reverted. From the discussion of problems of continuity, it may be expected that terrorism is most likely in those states that have experienced civil wars, dictatorships or revolutions in the twentieth century. As for problems of integration, terrorism is to be expected in countries with substantial unintegrated fringe parties and movements, to be more specific nostalgic parties, communist parties or right-wing extremist parties (fascist or neo-Nazi). Terrorism may also be expected in states where such parties have been explicitly banned. Further, as the theoretical perspective presented here holds that terrorism is a struggle over legitimacy, it is to be expected that terrorism appears in times when the legitimacy of the state is in crisis or is being redefined. Thus terrorism is to be expected in connection with constitutional crises, when terrorism may be used to influence bonds of allegiance and loyalty.

NOTES

1. Such a negotiated achievement of independence is of course not the only way of achieving independence. Naturally, detachment from the colonial power may occur through armed struggle or may occur peacefully through an unilateral declaration of independence.
2. See Drake (1996) for a discussion of conservative terrorism, a form of terrorism related to state loyal-terrorism.
3. It is a little-doubted proposition that terrorist groups are indeed small and isolated from their environments. Such an assumption is easily challenged however by pointing to terrorist groups with a relatively large membership and with extended interaction with its environment. This typically applies to nationalist terrorist groups appealing to nationalist minorities, but even groups like the Red Brigades had extensive contact with

workplaces and the fringes of the Italian political left. Moreover, dissension over ideology and strategy is a common trait in terrorist organizations. This implies that isolation is not complete and that members of terrorist groups are in fact able to orient themselves in relation to alternatives according to reactions or expectations from the environment.

4. Tilly (1985) points to the central role violence plays in European state-building to the point of using the words organized crime in the title of his article. This analogy nevertheless also illustrates the differences between today's organized crime and the legitimacy that developed in the relationship between state-building elites and the population they sought to control.

5. This is incidentally an important argument for those who claim that terrorism is immoral in democracies: other ways exist of expressing dissatisfaction and discontent, and achieving change.

6. When collecting data, the source was inspected for relevant events in all 18 countries. However, for two countries, Finland and Iceland, no events were found.

7. For a discussion of ethnicity and related terms see Connor (1978).

3. The Event Data Approach

The purpose of the present chapter is twofold. First, to look at the determinants of the data used and to discuss the event data approach, the type of empirical approach used in this investigation. This will be done by looking at the historical development of this particular data tradition, followed by a discussion of some central characteristics of this kind of empirical data collection. Attention is then directed at terrorism and event data research in a discussion of available data sources that may be used for research on terrorism in Western Europe. Second, the data set used further in the investigation will be presented and its possibilities and limitations will be discussed.

DETERMINANTS OF THE DATA USED

The type of data used in an investigation on terrorism is partly dependent on the availability of data sets and on the possibilities for collecting and structuring new data sets. These are important factors, concerning such things as the public availability of data and the costs involved in obtaining it. Ultimately however, what kind of data is used must be determined by the problem under scrutiny in the investigation. That is to say, it is the research question that determines what data to use. Without a clear idea of what we want to investigate, and what questions we want to answer, we will not resolve any problem relating to data. This is also stressed by Gurr (1988, p. 117) when he emphasizes the 'questions first procedure' by which theoretical concerns are logically prior to the empirical.

Thus the type of data used must be tailored to the specific needs of the investigation. The data must be suited for the research purpose, which means that it must be valid and reliable. Given this work's focus on the variation in terrorism between countries, a choice has been made to use the events data approach; this allows for describing terrorism in each country and allows for connecting levels and other attributes of terrorism to other characteristics of the countries included in the study. The choice implies structuring data from third parties according to a predetermined set of variables. Attention will now turn to a closer examination and discussion of the approach and type of data chosen for this investigation, the events data approach.

EVENT DATA: HISTORY AND DEVELOPMENTS

The development of the event data approach has progressed through three phases (Merritt et al. 1993, pp. 3–6). The first attempts came early in the twentieth century, at a time when most Western countries had gone through the process of industrialization. With industrialization followed the mobilization and organization of workers. This produced concern over the frequency of industrial unrest and disputes, in particular events such as strikes. It was deemed important to have knowledge about these events and the result of this was government-produced statistics on strikes (Merritt et al. 1993, p. 3; Franzosi 1989, p. 348). Somewhat later, Lasswell and Blumenstock studied social unrest and revolutionary activity in Chicago in the 1919 to 1934 period, based on recorded events such as communist meetings and demonstrations, strikes, arrests of radicals and so on (Merritt et al. 1993, p. 3). It is indicative of the common understanding of events throughout the three phases, that from the earliest data-gathering efforts, attention has been given to incidents that represent the unexpected or the breaks in the order to which people have grown accustomed.

The definite breakthrough of the event data approach had to wait until the 1950s. This new phase in event data research saw the initiation of several major research projects based on the collection of event data (Peterson 1972). The source of the new interest came from the increased preoccupation with political development processes, especially in the field of international relations (Merritt et al. 1993, p. 3). Attention was given to countries as units of analysis and information was collected on variables such as conflict and violence. In particular, it was the behaviour of countries in the field of foreign affairs, foreign policy decision-making, that was of interest (Andriole and Hopple 1984). Attention was given to a larger number of countries, and data sets may be classified as either regional or global in scope.[1]

First among the major event data projects was the Dimensionality of Nations (DOM) project led by Rudolph J. Rummel. Originally covering the years 1955, 1956 and 1957, the DOM project collected data on 13 variables of foreign and nine variables of domestic conflict for 77 countries (Rummel 1971, p. 49–53; Merritt et al. 1993, p. 4). The focus on international relations is strongly present in Charles A. McClelland's World Event/Interaction Study (WEIS), which mapped cooperation and conflict events (interactions) between pairs of countries (McClelland and Hoggard 1969, p. 714; Merritt et al. 1993, p. 4). A data set with an original regional focus on the Middle East, The Conflict and Peace Data Bank (COPDAB) developed by Edward E. Azar, was expanded to a global coverage of 'the actions, reactions, and interactions of nation-states' (Azar 1980, p. 146). Again, the events covered are those concerning cooperation and conflict between countries (Azar 1980, pp. 146–8, Merritt et al. 1993, p. 4). The development of these and other event data sets had a substantial impact on research. In one opinion, 'The explosion of event data collection in turn triggered an avalanche of quantitative analyses designed to test hypotheses about when, how, and why nations act and interact in the international system.' (Andriole and Hopple 1984, p. 295).

The *World Handbook of Political and Social Indicators*, first published in 1964, emphasized the internal characteristics and developments of countries more strongly, and provided measures on social protest and violence in addition to peaceful or routine events such as changes of government or elections (Russett et al. 1964; Taylor and Jodice 1983, p. xiii).

By the mid-1970s, interest in event data research was on the wane. An increasing amount of criticism had been levelled against the approach. These were for a large part directed against general features in the event approach, traits common to the method of collecting event data. One important criticism pointed to the distortions inherent in separating the flow of interaction into singular events. Other critical remarks pointed to the uneven reporting of events in the sources used to construct data sets, and to the potential dangers inherent in the reliance on one or just a few sources. More substantial criticisms were directed against the specific dimensions and variables of data sets (Merritt et al. 1993, p. 6; Andriole and Hopple 1984, pp. 297, 303). Moreover, the collection of event data had become increasingly costly and time consuming.

Recent developments in the event data approach, the third phase, do not entirely redirect the research focus. Rather, they concentrate on rationalizing the collection of data. Earlier, the major task in event data collecting was to read sources, which meant reading news sources on paper, searching them for events of the type covered by the project, and then manually coding the event according to a coding scheme. Obviously, much may be gained from employing computers – partially or wholly. This is the latest phase in event data collection. Two projects deserve mention. The Global Event-Data System (GEDS) project employs an on-line news source for the 'computer-assisted identification, abstracting, and coding of daily international and domestic events' (Merritt et al. 1993, p. 7; see also Davies and McDaniel 1993). It is felt that on-line sources offer coverage that is more complete and even compared to the newspapers and other paper-based news sources traditionally used by event data collectors. An additional advantage of using on-line reports of news agencies is that the selection of secondary news sources is sidestepped.

The output of the GEDS project is a set of core events that are further developed by six specialized projects. One of these specialized projects within the GEDS project, the Kansas Event-Data Sources for Central Europe and the Middle East (KEDS) experimented with a coding process that is fully automated (Merritt et al. 1993, p. 9; Schrodt 1993). That is, computers were programmed to read on-line news sources, scan for and select relevant events, and then code these events, without human intervention in the process. Though an interesting experiment, event data collection is generally a long way from a fully automated coding process. Researchers and data collectors still have to rely on manual – or personal – reading of sources and coding of events.

WHAT IS AN EVENT?

But then, we might ask, what is an event? When thinking of what an event is, we easily think of important happenings that had a decisive influence on countries or even changed the course of history. This is a way of defining the event which has much in common with the tradition of history writing that emphasized the great man: the conflicts that started wars, the conferences and treaties that ended them; these were the important events.

In Azar's work, the event was defined as 'Any overt input and/or output of the type "who does or says what to and/or with whom and when," which may have ramifications for the behavior of an international actor or actors.' (Azar et al. 1972, p. 373). This wide definition is operationally modified with the introduction of another element, requiring that an event must be recorded and published in an open source (Azar et al. 1972, p. 374). This typically means news sources.

As emphasized in McLelland and Hoggard's definition of the event, a distinction may be made between routine actions, which are of little interest, and unusual or extraordinary actions. The former are called 'transactions', the latter 'interactions', in McLelland and Hoggard's terms. Transactions are defined as 'items of actions that have become so numerous, so commonplace, and so normal to their situation that they are accounted for conventionally in an aggregated form, usually by some unit other than item frequency'. Interactions, on the other hand, are defined as 'single action items of a non-routine, extraordinary, or newsworthy character that in some clear sense are directed across a national boundary and have, in most instances, a specific foreign target' (McLelland and Hoggard 1969, p. 713). It was the interactions that made up the events to be researched. As we can see, the field of international relations left its mark on both Azar's and McLelland and Hoggard's definition of the event. It was assumed that by researching events in these terms, it was possible to gain information on the foreign policy decision-making of countries (Peterson 1972, p. 264).

However there is a different way of conceptualizing the event. The concept of the event was first comprehensively discussed by William H. Riker (1957). His point of departure was that the concept of the event is based on the fact that social reality is complex and constantly evolving. As a consequence, humans divide this reality into comprehensible pieces, known as events. Thus dividing social reality into events is a result of our need to impose order on a complex reality. Though social reality is made up of processes of continuous actions, we have to break it up into smaller units to be able to understand it. This implies imposing boundaries on the continuous stream of actions in reality, and is how events are formed. These boundaries are artificial, and this implies that the delineation of an event is subjective to some extent. This subjective element is limited to the fixation of the event in time and does not imply that the other contents of the event are also subjective.

In other words the boundaries of events are temporal, that is they define the point in time when events start and end. Imposing such boundaries helps us identify the three other essential components of the event: the actors, the actions and the targets. Thus an event may be defined, as Riker does:

> An event is the motion and action occurring between an initial situation and a terminal situation such that all and only the movers and actors of the initial situation (or the components into which they are subdivided or the constructs into which they are formed in the course of the event) are included in the terminal situation. (Riker 1957, p. 61)

What is important in research on events is to compare the situations at the beginning and the end of the event. The situation may be defined as 'an arrangement and condition of movers and actors in a specified, instantaneous, and spatially extended location' (Riker 1957, p. 61). It is the extent of the difference between the state of affairs at the end of the event as compared to the state of affairs at the beginning of the event, which is of interest in research on events.

Riker warned that ambiguity is a major difficulty for research on events (Riker 1957, pp. 62–70). Ambiguous events may result from a number of circumstances, most importantly the failure to define the time limits of the event properly and to identify the actors involved. The risk of ambiguity increases when working with large events. Such large events may involve many actors, and may also cover a great time span during which some actors may enter and exit as the event unfolds. Consequently it is difficult to delimit the event in time, and decide which actors are actually part of the event. Riker therefore recommended working with small events, which are easier to delimit precisely and are thus less likely to be subject to ambiguity (Riker 1957, pp. 62, 67–8).

At the micro level then, events are units of action, defined by time limits defining the beginning and end, and consisting of an actor, an action and a target of the action. This is in line with the definition of the political event presented by Taylor and Jodice:

An event is a noteworthy occurrence that represents a substantial departure from a previous pattern of behavior by a state and its constituent agencies, groups or individuals. It is specific in time and place and generally is a physical action, although verbal utterances and symbolic statements are sometimes called events. (Taylor and Jodice 1983, p. 8).

This implies, as we shall discuss in detail later, a crucial dependence on news sources. The news sources decide whether something is potentially registered as an event.

TERRORISM AND EVENT DATA

As we have seen above, many event data sets exist. Several of these concentrate on foreign affairs or international relations. Some, however, focus on domestic conflict. The *World Handbook of Political and Social Indicators* contains indicators on domestic political protest behaviour and domestic political violence bordering on terrorism (Taylor and Jodice 1983, pp. 19–47). Data has been presented for the 1948 to 1977 period. The indicators of political protest are protest demonstrations, regime support demonstrations and political strikes. Violent behaviour is covered in the indicators of riots, armed attacks and assassinations. The two latter categories are close to terrorism. The armed attacks category cover 'all organized political violence in the country' (Taylor and Jodice 1983, p. 37). Assassinations are counted separately and cover 'politically motivated murder of a national leader, a high government official, or a politician' (Taylor and Jodice 1983, p. 43). The political motive is established through the position and identity of the victim, because the motivation of the assassin is hard to establish. A number of properties are coded for the categories of political violence. These are properties such as target, issue, number of participants, the organizational base of participants, injuries, deaths, property damage, duration, location and geographical extent. Unfortunately the global scope of the *World Handbook* made it impractical to employ lists of actor organizations and groups for each country (Taylor and Jodice 1983, p. 53). Instead generic terms are used to indicate the ideological inclination of the actor. Consequently, interesting information about the organizational identity of armed attackers and the organized challenge in armed attacks is lost. Nevertheless the *World Handbook of Political and Social Indicators* has some indicators that may well have been used to study terrorism. The weakness is that, though the data set covers 30 years, it ends in the mid-1970s. That is, it covers only the first few years of one of the most interesting periods in West European terrorism.

Those who have set out to collect event data specifically on terrorism have often tended to construct and publish chronologies, lists of terrorist attacks and other important incidents ordered by date. Though chronologies on domestic terrorism exist, there is a tendency to concentrate on what is labelled 'international terrorism'. The term 'international terrorism' is usually explained as terrorist attacks in which more than one country is involved in one way or another, usually that a terrorist group from one country performs attacks in another. This is not always the case however, and other operationalizations may also be used, such as the rule that terrorism is international terrorism when a terrorist group consists of people from more than one country or when people from more than one country are found among the victims of terrorist violence. However it is not always clear what it is that makes a terrorism attack a case of international terrorism. Sometimes foreign funding or support, or just foreign ties of a looser or more informal kind, is invoked to put the label of international terrorism on a group or an attack. Even more loosely, international terrorism may be cast as 'terrorism abroad', seen from the point of view of the person using the term, even when wholly domestic in both perpetrators and victims.

One of the best-known chronologies is the RAND–St Andrews Chronology of International Terrorist Incidents. This chronology was originally developed and maintained at the RAND Corporation in the USA, but was later relocated to St Andrews University in the United Kingdom. In the RAND–St Andrews Chronology international terrorism is defined as 'incidents in which terrorists go abroad to strike their targets, select their victims or targets that have connections with a foreign state (e.g. diplomats, foreign businessmen, offices of foreign corporations) or create international incidents by attacking airline passengers, personnel and equipment. It excludes violence carried out by terrorists within their own country against their own nationals, and terrorism perpetrated by governments against their own citizens' (Hoffman and Hoffman 1996, p. 89). The chronology covers the period from 1968 and is regularly updated.

ITERATE, or International Terrorism: Attributes of Terrorist Events, is another data set on international terrorism. Again the time period covered runs from 1968. What makes terrorism international in this project is apparently that 'the action's ramifications may transcend national boundaries through the nationality or foreign ties of its perpetrators, its location, the nature of its institutional or human victims, or the mechanics of its resolution' (Mickolus and Heyman 1981, p. 154). The definition of international terrorism is quite loose, as evident from a comment in the code book to ITERATE in which it is said that 'While many of these attacks are considered to be domestic terrorism, such attacks are included if the terrorists traverse a natural geographical boundary to conduct attacks on the metropole, e.g. Northern Irish attacks on the main British island, Puerto Rican attacks outside the island, and attacks within Israel by Palestinian refugees' (Mickolus 1991, p. 4). While ITERATE seems to include some terrorist events relevant to this project, the emphasis is still too much on the border-transcending character of terrorism to be able to give a satisfactory picture of domestic terrorism conflicts.

Many more data sets exist, mostly covering limited periods of time or selected countries or conflict areas (Schmid et al. 1988, pp. 137–88). Official statistics offer yet more sources of data. However such sources are difficult to compare across countries, because they employ different counting and coding rules, naturally based in the legal frameworks of the different countries. Official statistics on terrorism or related behaviour exist for a number of countries, most commonly those that have experienced terrorism as a persistent problem over time.

What is needed to throw light on the questions raised by this project is a data set covering Western Europe for a substantial period of time, preferably the entire period since the Second World War. Such a data set is available in the Terrorism in Western Europe: Event Data (TWEED) data set.

TERRORISM IN WESTERN EUROPE: EVENT DATA

Why yet another event data set? The uses of statistics in terrorism research generally tend to repeat or reproduce the figures presented by other writers without any evaluation or discussion on how these figures came about, how they were produced or to what degree they can be trusted. Though many different perspectives and approaches to terrorism may be employed, we almost always return to the question of the magnitude of the problem. This boils down to figures on terrorism, most commonly the number of attacks or the number of deaths resulting from terrorist attacks.

What is TWEED?

The TWEED data set, which is collected and constructed by the author, contains information on terrorism-related events in West European countries. Data has been collected for the period from 1950 to 1995.[2] The coding scheme includes 18 West European countries, 16 of which returned events for the data set (see Table 3.1). In total, 10 239 events are included in TWEED. Of these, 87 per cent are actions by terrorist groups or actors, the remaining events are government actions directed mainly against terrorists.

For each event, both properties of the action and properties of the actors have been recorded.[3] As for the action side of the event, we find such recorded properties as the date on which the incident happened, the country where it took place, the identity of the actor, number of injuries and deaths, identity of the victims, types of action and government reaction. On the actor side, in addition

Table 3.1   Countries covered in the TWEED data set

Austria	Italy
Belgium	Luxembourg
Denmark	Netherlands
Finland [a]	Norway
France	Portugal
Germany (Federal Republic) [b]	Spain
Greece	Sweden
Iceland [a]	Switzerland
Ireland (Republic of)	United Kingdom

Notes:

[a] Did not return events.

[b] West Germany to October 1990, united Germany after October 1990.

to registering the identity of the actor, properties such as the actor's regional connection, ideological profile and attitude to the state have also been recorded. The long period of time that has been covered and the possibility for investigating the organizational terrorist challenge to the state through the identification of terrorist actors, is a major strength of the TWEED data set.

TWEED is based on a single news source, *Keesing's Record of World Events* formerly known as *Keesing's Contemporary Archives*.[4] Why has *Keesing's* been used as the source for the data set? *Keesing's* offers continuous coverage of international news since 1931. It was originally published in the Netherlands, in four languages, but is now published in England.[5] The emphasis in the coverage is to present essential and factual information on prominent or important political, social and economic developments in the countries of the world. This includes conventional developments in the political system such as elections and government changes, important policy developments, and so on, but developments concerning political opposition are also covered. Irregular political participation, such as political violence, is included in the coverage of political opposition activities.

Keesing's works from news sources, mostly newspapers, news magazines and news services, supplemented when needed by information from government or non-governmental sources. The editing of reports takes place after the event has unfolded, which gives the opportunity for editors to compare and evaluate the reporting of sources and to present not only condensed summaries of events, but also corrected, factual information.

Source Coverage: The Reliability of Event Data

Event data sets, including TWEED, are based on reported events, and as we have already seen this is actually incorporated into the operational definition of the event in Azar's approach. Collectors of event data sets are in other words dependent on open, publicly available sources. In practice this means news sources. One consequence of this fact is that the methodological discussion over event data has concentrated on the problem of source coverage, that is differences between sources in the reporting of events. Difficulties concerning the sources used to construct event data sets have been seen as a major source of low reliability for such data sets, and has lead to a fear that 'Contradictory findings in the field of events data analysis might be entirely due to the problem of "source coverage"' (Azar et al. 1972, p. 375).

There is no doubt that the sources used to compile event data sets have uneven coverage of events. Taylor and Jodice mention six difficulties with news reporting which may affect the reliability of the sources and consequently also the reliability of the event data set (Taylor and Jodice 1983, p. 178–279). First, sources may display sporadic sensitivity, which means that the source's selection procedures are not consistent and that they tend to report intensely on selected developments. Second, there is a tendency, related to the first factor, to report spectacular events or events that represent departures from the usual. For those who study political violence, this is not necessarily a disadvantage. To the contrary, it may imply that exactly those events we are interested in are in fact reported. Third, sources may have a regional bias leading to more attention given to particular areas or countries. Fourth, the type of event reported for one country may differ from the kind of event reported for another. Fifth, reporting may change over time, so that the attention and reporting of certain events may decrease. For those studying political violence, this represents an important problem in cases where political violence has become the order of the day. As violence erupts more and more frequently, the threshold for reporting might get higher. Sixth, reports on developments within a country may change over time. According to Taylor and Jodice (1983, p. 179), these six difficulties apply most strongly to news reporting on Third World countries and do not so much affect reporting on the Western world where coverage is more stable and continuous.

Sources, then, differ in the selection, presentation and interpretation of what happens. This is due to several reasons. On the one hand, the selection and the angle of presentation is influenced by the editorial policies and the ideological or political commitments of the news source. On the other hand, practical factors such as limitations of space, the availability of background information and news wire reports, or correspondents on the spot, is also of importance. When constructing event data sets, it is important to select sources that are adequate to throw light on the research questions posed and cover adequately the countries under analysis (Hazlewood and West 1974, p. 317). Two aspects have typically been discussed in two respects: the use of global versus regional sources, and the use of single versus multiple sources. The assumption is that coverage will be more complete, that is, more events will be reported and more information will be available for each event, when using regional and/or multiple sources.

The point of departure in the debate over global versus regional sources is that sources are either global in coverage – that is they aim at reporting events in all the countries of the world – or they are regional – that is they report on a selection of geographically neighbouring countries. The fact that event data sets tended to rely on one large source has been an important point for much of the discussion on source coverage. Often the source used to find events anywhere in the world was the *New York Times*, or the *New York Times Index*. This gives rise to the question of how correct a picture of events such a source will give when studying a region such as for instance the Middle East. It has then been suggested event data collectors either add a source with a specific regional interest or let the regional source replace the global source altogether.

The discussion above developed out of event data collections that aimed at collecting data for the world. However in our context with Western Europe as the primary area of interest, the same difficulties occur. The logic of the source coverage argument may thus be extended to regional versus national sources, and further to national versus local sources. It is practically always possible to move one step closer to the place where the event took place. In doing so, however, the number of relevant sources increases dramatically, and with it the cost in time and money of reading and coding sources. In parallel with the increasing number of relevant sources, the language skill requirements increase (except in cases when the study applies to regions of the world with a common language). In effect this makes it practically impossible to use national or local sources without adjusting – that is lowering – the number of countries under study.

As we have seen, the discussion over global versus regional sources rapidly develops into a discussion over single versus multiple sources. The arguments are similar: adding more sources will increase the number of reported events and the information available on these events. By adding sources it will be possible to achieve more complete coverage. Thus by using multiple sources it is more likely that the data collected will reflect the correct distribution of events in reality (Jackman and Boyd 1979, p. 435). Using more sources will make it possible to clarify what really happened, to sort out ambiguity and to present and collect complete and corrected information.

Investigations into source coverage have found evidence for differences in coverage. Azar et al. used eight different sources to collect a data set on events involving Egypt and Israel in the 1955 to 1958 period. They discovered, somewhat surprisingly perhaps, given the assumption that regional sources will report more events than global sources, that 'the *New York Times Index* reported twice as many events as the *Middle East Journal*.' (Azar et al. 1972, p. 380). Moreover sources did not report the same events.[6] Azar et al. concluded with a warning against using a single source for collecting event data sets, as the conclusions about the subject matter might be entirely explained by differences in source coverage.

On the other hand, Jackman and Boyd investigated the effect of using different sources in measuring mass political violence in 30 African countries. Information was collected from five sources, and different data sets were compared (Jackman and Boyd 1979, pp. 439–40). Their conclusions were that data sets collected from different sources, and using different numbers of sources, produce different results. However they also concluded that these differences cannot be entirely explained by source coverage, as differences in definitions and the procedures for coding events may also have an effect. Jackman and Boyd warn that the advantages of using multiple sources may easily be overestimated. Furthermore Hazlewood and West found that although the number of events was different when using different sources, the structures in the data set remained unchanged. This means that adding more sources will add more events, but will not lead to different conclusions as the structure in the data set is not changed. In a way, the event data collected represented a sample of events. These conclusions are supported by Taylor and Jodice.

All in all, selection of sources, whether one or many, global or regional, is based on a judgement of costs and benefits. What is important is to select the source that produces the best results with the resources available.

The Reliability of TWEED

The data set used here will be affected by the difficulties and effects of source coverage discussed in the preceding section. The data set, TWEED, is based on a single source, *Keesing's*, with global coverage, though some use it as a regional source because of its excellent coverage of Western Europe (Taylor and Jodice 1983, p. 182). *Keesing's* is generally judged to be a good source of information. Taylor and Jodice describe the source as 'an excellent source of data on domestic conflict as well as on foreign affairs,' and add that *Keesing's* is 'remarkably well organized and is easy to use'(Taylor and Jodice 1983, p. 12). These two researchers are of the opinion that 'Coverage of the Western world is certainly one of the journal's greatest strengths'(Taylor and Jodice 1983, p. 13). With the exception of national newspapers, there are no rival sources capable of presenting continuous coverage of all West European countries for the entire period following the Second World War.

Using *Keesing's* seems therefore to be a natural choice. TWEED aims at including all events falling under the operational definition of terrorism that are reported by *Keesing's*. Every volume from 1950 to 1996 has been examined carefully to uncover events.[7] Entries for the countries under investigation have been read, cross-references examined and indices checked. Coding, in three separate rounds, was done by a single coder.[8]

Still, the source used to construct TWEED is far removed from the close national or local perspectives of the many potential alternative sources. Thus we expect that under-reporting is taking place, so that fewer events are selected and reported in *Keesing's* than actually are taking place. As a consequence we may expect TWEED to provide conservative figures on West European terrorism. Nevertheless we do not expect this to be a major source of low reliability for TWEED. We are dealing with countries in Western Europe, countries which have had well-developed news media systems for the entire period we are looking at. Thus *Keesing's* has had good sources available to work from and is in turn a good source for researchers to utilize. *Keesing's* is attentive to developments in Western Europe, and has had a particular interest in reporting political violence for the entire period covered by our investigation.

Comparisons with other data sets confirms that the figures in TWEED are conservative. Compared to official statistics on terrorism in Italy, TWEED shows dramatically lower figures. Figures from the Italian Ministry of the Interior reports 14 591 terrorist attacks in Italy from 1969 to 1987 (Jamieson 1989, p. 20), which makes an average of two terrorist attacks every day for the entire 19-year period. TWEED, on the other hand, only reports 255 terrorist attacks. However the difference is less dramatic than appears at first sight. The Interior Ministry figures are based on a loose definition of terrorism that includes vaguely defined attacks on civil servants and the 'authority of the state'.[9] The Italian example demonstrates how difficult it is to base comparisons between countries on official statistics.

Compared to the figures on armed attacks in the *World Handbook of Political and Social Indicators,* TWEED again produces lower figures, as shown in Figure 3.1. TWEED consistently reports fewer terrorist attacks than the armed attacks reported by the *World Handbook* (Taylor and Jodice 1983, pp. 39–42). For some of the countries differences are substantial, for instance the differences in figures for the United Kingdom. However it should be emphasized that the two data sets agree on the ranking of the four countries worst hit by violence (the United Kingdom, France, Italy and Spain). Within the group of countries in the middle range when it comes to the number of attacks, TWEED is in disagreement with the *World Handbook* on the ranking of the countries. The *World Handbook* ranks Greece and Ireland before Portugal and Germany, whereas TWEED ranks Portugal and Germany before Greece and Ireland. It should be noted however that the differences between the countries in this

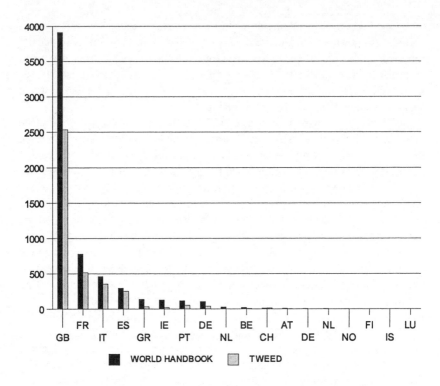

*Figure 3.1   Number of armed attacks according to World Handbook of
             Political and Social Indicators and number of terrorist attacks
             according to TWEED in West European countries, 1953–77*

group are small in both data sets.

Differences in definitions may again be one source of divergent figures, as the
armed attacks category may encompass more than terrorist attacks. The *World
Handbook* figures for armed attacks include, for instance, attacks carried out by
government actors. In cases where non-state actors initiated an attack and the
government agents responded violently, the *World Handbook* coded two
events, of which the state action formed a separate event unit (Taylor and Jodice
1983, pp. 29, 37–8). This may explain the differences in the figures between the
two data sets, not least for the United Kingdom where the conflict in Northern
Ireland has been so important. However the *World Handbook* used more
sources than TWEED, and that may also explain the differences.

A second possible bias, reporting favouring the large countries, is not likely
to be a major source of low reliability for the TWEED data set. Until 1988, when
a separate publication was set up to cover the United Kingdom in detail,

Keesing's reported more extensively on the United Kingdom than on other countries. From 1988 on, the United Kingdom is given coverage in the same manner as other countries. It should be added that the extensive coverage prior to 1988 mainly focused on parliamentary affairs, and thus has little effect on the reporting of political violence. The reporting of all countries covered by TWEED was stable and continuous throughout the years we are interested in.

Extensive reporting of selected actors or events may be a third possible source of bias. Reporting is likely to favour those actors that fought their way into the political arena, that is the organized terrorists that persist over time rather than the sporadic individual terrorist. Thus under-reporting is likely to affect sporadic attacks without organized backing that do not kill, and inflict little or no injuries, or cause little damage. On the other hand, we expect attention towards organized terrorist groups to be good, and we judge TWEED to be a reliable source of their activities.

Another aspect of this bias in reporting of events is the uneven coverage of acts of terrorism. Reporting on terrorist events will be influenced by the magnitude of the event in terms of deaths, injuries or damage, or may be influenced by the social status of the victims of violence. Attention is likely to increase with the social status of the victims and also increase with the number of victims. *Keesing's* directs most attention to terrorist events aimed at national political figures and leading businessmen. These are the events that get an attention of several pages. Other events may be described in a sentence or two.[10] As the latter are the more numerous, this means that there are limits to how much information we are able to extract from *Keesing's*. At any rate, *Keesing's* always reports basic and factual information about events, such as where and when the event took place, how many people were killed, who claimed responsibility for the attack, or who other actors attributed responsibility to. It is this kind of factual information that has been recorded in the TWEED data set, and the reliability is expected to be high.

Though we should be aware of the effects of source coverage, we nevertheless conclude that TWEED has acceptable reliability. It employs a source that offers continuous coverage of the region of interest, a source that directs attention to developments of both a regular and an irregular nature. Though details available may be scarce, and under-reporting may be a problem, the source used by TWEED, *Keesing's*, is a unique source which is ideal for compiling a multi-country data set.

CONCLUDING REMARKS

This chapter discussed the event data approach in general, looked at its fundamental assumptions, traced its history and development and looked at sources of uncertainty for event data sets. More specifically, the TWEED data set was discussed and some of its strengths and weaknesses were pointed out. TWEED offers data on terrorism for 18 countries in the time period from 1950 to 1995 in which it is possible to identify the organizational terrorist challenge. Such a data set is not available anywhere else. TWEED offers benefits compared to the one-country, one-actor or one-action approach in that it permits a broader comparative approach in which terrorism in several countries can be studied over time. We do not argue the superiority of the data set, but argue the possibility of pursuing what we feel is a neglected approach in the study of terrorism: the comparative approach.

NOTES

1. A third type of data set, the event-specific data set, takes a specific important event as the point of departure and event data is collected for the events that occurred before this decisive event (Merritt et al.1993, p. 4).
2. Originally the data set covered the 1950 to 1990 time period (cf. Engene 1994, p. 65), but was afterwards updated.
3. For the original Norwegian language coding scheme, see Engene (1994, pp. 247–75).
4. The publication, usually known only as *Keesing's*, changed name in 1986. Pages have been numbered continuously since publication started, and when referring to *Keesing's* in the present work, only the page number will be quoted.
5. The editorial team has been based in England since 1989. The original languages of the publication were Dutch, English, French and German. There are still Dutch and German editions, as well as a separate American edition (*Facts on File*).
6. In fact only 9.7 per cent of all recorded events were reported in both the *Middle East Journal* and the *New York Times Index* (Azar et al. 1972, p. 381).
7. The 1996 volume was examined for events taking place in 1995. *Keesing's* is always some months behind in its coverage and it also sometimes provides coverage summarizing events taking place over a longer period of time.
8. This single coder is the author of the present work.
9. See Merkl's (1986, pp. 359–60) discussion on the reliability of official statistics in the Italian case. Some alternative figures on terrorism in Italy are also presented there.
10. The reporting of some of the killings of the Rote Armée Fraktion and Brigate Rosse compared to the events of the Basque provinces or Northern Ireland may demonstrate these differences in coverage. See *Keesing's* pp. 28918–28924 for the coverage of the killings of Siegfried Buback, Jürgen Ponto and Hanns-Martin Schleyer by the RAF and *Keesing's* pp. 29053–29056 for the kidnapping and killing of Aldo Moro by the BR. Compare with the coverage of events in Northern Ireland, for instance *Keesing's* pp. 27419–27420 or in the Basque provinces *Keesing's* pp. 28936–28937.

4. A Regional Empirical Overview

In order to discover the general patterns and developments concerning terrorism in Western Europe since 1950, this chapter will present a general overview of the evidence collected on terrorism for the region as a whole. First we will look at the occurrence of terrorism over time, terrorism with both an internal and an external origin. Then we will then look closer at other characteristic patterns of domestic terrorism, such as the intensity of violence and the ideological tendencies behind the terrorist violence. Finally, by presenting aggregate evidence on dimensions concerning perpetrators, the chapter will address the question of the degree to which terrorism in Western Europe has presented an organized challenge to the states.

TERRORISM: INTERNAL AND EXTERNAL

From 1950 to 1995, according to the TWEED data set, West European terrorists have been responsible for 8916 terrorist attacks causing a total of 2777 deaths. The figure for the number of attacks is influenced by a high number of firebombs, 14 per cent of all domestic terrorist attacks in Western Europe in the 1950 to 1995 period were firebombs (see Table 4.1). Many of these attacks were of the Molotov cocktail type, which had to be registered in the data set because not enough information was available to justify excluding them. Firebombs may be dangerous and lethal in some circumstances, for instance when thrown into a building. In other situations they cause little damage and represent a modest threat, as when demonstrators throw petrol bombs landing in a street. A majority of the firebombs included in TWEED were thrown in conjunction with demonstrations and protest, almost all of them in the United Kingdom (the Northern Ireland conflict). Later in this work we will exclude from the analysis firebombs for which there is only an unidentified perpetrator and also firebombs that do not kill or injure. This is done to avoid difficulties of bias involved if these events are included.[1]

Compared with the annual figures of domestic or within-region terrorist attacks, relatively few international terrorist attacks have taken place in Western Europe. In Figure 4.1 figures are presented for the annual number of domestic (1950–95) and international terrorist attacks (1968–91) in Western Europe. The

Table 4.1   Types of terrorist attacks, 1950–95, TWEED

Type of attack	Percent of all attacks	Percent of all attacks, all firebombs excluded
Bombs, explosions	39.4	45.8
Armed attack	18.5	21.5
Firebombs	14.0	–
Car bombs	1.7	2.0
Fires	0.9	1.1
Kidnaps	0.9	1.0
Letter bombs	0.7	0.8
Other attacks	0.7	0.8
Rockets, grenades	0.3	0.3
Unsuccessful attacks	1.2	1.4
Missing data	21.9	25.4
Total	99.9	100.1
	N = 8916	N = 7665

figures for the international attacks are from the ITERATE III data set mentioned earlier,[2] and include attacks by actors with origins outside the 18 West European countries covered by the analysis in the present work.[3] These figures are compared to the terrorist events from the TWEED data set, adjusted for low-intensity firebomb attacks from unidentified actors that did not kill or injure. As we can see, the level of terrorist violence from actors originating from outside the region is considerably lower than that for within-region terrorism. In fact, domestic terrorism totally dominates the terrorism scene in Western Europe as far as the volume of terrorist attacks is concerned.

International terrorism also seems to have been a comparatively stable element once appearing in Western Europe, though international terrorism rose to a peak in 1972 and levels of violence of this kind rose somewhat again in the years from 1980 to 1987. In comparison, internal or domestic terrorism produces a higher level of violence, but one that is much more fluctuating. While the extra-regional international terrorism is more or less stable, domestic terrorism shows a peak in the early 1970s and again in the early 1980s. We also note the outbursts of domestic terrorism, though the volume is lower than in the campaigns of later decades, from 1956 to 1959 and again from 1961 to 1962. The level of domestic terrorism is remarkably lower towards the last year for which figures are available, 1995, than in the decades following 1970.

We cannot say exactly when extra-regional international terrorism appeared

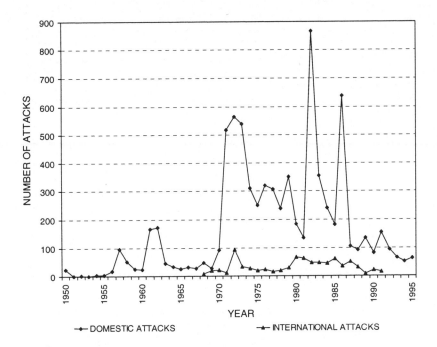

Figure 4.1   *Number of international terrorist attacks per year according to ITERATE III, 1968–91 (N = 811), and number of domestic terrorist attacks per year according to TWEED, 1950–95 (N = 7743), corrected for firebombs*

in Western Europe, as the ITERATE figures are from 1968 onwards only. We note however that for the two years prior to 1970, figures for the two types of terrorism are close to each other. Often, 1968 is seen as the starting point of terrorism, domestic as well as international.[4] The TWEED figures indicate that this is not entirely justified as far as internal terrorism is concerned, since important domestic terrorist campaigns took place before that year. We are thus, from this data, in no position to say that domestic terrorism is a consequence of the introduction of this method of political struggle to Western Europe by extra-regional actors taking acts of international terrorism into Western Europe. Thus we should be careful in suggesting that the domestic terrorism of the West European countries is a result of contagious international terrorism originating with infectious neighbouring regions.[5]

The distribution of deaths resulting from international and domestic terrorism, by year, is presented in Figure 4.2. Again, the level of within-region (or domestic) terrorism is generally higher than the level of international terrorism.

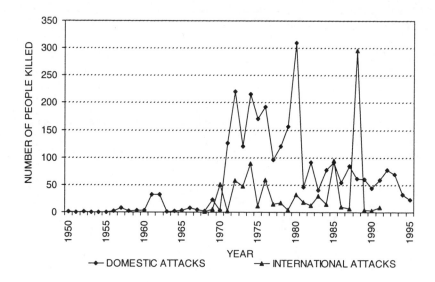

Figure 4.2   *Number of people killed in international terrorist attacks per*
year according to ITERATE III, 1968–91 (N = 899), and
number of people killed in domestic terrorist attacks per year
according to TWEED, 1950–95 (N = 2777)

However we note larger variations in the levels of deaths caused by international terrorism, and we also note that for a selection of years deaths caused by international terrorism approach, and even surpass, the number of deaths caused by domestic terrorism. This indicates that while the number of international terrorist attacks is lower compared with the number of attacks with origin within Western Europe, international terrorism tends to strike hard when occurring. The dramatic death toll of international terrorism in Western Europe for 1988 for instance is the result of a single incident in which an airliner was struck by an explosion and hit the ground in a village in the United Kingdom.[6]

The number of people killed in incidents of domestic terrorism in Western Europe remained low throughout the 1950s and 1960s, with the exception of two years in the early 1960s and one year in the late 1960s. Death tolls resulting from domestic terrorism increased dramatically from 1971 onwards. The number killed per year remained high for a decade, peaking in 1980 with 310 deaths resulting from domestic terrorism in the West European countries. As many as 85 of these were killed in the worst incident of domestic terrorism recorded in the TWEED data set, the bomb that exploded at the railway station in Bologna in Italy. After 1980 the number of people killed per year is lower, with the 1994 and 1995 figures

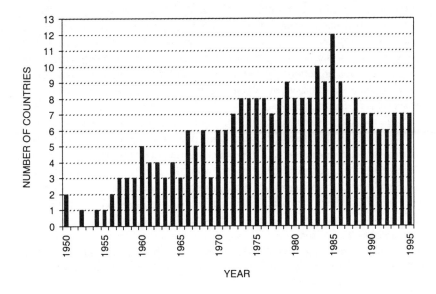

Figure 4.3   Number of West European countries affected by domestic acts of terrorism by year according to TWEED, 1950–95

back at the levels of the peak years of the 1950s and 1960s.

If we look at the number of countries affected by internal (domestic) terrorism each year, as in Figure 4.3, we note that with increased levels of terrorism in terms of activity, more countries are involved. Thus terrorism may be said to be a problem that spreads to more countries over time. Once again the early 1970s represents the years when more countries got involved, but it is 1985 that represents the year in which the problem peaks in terms of the number of countries affected by terrorist actions. In 1985, 12 out of 18 countries covered by the TWEED data set experienced one or more terrorist attack. The number of countries affected by domestic terrorism subsequently dropped somewhat.

What made 1970 or thereabouts such an important turning point for terrorism, external and internal? One reason might be increased opportunities for people to take advantage of terrorist techniques, that is 'permissive causes' in Crenshaw's terminology. Technologically it might have become easier to acquire the capacity to carry out terrorist actions, for instance through new types of explosives. Furthermore, the 1960s marked a turning point in the development of television that was soon taken advantage of by terrorists. In this respect the three coordinated aircraft hijacks by the Popular Front for the Liberation of Palestine (PFLP) in September 1970 set an unprecedented example of what terrorists could achieve, not only operationally but also in having their actions and views distributed worldwide. Television played a crucial part in this (Schmid and de Graaf 1982, pp. 28–9; Bjørgo and Heradstveit 1993, p. 127). The PFLP and the media organizations used each other for mutual benefit. The publicity created by this spectacular action – the three aircraft were blown up in front of the television camera – may have served to make terrorism a more attractive mode of action for potential terrorists.

Nevertheless the possibilities of terrorism created by advances in technology will not be turned into terrorist action unless there are people motivated towards the use of such means. Again the years immediately before and after 1970 represent an important turning point, with the increased radicalization of students. Some groups were more radicalized than others, and a few turned to terrorism. Moreover, the radicalization of students left its mark on segments of the population that so far had been mobilized by conservative or even fascist ideologies. Whereas the mobilization of national minorities through the 1950s and 1960s had been right-wing, for instance in South Tyrol, mobilization on the part of national minorities turned increasingly left-wing in the wake of the student revolt (Allardt 1979, pp. 19–22; Beer 1977, pp. 145–6). The mobilization of national minorities, peaceful as well as violent, only increased throughout the 1970s.

TERROR BY DESIGN: THE INTENSITY OF TERRORIST ATTACKS

Noting the high frequency of domestic terrorist attacks in Western Europe, especially since the 1970s, it is somewhat surprising to learn that only just above a quarter of the attacks, 27 per cent, inflict injury or death on people. Moreover, still fewer attacks, 19 per cent (adjusted for firebombs), are lethal. Again, the decade following 1970 stands out as particularly violent. As violence levels rise, so does also the number of attacks that leave people dead. These figures raise some questions. Considering the fact that only one attack in five kills, can we then say that terrorists aim to kill? And further, are terrorists out to kill as many people as possible?[7]

The terrorist's ability to kill is determined by several factors. The type of attack, based on the type of arms employed, may influence both the possibility of killing and the death toll. As we have seen from Table 4.1 above, terrorists carry out mainly two kinds of attacks. Firstly and most prominently, terrorists use bombs and other kinds of explosives, and secondly and less prominently, but still significantly, terrorists use armed attacks.[8]

Typically the bomb attack involves little risk for the terrorist themselves of

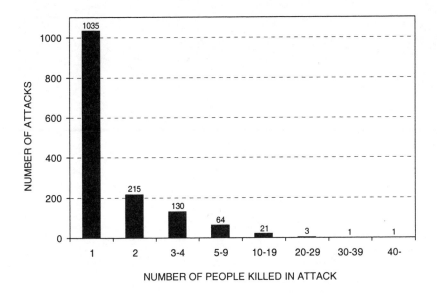

Figure 4.4 Lethality of terrorist attacks: number of people killed in terrorist attacks that resulted in loss of life, 1950–95, TWEED (N = 1470)

getting killed or injured, but the acts may inflict much damage on the victims of violence. How much damage, depends on where and when the bomb is set off. Whilst more than 90 per cent of ordinary bombs do not kill at all, those bombs placed in cars kill in more than half of cases. Where there are cars there is traffic and where there is traffic there are people. Thus the bomb may be designed to kill many people, not only by its explosive power, but also by being placed at a time and in a place which the terrorists know will be crowded. This is not to say that terrorists do design bomb attacks in such a way. Quite the opposite, some terrorists are actually known to design their attacks to inflict as little personal death and injury as possible by setting off bombs against material targets or in public places at night when no or few people are around. Some of the groups that are not alien to taking life are known to give warnings ahead of attacks, so that the scene of the attack can be evacuated. Nevertheless predicting precisely the outcome of a bomb attack in terms of death and injury is difficult for terrorists, as there are so many factors that they cannot control, and therefore the bomb attack always involves the risk to the life of people. That is part of the reason why bombs are set off.

The design element may be stronger in the armed attack type of terrorist act.

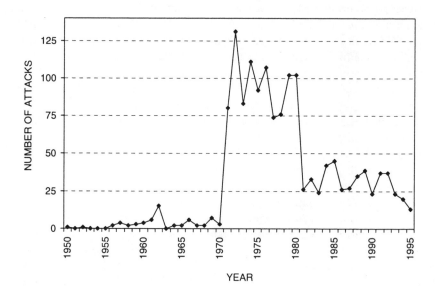

Figure 4.5   Number of attacks causing death by year, 1950–95, TWEED
            (N = 1470)

Here terrorists themselves are present during the attack and risk more in terms
of personal death and injury – and arrest – compared to the bomb attack,
especially if attacking a high-security target. If we look at the TWEED data, we
see that whereas only one bomb in ten results in the death of a victim, armed
attacks are much more likely to kill: 43 per cent of the armed attacks performed
since 1950 in Western Europe left people dead. Nevertheless, even with the
knowledge that armed attacks are more lethal than terrorist bomb attacks, we
must conclude that the intention to kill or maim seems not to be present in all
terrorist attacks, not even a majority of these attacks.

We may then ask: when terrorists are out to kill, are they out to kill as many
people as possible? The material available to us, TWEED, does not support the
assumption that terrorists are out to kill as many people as possible. We know
already that only one terrorist attack in five in Western Europe kills people. From
Figure 4.4 we can see how many people are killed in the lethal attacks. It is
evident from the figures that even the lethal attacks are limited in scope. Of these
attacks, about 70 per cent kill one person only, and a further 14.6 per cent kill two
people. We are left with 6 per cent of the attacks with a death toll of five people
or more. In the entire period under investigation, five attacks caused more than
20 deaths, the worst of which took the lives of 85 people. Although three of the

five most lethal attacks took place in 1980 and another in 1987, there is no clear evidence in the TWEED material to suggest that lethal attacks are becoming more frequent. As can be seen from Figure 4.5, the number of attacks that caused death fell sharply after 1980. Again the 1970s stand out as the violent decade.

In other words, the overwhelming bulk of terrorist attacks does not kill. Those that do kill, take the lives of relatively few people. The highly lethal terrorist attacks are known, but relatively uncommon. If the purpose is not to kill as many as possible, or even not to kill at all, what then is the point of setting off bombs or carrying out armed attacks? We recall from the definition in Chapter 1 and the figures in Chapter 2, that the victims terrorists aim their violence at are not the ones they seek to influence by a political message. The violence is used to gain attention in order to provoke some sort of reaction from various groups in society. Getting that attention does not necessarily require maximizing the death toll. Striking indiscriminately by maximizing the death toll will maximize attention. Such acts will create much noise. That however may also be a drawback for some terrorists. The risk is that the violence and mayhem overshadow the political message. Terrorist acts are thus designed to kill many in cases when the terrorists do not want to distribute a particularly complex political message, when they are indifferent to the outcry, or are aiming at provoking exactly that kind of negative response. By striking selectively, the terrorist may want to maximize attention towards the actor and not the act itself, leaving more room for designed publicity. Striking selectively means creating minimal mayhem by striking symbolically important targets, or it involves hitting at socially or politically prominent targets.[9] It is no coincidence that terrorist abductions (kidnaps), though such acts only makes up 1 per cent of the events, are among the terrorist acts that get the most attention.[10]

IDEOLOGICAL TENDENCIES OF TERRORIST ACTORS

Attempting now to take one step closer to identifying who the responsible terrorist actors are, we can break down the annual figures for the number of terrorist attacks by the ideological tendency of the acting group. To do this we have employed rough categories, firstly making a distinction between actors ideologically belonging on the extreme left and extreme right, and secondly making a distinction between actors motivated by these ideological tendencies and those motivated by extreme nationalism on the behalf of national minority groups, ethnic terrorism for short. Though the ethnic nationalists, as mentioned before in this chapter, may also be ideologically at home at the extreme right or extreme left of the political spectrum, they are treated as a separate category here because of the overshadowing emphasis on national liberation in their platforms.

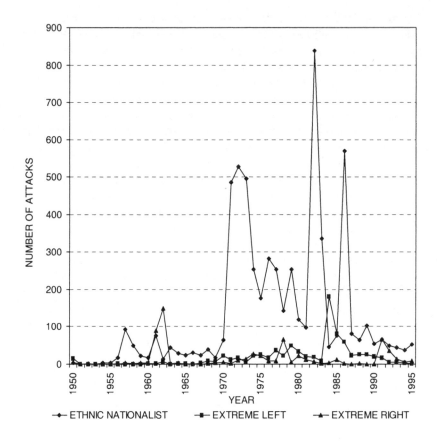

*Figure 4.6   Number of attacks by ideological tendency of actor, 1950–95,
          TWEED (N = 7517)*

A breakdown according to ideological tendencies, as in Figure 4.6, shows that terrorism inspired by ethnic nationalism is the dominant type of domestic terrorism in Western Europe since 1950. Of the total number of acts of terrorism, adjusted for firebombs, 78.3 per cent, were committed by ethnic nationalist terrorists. The remaining acts are divided between left-wing extremists, responsible for 10.2 per cent of the total, and right-wing extremist terrorists who are responsible for 8.1 per cent of the total.[11] The picture remains largely the same when we look at the breakdown of killings. Of the killings for which identifying the ideological position of the actors is possible,[12] the ethnic nationalists were responsible for a little more than 78 per cent. However, the position of the extreme right and extreme left is now reversed. The right-wing extremists were responsible for 13.2 per cent of the killings, while the extreme left actors lay claim to a little more than 8 per cent of the killings for which the actors were ideologically categorized.

Ethnic nationalist terrorism is dominant throughout the period under investigation, with the exception of two or three years. The dramatic increase in levels of terrorism from 1971 onwards is due largely to activities by terrorists ideologically belonging to the ethnic nationalist camp. The levels of activity vary year by year, largely due to the special operating patterns of some groups that strike with a large number of attacks when they enter the scene, only to return to a low level of activity until the next time.

Terrorism from the extreme right and extreme left shows a somewhat cyclic pattern. Terrorists from the extreme right were responsible for the brief but powerful outbreak of ideological (as opposed to ethnic nationalist) terrorism in the early 1960s. When levels of terrorist violence rose following 1970, the extreme right and extreme left were about equal in terms of performing terrorist attacks. Then the terrorist actors on the extreme left dominated the scene from the late 1970s and through the 1980s (with 1978 as a clear exception). Right-wing extremist terrorism then overtakes terrorism from the extreme left from 1991 onwards. Towards the turn of the century, however, there is no clear sign that the cycle of ideological terrorism has again turned to the extreme right. Rather, in the 1990s all forms of domestic terrorism in Western Europe remains at a relatively low level.

ORGANIZED TERRORISM: CHALLENGING THE STATE

The preceding sections of this chapter revealed that levels of terrorist violence have been considerable, especially since the early 1970s, but also earlier. Looking at the distribution of the number of terrorist organizations active each year in the 1950 to 1995 period, as in Figure 4.7, the impression of the early 1970s as an important turning point is confirmed. From 1970 onwards the number of terrorist groups active each year climbs rapidly, peaking in 1975, then climbing again to another peak in 1980 before dropping considerably, only to regain and reach the highest number of terrorist groups recorded as active in the TWEED data set in 1985. That year as many as 30 domestic terrorist groups were active in the West European countries. Despite variations, the number of active groups per year remained high throughout the 1980s. The number of active terrorist groups per year then fell considerably, and has been markedly lower in the 1990 to 1995 period.

As we have seen, as many as up to 30 terrorist groups have been committing acts of terrorism in a single year. However, though levels of terrorism are high

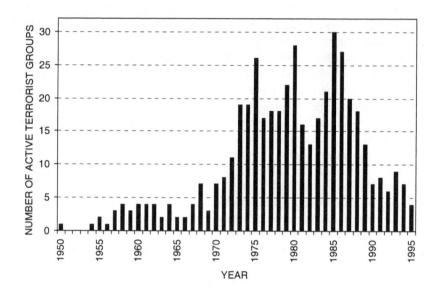

*Figure 4.7   Number of active domestic terrorist groups by year, 1950–95,
               according to TWEED*

in terms of the number of acts or number of people killed in terrorist acts, it
remains to be seen how well organized this terrorist activity is. Are the many
terrorist acts and terrorist killings in Western Europe just a result of random
violence from unknown or unorganized actors, or is there a concentration of
action capacity to the organized terrorist groups briefly mentioned at the start
of this section? This is really a question of how well organized the challenge and
attack against the state is on the part of terrorist actors. We will try to answer the
question by first looking at how large a part of the activity can be ascribed to
organized terrorists, and secondly by looking at the activity levels of terrorist
groups and their ability to survive over time.

The Capacity to Act and Inflict Death

A total of 188 name-carrying terrorist groups were identified in the TWEED data
set. These groups were responsible for 63.3 per cent of the total number of
terrorist actions (corrected for firebombs) and about the same share of the
killings resulting from acts of terrorism (63.6 per cent). This means that TWEED
includes a large number of acts and killings in which the responsible actor was
not identified with a proper name. This category of terrorist acts falls in two

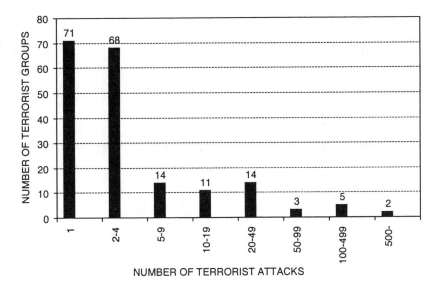

Figure 4.8   *Activity levels of terrorist groups: number of terrorist actions by*
            terrorist groups, 1950–95, TWEED (N = 188)

types. First, there are the acts in which the data source identifies the ideological
tendency or general political background attributed to the actor. This means that
we are told the actor in a particular terrorist event was right-wing extremist or
belonged to a particular side in a regional conflict (for instance a separatist of
some kind). These politically, but not organizationally, identified acts make up
15.7 per cent of the total number of acts. This leaves 21.3 per cent of the acts
with actors really unknown or unidentified, meaning there was no claim of
responsibility on part of a terrorist actor reported, and further that no attribution
on the part of authorities or observers was reported.[13]

Hardly all of the identified terrorist groups are of the same calibre. Of the total
number of 188 terrorist groups registered with TWEED, 86 were responsible for
killing people as a result of their actions (a further 18 injured people but did not
kill). This leaves a considerable number of groups, 83 in all or 44.2 per cent of the
total, that did not kill or injure people. This further suggests that the capacity of
groups is uneven and that the organizational challenge to the state should be
further investigated. We shall therefore take a closer look at the activity levels,
in terms of action levels and the number of killings committed, and the durability
of terrorist groups in terms of number of years in existence. These factors may
suggest the different levels of capacities of terrorist groups, and the differences
in their ability to organize in a way that maintains their activities over time.

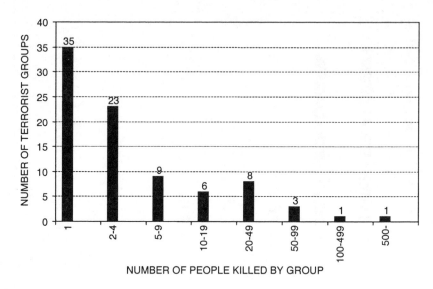

*Figure 4.9   Lethality of terrorist groups: number of people killed by
              terrorist groups, 1950–95, TWEED (N = 188)*

The activity levels of terrorist groups, that is the total number of terrorist acts
committed by them, is presented in Figure 4.8. We are immediately struck by the
large number of groups with a very low level of activity. More than one-third of
the total number of identified terrorist groups only carried out a single terrorist
act. A further third of the total were responsible for two to four acts, still a low
level of activity. Nevertheless, Figure 4.8 also reveals that there is a core of
groups with a considerable capacity to act and which have a high activity level.
For instance, seven groups in the data set are registered with 100 attacks or
more. So while the great number of terrorist groups has a low level of action
capacity, there are a number of terrorist organizations capable of striking
frequently. The ten groups with 50 or more terrorist actions on their record are
together responsible for 60.9 per cent of the terrorist acts carried out by terrorist
organizations identified by name.

As mentioned briefly above, 86 of the 188 identified terrorist groups were
responsible for taking the lives of people hit by the violence instigated. In Figure
4.9 we can take a closer look at the variations in the lethality of terrorist groups,
measured as the number of people killed by terrorist groups in the data set.
Again we note the dominance of the low-level groups. Aside from the 102
groups that did not kill anyone at all by their acts of terrorism, that is more than
half the groups (55.1 per cent of the total number), 35 groups killed one person

only. These single-killing groups make up 18.6 per cent of the overall number of groups, and as much as 40.7 per cent of those groups that did kill. Only 19 groups (10.1 per cent of the total, 22.1 per cent of the groups responsible for killing at least one person) are responsible for killing ten people or more. However, these 19 high-lethality groups are responsible for the deaths of more than 90 per cent of the people killed by terrorist groups identified by name, which is close to 58 per cent of the total number of killings. This indicates a set of groups that represent a remarkable challenge to the state in terms of their capacity to inflict death on members of society.

The Durability of Organized Terrorism

Turning now to the durability of organized terrorism, we shall have a closer look at the period of existence of the terrorist groups identified by name in the TWEED data set. The data set allows us to measure two aspects of durability of a terrorist group. First, we may look at the number of years in which the terrorist group has carried out acts of terrorism. Second, we may look at the period in which the group has been active, or in other words the number of years between the first act of the group and the last act recorded in the data set.[14] This means that years of inactivity are counted in the measure for period of activity. It is here reasoned that though the terrorist organization does not carry out any attacks, it is nevertheless still in existence. The two ways of looking at the time span of terrorist groups are presented in Figure 4.10.

Looking at Figure 4.10, we are again struck by the relatively high number of short-lived groups. A total of 122 out of 188 registered terrorist groups (64.9 per cent) are registered as active in one year only, while a further 29 groups (15.4 per cent) spread their activities over two calendar years. We note that the figures for the period of activity are higher than for they are for the years of activity, suggesting a tendency for longer-lived groups to take breaks in their campaigns. It is interesting to note however that 84.6 per cent of all identified terrorist groups are gone within four years of their first registered terrorist act measured by their period of activity. Thus we are again left with a smaller group of longer-lived terrorist groups with a staying power that can be quite astonishing. Considering that these are groups that are fighting within modern democracies and against resourceful states, it is remarkable to find as many as 16 groups that have been active for more than a decade. Five of these have kept up their struggle for more than 20 years, though only two of them can point to 20 or more activity years.

Most of the groups with the longest period of existence belong to the ethnic nationalist camp. Some of the terrorist groups issued from the extreme left have

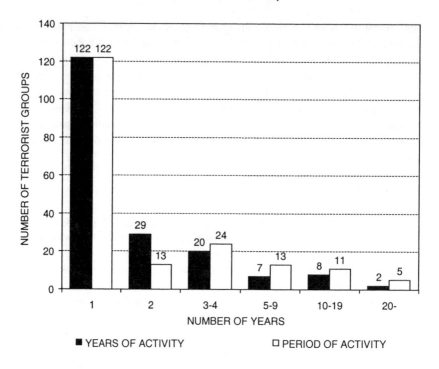

Figure 4.10 The durability of organized terror: years and period of activity of terrorist groups, TWEED (N = 188)

also proved to be capable of surviving for a long period of time. The terrorists on the extreme right however are characterized by more shifting organizational structures, and only few of them manage to survive for a longer period of time. It should here be remembered, though, that terrorist groups of the extreme right are more difficult to identify and trace than the groups belonging on the extreme left or among the ethnic nationalists. Groups on the extreme right are generally small and with a diffuse organizational structure. We may have been able to establish a different picture of terrorism from the extreme right if we could trace the genealogies of these groups, that is trace succeeding groups. Nevertheless, the TWEED data set contains no right-wing terrorist groups with more than seven active years, though two of these right-wing extremist groups have a period of activity of ten years. The comparatively weaker continuity of terrorist groups of the extreme right may be explained with reference to the discussion in Chapter 2 concerning the relationship of state-loyal terrorism to the state. Extreme right-wing terrorism finds itself in a situation in which it on the one hand accepts, indeed even admires, the state and its apparatus of authority, and on the other hand is dissatisfied with state policies. Reconciling attacks on the powers of the state is ideologically difficult while simultaneously wanting the state powers and rights to be increased and respected.

The pattern revealing itself is that of a terrorist threat from a limited number of organized terrorist groups. The majority of terrorist groups carry out few actions, kill few people or none at all, and disappear after a short time. The explanation to this may again be sought in the theoretical perspective on terrorism explained and discussed in Chapter 2, more specifically in the relationship of terrorism to the state. Terrorism aims at influencing the bonds of loyalty and allegiance in a political system. When terrorist groups act to achieve such an influence on the structures of loyalty and allegiance, they overstep the threshold of violence and the state reacts by attempting to control these unauthorized actions (Crelinsten 1987a, p. 15). The large number of terrorist groups responsible for a low number of actions, and which are low intensity in terms of harm inflicted, indicates that many of the groups using terrorism originally operated in the grey area between legal and illegal opposition. What is more important, the evidence from the TWEED data set suggests that once these groups cross the border into illegal violent opposition by means of terrorism, they collapse. Based on the theoretical perspective pursued in this work, we assume that this is due to a lack of a basis of legitimacy, that is support from segments of society. This support is not strong enough in most cases to support a prolonged or sustained campaign of terrorism. Those sympathizers the group may have had originally have not completely broken their bonds of allegiance and loyalty to the state, and revert to the side of the state once the opposition group steps over the threshold of violence and the state reacts by activating its control apparatus. The use of terrorist violence then strikes back at the terrorist group.

THE PRESENCE OF TERRORISM IN WESTERN EUROPE

In the general introduction to the patterns of terrorism in Western Europe presented in this chapter, we have seen that terrorism has had a strong presence in the region, especially from the early 1970s onwards. However, we have also noted the occurrence of terrorism before that, particularly in the late 1950s and early 1960s. The volume of terrorist acts and the total death toll from domestic terrorism is so high that one is tempted to establish that terrorism is a significant problem for the countries in the region. However that would be premature, as the possible variations in terrorism between countries are yet to be mapped. Nevertheless we also note that though a large portion of the terrorism perpetrated within the region is done by unidentified actors, there remains a strong organizational presence in terrorism that makes it all the more of a serious threat to the established institutions and to the political system. All this makes it even more important for us to look closer into the differences between countries when it comes to terrorism, and to relate the patterns we may discover to the theoretical perspective developed earlier in this work.

NOTES

1. Only 27 firebomb acts caused death or injury. A total of 63 firebombs had known terrorist groups behind them (that is groups identified by name).
2. The ITERATE III, or International Terrorism: Attributes of Terrorist Events, Version 3, data set was acquired from Vinyard Software in Virginia, USA.
3. The ITERATE data set includes a great number of West European terrorist groups, some mostly operating within their own country, others transcending borders. All actors with origins in the 18 West European countries were excluded when the numbers for Figure 4.1 were made. Thus the figures are for attacks in which terrorists from countries outside Western Europe travel to the West European countries to perform terrorist attacks.
4. For instance the ITERATE data set starts with the year 1968, so does the Rand–St Andrew Chronology of International Terrorism.
5. See Brosius and Weimann (1991) and Picard (1986) for critical discussions of the contagion model of the causes of terrorism.
6. This incident is known as the Lockerbie incident, so named after the village in Scotland where the airliner hit the ground. While most of those killed were aboard the plane, people on the ground were also killed in the attack.
7. More and more concern, even fear, seems to be directed at the possibility of terrorists acquiring weapons of mass destruction. Lying behind this concern, it seems, is the assumption that terrorists are out to kill as many people as possible and that they are therefore eager to possess nuclear, chemical or biological weapons.
8. For as many as a quarter of the attacks, no information was available in the source to make it possible to determine what kind of attack had taken place (see Table 4.1 missing data). Probably many of these attacks were either bombs and other explosives or armed attacks, though the description of the event only stated an attack had taken place.
9. For instance by targeting a prominent politician. The action against Spanish prime minister Carrero Blanco in December 1973 springs to mind as an example.
10. Recall for instance the attention and media coverage created by the abduction and subsequent killing of Gerold von Braunmühl, Siegfried Buback, Peter Lorenz and Hanns-Martin Schleyer in Germany, and Aldo Moro in Italy.
11. A total of 3.4 per cent of the acts were committed by 'others' or had missing data on this variable.
12. Of the total number of killings, it was only possible not to categorize according to ideological position 6 per cent of the killings.
13. Most of these acts with no claim or no attribution of responsibility took place in the Northern Ireland conflict of the United Kingdom.

14. Naturally a more specific measure of the life span of terrorist groups would be to look at the date of foundation for the groups, possibly corrected for the date when the group definitely decided to use terrorism as a means of struggle. This kind of information is generally not available in *Keesing's* and is consequently not included in the TWEED data set. One would probably have to turn to the literature on specific groups, reference works and handbooks, to decide on the year of formation or the year of adoption of terrorism as a means of struggle for the individual terrorist groups. It should be noted however that some groups make themselves known to the world by committing acts of terrorism, and that little is known about their histories or their internal policy processes.

5. Patterns of Terrorism in West European Countries

This chapter will analyse the patterns of terrorism in West European countries on the macro level. An attempt will be made to investigate possible systematic relationships between variations in terrorism in the countries under scrutiny and the factors argued (in Chapter 2) to influence the occurrence and volume of terrorism. The relationship of terrorism to democracy and freedom will be discussed first, then the discussion will turn to the question of the importance of various socio-economic explanatory factors for the occurrence and extent of terrorism. Finally, the relationship between terrorism and problems of legitimacy will be discussed.

These independent variables will be related to measures of terrorism derived from the TWEED data set. On the one hand we will look at various measures of the occurrence of terrorism. Occurrence for each country will be measured in terms of the number of terrorism acts recorded, the number of deaths resulting from acts of terrorism and the number of years marked by acts of terrorism. On the other hand, we will further look at the extent of the terrorist challenge that a country has been exposed to, in other words organized terrorism. The terrorist challenge will be measured in terms of the number of terrorist groups recorded, the number of groups responsible for killing people (lethal groups) and the number of established groups, that is groups with a substantial capacity to kill or ability to survive. These established groups are the serious terrorist organizations that have survived for five or more years or that have killed ten or more people. For all measures, we have corrected the figures to exclude firebombs that did not kill or injure, or had no organizationally identified perpetrator.

The analyses in this chapter will make a distinction between acts of terrorism with an ethnic nationalist background and other acts of terrorism, out of convenience named ideological acts of terrorism. This is partly because a theoretical distinction was made between various sources of terrorism, one of these being ethnic heterogeneousness. Another reason is that the dominance of ethnic terrorism is in danger of overshadowing other kinds of terrorism so that possible relationships may be obscured.

TERRORISM AND THE RIGHTS OF MAN

As we have seen in Chapter 2, democracy is portrayed as a facilitating condition of terrorism. The argument is frequently cast in terms of democracy versus dictatorships. This distinction is less fruitful in the context of the present analysis, because as of the end of the period under investigation in this project, all the countries under scrutiny were democracies; although two of them, Spain and Portugal, experienced long-standing dictatorships originating before the Second World War, and a third, Greece, had a period of military dictatorship in the late 1960s and early 1970s. Thus these three countries reached the democratic stage only in the latter half of the period under investigation. However we may also find differences between political systems in terms of levels of democratic development. Rights and freedoms are differently distributed even in democratic political systems and this may be argued to be related to terrorism. A poor human rights record for a political system with basically democratic political institutions, and poorly developed freedoms in various fields, may be a source of terrorism. Is there a connection between human rights standards, levels of freedom, levels of democracy, and the occurrence and extent of terrorism?

Terrorism and Human Rights

Table 5.1 presents the correlation coefficients for the relationship between the levels of human rights in the countries and the occurrence and extent of terrorism.[1] Variables measuring human rights standards are never straightforward. The variable used here is the human rights index developed by Charles Humana and is based on a set of indicators concerning political and social rights in countries as measured against the human rights standards expressed in international agreements (Humana 1992, pp. xii–xiv, 3–10).[2] Countries are given a score, with 100 as the maximum possible score. Towards the end of the time period under investigation, all West European countries have a very high score on the human rights index. The poorest record is a score of 87, while some countries are close to the best score possible with 98 points. This record is the result of a development, as some countries have actually improved their human rights record in recent years. The measures for terrorism are correlated with the human rights index for the countries as of 1980, the year for which data is available. The figures are those of Humana, as listed in Lane et al. (1997, pp. 120–21). Thus the human rights status of countries in 1980 is taken as indicative for the period under investigation, an assumption that is of course not unproblematic in light of the democratization that occurred in countries such as Greece, Portugal and Spain. This development also involved improvement of the

Table 5.1 *The relationship (r_{xy}) between human rights in 1980 and terrorism 1950–95, TWEED*

		Occurrence of terrorism			Extent of terrorism		
		Number of					
		acts	people killed	terrorism years	terrorist groups	lethal terrorist groups	established groups
Human	All	-0.06	-0.06	-0.47	-0.65	-0.60	-0.23
rights	Ethnic	0.02	0.02	-0.24	-0.31	-0.31	-0.06
	Ideologic	-0.52	-0.33	-0.61	-0.72	-0.55	-0.43

human rights practices in these countries. Using the human rights index for 1980 may therefore produce indications of a weaker relationship between terrorism and levels of human rights than might otherwise have been expected. Nevertheless, the relationship is worth exploring.

The relationship between levels of human rights and the occurrence of terrorism is not unambiguous. When considering all acts of terrorism, there is no correlation for the number of acts or the number of people killed, but there is a fairly strong negative correlation between the number of terrorist years and the level of human rights. The picture is much the same when we look at ethnic terrorism, although the negative correlation between human rights and terrorist years is weaker. A different picture emerges when we single out ideological terrorism. Here the correlations are stronger for all three measures of the occurrence of terrorism. The correlation coefficients are negative. This means that the occurrence of ideological terrorism is high where the levels of human rights are low, as we expected theoretically. This relationship is reinforced when we look at measures for the extent of terrorism, that is when we direct the attention to the organized terrorist challenge. Here we find strong negative correlations between terrorism and levels of human rights, especially for the measures for the number of groups and number of lethal groups. However the association between human rights and established terrorist groups is weaker.

The pattern that terrorism appears where the human rights record is poorer is strongest for ideological terrorism, although it is nevertheless also present for ethnic terrorism. This supports the notion that terrorism is related to the level of

Table 5.2   *The relationship (r_{xy}) between freedom in 1975 and terrorism 1950–95, TWEED*

		Occurrence of terrorism			Extent of terrorism		
				Number of			
		acts	people killed	terrorism years	terrorist groups	lethal terrorist groups	established groups
Freedom	All	0.04	0.18	0.31	0.47	0.51	0.16
	Ethnic	0.00	0.13	0.30	0.38	0.47	0.16
	Ideologic	0.30	0.15	0.35	0.39	0.28	0.06

human rights, and that this is especially true for ideological terrorism. Moreover we may interpret the stronger correlation between human rights levels and the measures for organized terrorism as support for the claim that poor human rights records are especially important to explain the possibility for terrorist groups to survive. However we should also consider the possibility that terrorism is a factor contributing to a low score on the human rights index. Acts of terrorism frequently produce calls for stronger measures to eradicate the problem, and some of the measures employed in the fight against terrorism are such that limit civil rights.

Terrorism and Freedom

Whereas the human rights index referred to above includes a certain number of social rights, along with basic political rights, we may also narrow our attention to the political rights citizens enjoy. In Table 5.2 are presented correlation coefficients for the relationship between the levels of freedom in 1975, as reported by R.D. Gastil (Lane et al. 1997, pp. 120–21), and the measures for the occurrence and extent of terrorism. The freedom index is based on an evaluation of the overall situation concerning civil liberties and political rights in a country. When a country gets a high score on this index, it means that the level of freedom is low. Again, we assume that the status of countries in a certain year, this time 1975, is indicative for the whole period under investigation. We assume theoretically that low levels of freedom create a breeding ground for terrorism.

Following this assumption we may expect positive correlation coefficients.

The correlations presented in Table 5.2 show that there is no association between freedom and the occurrence of terrorism in general. The exception is the measure for the number of terrorism years, which correlates moderately with the freedom index and indicates a tendency for terrorism to occur in countries with a low level of freedom. It is interesting to note that the association between the occurrence of ideological terrorism and levels of freedom is stronger than the association between the occurrence of ethnic terrorism and freedom, indicating the possibility that levels of freedom are most important for the occurrence of ideological terrorism.

Again, correlations tend to be stronger when looking at the relationship between freedom and the measures for organized terrorism, indicating that organized terrorism is stronger in countries with lower levels of freedom. This is especially so for the measures of number of groups and number of lethal groups, but less so for the number of established terrorist groups (those with a long life or large capacity to kill). Correlations are actually fairly high for the two first measures of the extent of ethnic terrorism.

We may conclude that terrorism does not seem to be positively related with freedom. It is not the countries with the highest levels of freedom that get the highest levels of terrorism. Rather, terrorism seems to be related with lower levels of freedom.

Terrorism and Democracy

Measuring democracy requires attention to be directed towards political institutions, as well as the fundamental civic and political rights of citizens. In Table 5.3 correlations are presented for the relationship between measures of democracy early in the period under investigation, and measures of the occurrence and extent of terrorism in the period as a whole, giving an indication of how political conditions at this early point might influence later events. The democracy index is based on an evaluation of the degree of fairness of the political institutions (elections, legislative, executive) and fundamental political rights fundamental to a freely functioning opposition such as freedom of organization and freedom of the press (Bollen 1980, pp. 387–8). The higher the score on this index, the higher the level of democracy. Scores for 1960 have been used. Whereas many West European countries made a high score, indicating a high degree of democracy in 1960, other countries – notably Spain and Portugal, both of which were dictatorships at the time – scored fairly low. Using data for 1960 is theoretically in keeping with the arguments put forward in Chapter 2, that the political circumstances at an early point in time may have consequences at a much later date, or in other words that low levels of democracy early in the period contribute towards creating a breeding ground for terrorism, the results

Table 5.3   *The relationship (r_{xy}) between democracy in 1960 and terrorism 1950–95, TWEED*

		Occurrence of terrorism			Extent of terrorism		
		acts	people killed	terrorism years	terrorist groups	lethal terrorist groups	established groups
Democracy	All	-0.09	-0.23	-0.37	-0.49	-0.56	-0.21
	Ethnic	0.04	-0.18	-0.35	-0.45	-0.54	-0.21
	Ideologic	-0.34	-0.15	-0.42	-0.38	-0.27	-0.09

of which manifest themselves in later years.

As shown in Table 5.3, when considering the occurrence of terrorism overall without regard to its ethnic or ideologic origins, we find correlations that are negative though moderate. That indicates a certain tendency for high levels of terrorism in the period as a whole to be associated with low levels of democracy early in the period. The exception is the relationship between democracy and the number of terrorism acts, which is weak, indicating that the level of democracy is not systematically related to the occurrence of terrorist acts. However we see that there is a stronger tendency for countries with a low level of democracy to experience more years with the occurrence of terrorist actions. We also note that correlations are again negative and generally stronger when we consider the relationship between the level of democracy and the extent of terrorism (all acts considered). This may indicate that a low level of democracy is especially important for the organizational character of terrorism. Those countries with a low level of democracy tend to have the higher number of organized terrorist groups, though the level of democracy tends to play a lesser part in terms of established groups.

The patterns just mentioned are by and large the same when we look at the relationship between levels of democracy and the occurrence and extent of terrorism with ethnic origins. However we note a somewhat different picture when attention is directed to ideological terrorism. In that case there is a negative association between the level of democracy and the occurrence of terrorism, especially as measured in terms of the number of terrorist acts and the number of terrorist years. Thus it may seem that terrorism ideologically originating on the extremes of the left–right dimension tends to be associated with countries that had a low level of democracy in 1960. On the other hand, the association between democracy and the extent of ideological terrorism is weaker than for ethnic terrorism, though the correlation coefficients for the relationship between democracy and the number of groups and number of lethal groups are moderately negative.

The correlation coefficients presented in Table 5.3 are all negative and show that there is a tendency, though sometimes moderate, that low levels of democracy in 1960 go together with high levels of terrorism. This tendency is strongest for the measures of the extent of terrorism. In other words, organized terrorism tends to be strongest in countries scoring lower on the index of democracy. Also there is a pattern to the effect that ethnically inspired terrorism, measured in the extent of terrorism, displays a stronger association to levels of democracy than ideological terrorism. The relationship is the opposite for the occurrence of terrorism.

Our analysis in this section demonstrated that terrorism seems to be systematically related to various measures of freedom and democracy. The tendency is for low levels of freedom, human rights and democracy to be associated with high levels of terrorism. There is also a tendency, though, for this to be especially true for ideological terrorism, and it may be that ethnically inspired terrorism is not to the same extent dependent on factors like freedom, human rights and democracy. Nevertheless these findings suggest that the relationship between terrorism and democracy, theories of which were discussed in Chapter 2, is not a simple one and that care should be taken in specifying under what circumstances democracy may act as a facilitating condition for democracy.

TERRORISM AND SOCIO-ECONOMIC FACTORS

As we have seen in Chapter 2, various socio-economic variables have been proposed as causes of terrorism. The social changes that follow economic growth lead to changes in established cultural norms and in the patterns of social organization. This may create situations in which people find themselves in new or changed situations for which norms and organizations have not yet fully developed. This may also apply to social integration and the norms of conflict regulation and rules for solving disputes. In the end, economic modernization may create conflicts that lead to terrorism. Further, real or perceived social injustices may also contribute to conflicts leading to terrorism. One measure of social injustice is the distribution of income in a country. We

*Table 5.4   The relationship (r_{xy}) between growth in real GDP 1960–68
              and terrorism 1950–95, TWEED*

		Occurrence of terrorism			Extent of terrorism		
		Number of					
		acts	people killed	terrorism years	terrorist groups	lethal terrorist groups	established groups
Economic	All	-0.01	-0.04	0.43	0.64	0.55	0.14
growth	Ethnic	-0.10	-0.13	0.17	0.24	0.21	-0.04
1960–68	Ideologic	0.54	0.37	0.61	0.78	0.60	0.40

will try to find out what the relationship is between income distribution and terrorism. Finally, we will pay some intention to the possible influence the development of the post-industrial society has on terrorism. Is terrorism a phenomenon that is tied to the post-industrial society?

Terrorism and Economic Modernization

Economic growth is one indicator of modernization. Table 5.4 presents correlation coefficients for the relationship between growth in real GDP for the years 1960 to 1968 (annual averages) and measures of terrorism. The figures for growth in real GDP are originally from *OECD* statistical sources, and are available for all countries under scrutiny (Lane et al. 1997, p. 64). The argument underpinning the analysis is that socio-economic developments early in the period may produce consequences in terms of terrorism that are only manifested later in the period under investigation.

As we can see, when all kinds of terrorism are considered there is no association between change in real GDP and the occurrence of terrorism measured in the number of acts committed or the number of people killed. However, we note a positive association between economic growth and the number of terrorism years. So while terrorism does not seem to have an influence on the number of acts or people killed, it does seem to influence terrorism as a persistent phenomenon over time. In countries where change in real GDP in the 1960s was high, the tendency is that these countries also experienced a higher number of years exposed to terrorism.

When looking at the relationship between change in real GDP and the extent of terrorism, we note strong correlation for two of the measures. Where the level of change was high in the 1960s, there tend to be a higher number of groups, and a higher number of groups that killed people. However the relationship with the number of established groups is weak. Nevertheless, modernization seems to have a notable influence on the organized challenge of terrorism. Terrorism's organizational base seems to be stronger in those countries which experienced the strongest economic growth in the 1960s.

However when we make a distinction between ethnically and ideologically inspired terrorism, we note that there is no association between modernization and the occurrence of ethnic terrorism, and we find only a weak association between modernization and the extent of ethnic terrorism. The impact of modernization is strong however on ideological terrorism. For ideological terrorism, we find consistently positive and strong to moderate association between change in real GDP and all measures of the occurrence and extent of terrorism. We may conclude then that modernization seems to be most important for terrorism inspired by the traditional ideologies.

Terrorism and Income Distribution

One way to measure economic differences in a society is to look at the distribution of the national income. In Table 5.5 one such measure, the percentage of the national income going to the top 20 per cent of the population, has been related to the occurrence and extent of terrorism. It should be noted that the figures, which are based on statistics from the World Bank and reported in Lane et al. (1997, pp. 24–5), are only available for some of the 18 countries we are dealing with. Data is missing for four countries (Austria, Greece, Iceland and Luxembourg), which reduces the value of the investigation into this particular relationship somewhat. The information concerning income distribution measured as the percentage of the national income going to the top 20 per cent of the population, is mostly from the late 1970s and early 1980s, and the status of income distribution for these years is taken as indicative for the period under investigation.

We can see from Table 5.5 that there are strong correlations between income distribution and two of the measures for the occurrence of terrorism; those for the number of acts and the number of years. This suggests that terrorism tends to occur in high levels in those countries in which income is most unevenly distributed. Somewhat puzzlingly, this is not the case for the third measure of the occurrence of terrorism, the number of people killed. This may reflect the fact that a high volume of terrorist acts is not necessarily followed by a high death toll (as discussed in the preceding chapter). Nevertheless terrorism also tends

*Table 5.5   The relationship (r_{xy}) between income distribution in the late
1970s and early 1980s and terrorism 1950–95, TWEED*

		Occurrence of terrorism			Extent of terrorism		
		Number of					
		acts	people killed	terrorism years	terrorist groups	lethal terrorist groups	established groups
Income	All	0.33	0.05	0.44	0.55	0.48	0.21
distribution	Ethnic	0.25	-0.04	0.25	0.31	0.06	0.10
	Ideologic	0.67	0.43	0.52	0.62	0.67	0.32

to be better organized in those countries in which income is unevenly
distributed. The correlation coefficients are strong for the relationship between
income distribution and the measure for the number of groups and the number
of lethal groups, though the correlation with the number of established groups
is only moderate.

Again we note that the relationship under scrutiny is strongest for ideological
terrorism as opposed to ethnically inspired terrorism. While the association
between income distribution and terrorism is generally moderate to weak for
ethnic terrorism, the analysis produced consistently positive and mostly strong
correlations for ideological terrorism. It is perhaps not surprising that inequalities
in income distribution are more closely connected with ideological terrorism than
with ethnic terrorism. However in some cases ethnic cleavages may coincide
with social cleavages based on distribution of economic goods.

Thus the results of the analysis indicate that those countries in which income
is most unevenly distributed also tend to have higher levels of occurrence of
terrorism and more extensive organized terrorism. This was as expected
theoretically.

Terrorism and the Post-Industrial Society

As we saw in Chapter 2, there are those who attempt to explain terrorism by
relating it to certain types of society. According to this argument, terrorism
appears in the pre-industrial and post-industrial types of society. This, it is

Table 5.6   *The relationship (r_{xy}) between unionization in 1975 and terrorism 1950–95, TWEED*

		Occurrence of terrorism			Extent of terrorism		
		Number of					
		acts	people killed	terrorism years	terrorist groups	lethal terrorist groups	established groups
Union	All	-0.41	-0.19	-0.6	-0.72	-0.58	-0.4
membership	Ethnic	-0.34	-0.12	-0.44	-0.53	-0.36	-0.25
	Ideologic	-0.61	-0.3	-0.61	-0.64	-0.47	-0.46

argued, is because social organization, and especially solidarity, is weaker in these two societal categories. Two variables will be used in an attempt to find out whether terrorism in post-war Western Europe may be said to be related to the post-industrial type of society. These variables are the degree of unionization and the percentage of the GDP originating from the services industries.

The argument is that terrorism will not occur in societies with strong labour unions. In Table 5.6 the degree of unionization is correlated with measures for the occurrence and extent of terrorism. The variable for unionization measures the percentage of the labour force with membership in a labour union. One problem with figures for union membership on the national level is the lack of information for several countries. Sources from which figures are available for as many countries as possible have been used. Information is not available for one country (Iceland). Figures are for 1975 and originate from OECD sources as provided in Lane et al. (1997, pp. 26–7). In the analysis the status of unionization in 1975 is taken as indicative for the entire period under investigation.

From Table 5.6 we can see that there is a negative association between the degree of unionization and the measures for terrorism overall. Correlations are mostly strong for both the occurrence and extent of terrorism. Thus terrorism seems to be a problem in those countries that have a low level of unionization. This is as expected theoretically. We also note that although correlations are weaker, the same tendency is present for ethnically inspired terrorism. This is perhaps somewhat surprising, but indicates that strong unions may even

Table 5.7   *The relationship (r_{xy}) between tertiary-sector importance in 1980 and terrorism 1950–95, TWEED*

		Occurrence of terrorism			Extent of terrorism		
		Number of					
		acts	people killed	terrorism years	terrorist groups	lethal terrorist groups	established groups
Third	All	0.16	0.14	-0.26	-0.22	-0.24	0.04
sector	Ethnic	0.23	0.20	0.09	0.11	0.12	0.19
share	Ideologic	-0.46	-0.31	-0.49	-0.42	-0.48	-0.26

influence the presence of ethnic terrorism. Stronger correlations are produced for ideological terrorism, which is as expected theoretically. Overall these results strengthen the idea that there may be a relationship between the type of society and terrorism. It is those countries that have stronger unions that have the lower levels of terrorism.

Nevertheless a society may be dominated by industrial production even when the degree of unionization is low. In Table 5.7 measures for the importance of the tertiary sector (services) have been correlated with measures for the occurrence and extent of terrorism. Figures originating from the World Bank and collected from Lane et al. (1997, p. 57), are from 1980 and are available for all countries except one (Switzerland). The percentage of the GDP originating from the services sector is then an indication of how strong the industrial production is. The service sector is expected to expand at the expense of the agricultural and industrial sectors in the post-industrial society. Following the arguments about the relationship between the type of society and terrorism, we expect the levels of terrorism to be highest in cases where the features of the post-industrial society are highest; thus we expect terrorism to be a problem where the share of the services industries in the GDP is the highest.

However more of the opposite relationship turns out to be the case, as can be seen from Table 5.7. Generally there is no or only a very moderately weak, association between share of the services sector in GDP and the occurrence of terrorism, in all cases regardless of ethnic or ideological origin. For the occurrence of terrorism, two of the relationships turn out positive, but only weak, while the third is still weak but is negative. Turning our attention to the extent of terrorism, two relationships are negative, but weak, while the third is positive but so weak that we cannot say there is systematic association between the two variables.

For ethnic terrorism, the analysis produced consistently positive correlation coefficients, but these are all weak. This means that again, there is little evidence to say that terrorism is systematically a problem appearing in countries with strong services sectors. The strongest indication that this is not true at all is produced when looking at the relationship between ideological terrorism and the tertiary sector's share of the GDP in 1970. Here correlation coefficients are consistently negative, and several of them are quite strong. This is the case for both the occurrence and the extent of terrorism. This means that we are faced with a situation in which terrorism tends to occur most forcefully in those countries that have weaker tertiary sectors, and by implication, are not so typical post-industrial societies. This is contrary to what was expected theoretically.

In sum then it is difficult to see any consistent pattern to the effect that the post-industrial society favours terrorism. One measure, degree of unionization, suggests there is a relationship, with a high degree of unionization working against the occurrence and extent of terrorism. On the other hand, it tends to be the case, especially for ideological terrorism, that terrorism is associated with societies in which the tertiary sector is weak. This goes against the suggestion that terrorism is related to the post-industrial type of society. In a similar way economic modernization, measured as growth in real GDP, turned out to be particularly associated with ideological, terrorism whereas the results of the analysis were not so clear-cut for terrorism overall and for ethnic terrorism. When looking at the relationship between income distribution and terrorism, we also found that the association was strong for ideological terrorism, indicating higher levels of terrorism in those countries in which income is most unevenly distributed. These results would indicate that socio-economic variables are especially important when explaining ideological terrorism.

TERRORISM AND THE PROBLEMS OF LEGITIMACY

We will now look further into the relationship between terrorism and the three problems of legitimacy discussed in Chapter 2. It was argued that certain aspects of a country's political history, in particular disruptive experiences like civil wars, dictatorships or revolutions, may contribute to challenging the state's legitimacy and consequently also contribute to the outbreak of campaigns of terrorism. We also argued that difficulties in integrating fringe groups, either because these have themselves decided to withdraw from fully fledged participation or because

*Table 5.8   The relationship (r_{xy}) between ethnic fragmentation (1970s)
and terrorism 1950–95, TWEED*

		Occurrence of terrorism			Extent of terrorism		
		Number of					
		acts	people killed	terrorism years	terrorist groups	lethal terrorist groups	established groups
Ethnic	All	0.33	0.34	0.28	0.27	0.26	0.33
fragmen-	Ethnic	0.35	0.34	0.47	0.48	0.45	0.38
tation	Ideologic	0.03	0	0.03	0.01	-0.11	0.09

these groups are actively blocked from participation, may have a similar effect on the legitimacy of the state and the appearance of terrorism. Finally, it was argued that ethnic divisions within a state might also be a contributing factor causing a state's legitimacy to be challenged, and thus create a basis on which to build a campaign of terrorism. We will now examine whether these patterns reflecting these relationships may actually be said to be present in the empirical material at our disposal.

Terrorism and Ethnic Diversity

Table 5.8 presents correlation coefficients for the relationship between ethnic fragmentation and the occurrence and extent of terrorism. Though ethnicity may be based on several shared characteristics in a group, we will use an index for the ethno-linguistic fragmentation of the 18 West European countries in the 1970s. The data is taken from Lane et al. (1997, p. 21).[3] This index, which varies from 0 to 1, indicates the probability that two people that have been randomly sampled from a population turn out to belong to different ethno-linguistic groups. Countries that are linguistically homogenous will have a low score on the index, while linguistically heterogenous countries will have a high score.

It is clear from Table 5.8 that there is a moderate to strong association between ethnic diversity and terrorism overall. Correlation coefficients are all positive. The positive association is present both for the occurrence and the extent of terrorism, indicating that the ethnically most diverse countries tend to have more terrorism than the ethnically homogenous countries. As would be expected, the pattern is the same for ethnic terrorism. There is no systematic association present between the ethnic diversity measure and the measures for the occurrence and extent of ideological terrorism. This means that ideological terrorism may be seen as unrelated to the ethnic composition of countries. Ethnic terrorism is consistently positively correlated with ethnic diversity. The more ethnically diverse a country is, the more terrorism there seems to be. However that is not entirely true. Coefficients are moderate to strong, and one may ask why they are not stronger. It seems that there must be ethnically diverse countries without much terrorism, and that other factors than just diversity play a part in producing ethnic terrorism.

Terrorism and Problems of Continuity

Judging which countries have experienced problems of continuity must be based on an assessment of each country's political history and development. Those countries that have problems of continuity have all experienced disruptive political events, typically civil wars, revolutions or dictatorships. Earlier in this work we argued that such factors may contribute to the launching of challenges to the state's legitimacy long after these events were actually experienced. This may then also contribute to the outbreak of terrorism. The problems of continuity variable is a dichotomous variable, simply distinguishing between those countries that we judge to have problems of continuity from those that have not. It is still possible to use a variable like this for the kind of statistical analysis we so far have performed in this chapter.[4]

When looking at the relationship between problems of continuity – that is the existence of seriously disruptive political events in a country's history – and terrorism, as we have done in Table 5.9, we can see that there is no clear pattern when we use terrorism overall as the dependent variable. For the occurrence measures of terrorism in general, there is no association or only a weak association for the number of acts in total and the number of killings in total. However, there is a strong association indicating that though the presence of problems of continuity in a country are not associated with the volume of terrorism, there is a tendency for those countries which have experienced the disruptive political developments that produce problems of continuity to have experienced terrorism more frequently. In other words, terrorism seems to be a more persistent problem in the countries with problems of continuity. We also note that these countries tend to have more groups, both overall and in terms of groups that have killed people. Associations here are strong. However we note that the association between problems of continuity and the number of established groups is only weak to moderate, which indicates that when looking at terrorism in general the countries with a troubled political past do not turn out

Table 5.9   *The relationship (r_{xy}) between problems of continuity and terrorism*

		Occurrence of terrorism			Extent of terrorism		
				Number of			
		acts	people killed	terrorism years	terrorist groups	lethal terrorist groups	established groups
Problems	All	0.1	0	0.42	0.49	0.48	0.18
of	Ethnic	0.01	-0.14	0.12	0.17	0.08	0
continuity	Ideologic	0.63	0.47	0.63	0.59	0.63	0.47

to be generally more exposed to long-lived terrorist campaigns from established terrorist groups than countries without problems of continuity.

These results are to a large extent determined by the fact that ethnic terrorism shows no, or only a weak association with problems of continuity, both for the occurrence variables and for the extent variables. From these results we can only conclude that ethnic terrorism is unrelated to problems of continuity.

It is when we look at ideologic terrorism that a pattern of strong association between the occurrence and extent of terrorism and problems of continuity is produced. Associations are consistently strong, as can be seen from the bottom row in Table 5.9. This applies to measures of the occurrence of terrorism, as well as to the organized extent of terrorism. Ideological terrorism turns out to be much more sensitive to historical factors in the development of the political systems than ethnical terrorism. It is those countries which have experienced a troubled political past that also experience high levels of terrorist attacks, many deaths and terrorism over a long period of time, and which have a high number of terrorist groups, frequently lethal and likely to succeed in establishing themselves for years.

The strong positive association between problems of continuity and ideological terrorism is as we expected theoretically. Nonetheless it is perhaps not unreasonable to expect ethnic terrorism to show a stronger positive association with the complex of problems of continuity. When this is not the case, it indicates that ethnic terrorism tends to occur also in multi-ethnic countries that have not experienced a troubled political history.

Table 5.10   The relationship (r_{xy}) between problems of integration and terrorism

		Occurrence of terrorism			Extent of terrorism		
				Number of			
		acts	people killed	terrorism years	terrorist groups	lethal terrorist groups	established groups
Problems	All	0.21	0.05	0.58	0.68	0.64	0.33
of	Ethnic	0.10	-0.07	0.25	0.30	0.18	0.06
integration	Ideologic	0.81	0.59	0.79	0.77	0.78	0.64

Terrorism and Problems of Integration

Previously in this work we discussed how difficulties in integrating groups at the political fringes may contribute to creating challenges to the legitimacy of the state and thus also help produce terrorism. In Table 5.10 we present correlation coefficients for the relationship between problems of integration and the occurrence and extent of terrorism in the 18 West European countries. Countries have been categorized as either having or not having problems of integration on the basis of the presence of anti-system parties, that is parties that are not fully integrated into the mainstream political process. This may be, as we have noted, because these parties have themselves decided to stay outside the usual processes and patterns of cooperation with other political parties, or because other political actors exclude them from cooperation and power sharing. Specifically, we have on the one hand counted fascist or extreme right-wing parties with parliamentary representation as constituting a problem of integration.[5] On the other hand, we have also counted communist parties with substantial and lasting electoral support (more than 10 per cent) as also representing a problem of integration. Both kinds of parties may be viewed as anti-system parties in that they demand radical regime change. Countries faced with one or both of these kinds of challenges have been classified as having problems of integration.

When looking at the relationship between terrorism in general and problems of integration, we again discover no clear-cut pattern. While there is no association between the number of people killed as a result of terrorism overall and problems of integration, the association is stronger, but still only moderate, for the number of acts in total, but strong for the number of years. Acts of terrorism thus seem to be a somewhat more recurrent phenomenon in countries that experience problems in integrating groups into the mainstream political process, though these countries do not seem to be equally hard hit in terms of death toll. This reminds us of the relationship between acts and deaths discussed in the previous chapter: acts of terrorism do not always kill. Nevertheless we are faced with an indication that there may be a relationship between problems of integration in a country and the occurrence of terrorism. This impression is reinforced when turning our attention to the extent of terrorism. Here, associations are stronger, especially for the number of groups and the number of lethal groups. The association is somewhat more moderate when looking at the relationship between the number of established groups and problems of integration. When looking at the extent of terrorism, then, it seems terrorism is also more persistent in the countries that experience problems of integration.

When we introduce the distinction between terrorism motivated by ethnic nationalism and ideological considerations, a pattern similar to that found for problems of continuity appears: it is ideological terrorism that is more strongly associated with problems of integration, whereas ethnic terrorism is not clearly associated with this dimension. Associations tend to be weak or not present at all for the relationships between the occurrence and extent of ethnic terrorism and problems of integration. Only a couple of relationships can display moderate correlation coefficients, one of them for the relationship between the number of terrorist groups and problems of integration. Nevertheless we are not in a position to say that ethnic terrorism is systematically associated with problems of integration in the West European countries.

On the other hand, associations between problems of integration and the occurrence and extent of ideological terrorism are generally quite strong for all the measures we have used, including the number of people killed as a result of acts of terrorism. This indicates that terrorism tends to occur, and hit the hardest, in countries that experience difficulties in integrating fringe groups into the political process, whereas countries that do not experience these difficulties do not experience terrorism either. It also seems to be the case that the extent of ideological terrorism is strongly associated with problems of integration. Again the associations are quite strong for all measures, suggesting problems of integration in countries play a part in laying the foundation for terrorism.

THE SOCIAL AND POLITICAL ORIGINS OF TERRORISM

The analysis made at the beginning of this chapter showed terrorism to be systematically related to measures of freedom and democracy. We found a tendency for low levels of freedom, human rights and democracy to be associated with high levels of terrorism in the West European countries included in the analysis. The pattern is especially strong for ideological terrorism, indicating that ethnic terrorism is not as strongly dependent on political factors like freedom, human rights and democracy.

The analysis also demonstrated that growth in real GDP, the measure we used for economic modernization, is especially associated with ideological terrorism. However the results of the analysis on this point were not so unambiguous for ethnic terrorism, producing a weaker relationship between economic modernization and terrorism overall. Nevertheless we may conclude that ideological terrorism seems to be more associated with countries that have experienced stronger economic growth. When turning our attention to another socio-economic factor, that of income distribution, we found a tendency for higher levels of terrorism in those countries in which income is most unevenly distributed. Again the relationship was strongest for ideological terrorism.

When looking at the effect of the post-industrial society upon terrorism, it was difficult to discern any consistent pattern in the results of the analysis. Looking at the relationship between the degree of unionization and terrorism suggests a high degree of unionization in a country works against the occurrence and extent of terrorism. At the same time we found that terrorism is not associated with societies in which the tertiary sector is strong. In our view this does not support the suggestion that terrorism is related to the post-industrial type of society.

Despite the somewhat varying results presented in this chapter, we may conclude that political and social injustices, as well as rapid economic growth, may play a part in stimulating terrorism in the West European countries in the last 45 years. Terrorism shows signs of being associated with both political and socio-economic factors. The results of the present analysis indicate that socio-economic variables are especially important when explaining ideological terrorism.

As for the relationship between ethnic diversity and terrorism, the analysis showed that there is a moderate to strong association. While ideological terrorism, not unexpectedly, turns out to be unrelated to the ethnic composition of countries, ethnic terrorism is consistently and positively correlated with ethnic diversity. This means that the ethnically diverse countries tend to have more terrorism than the ethnically homogenous countries. Further, the analysis showed that there are strong positive associations between problems of continuity and ideological terrorism. In other words terrorism, especially ideological terrorism, tends to emerge in countries that have experienced a particularly troubled development to democracy. Similarly we found strong associations between problems of integration and the occurrence and extent of ideological terrorism. This is an indication that terrorism, and again especially ideological terrorism, tends to hit hardest in countries that have difficulties in integrating political fringe groups.

In conclusion we may say that political and social injustices, as well as rapid economic growth, may play a part in stimulating terrorism. In the next chapter we will have a closer and more detailed look at the development of terrorism in the West European countries. We will look at the different levels of terrorism in the countries. Further, we will have a closer look at the political issues terrorism derives from. We will relate the organized terrorist challenge to the problems of legitimacy we have argued may be important contributing factors to the occurrence and extent of terrorism.

NOTES

1. In this and the following tables reporting correlation coefficients in the present chapter, no tests of significance will be reported. This is because tests of significance are based on the relationship of a random sample drawn from a known population. Significance tests are used to determine how confident we can be that the random samples we use for analysis are not produced by chance. In our case, we are using states as units of analysis and all states covered by the research question are included in the analysis. Consequently we do not operate with a random sample in our analysis. Rather we are dealing with the entire population of units of analysis that we want to say something about. This makes tests of significance less relevant to the present analysis.
2. The international agreements are the Universal Declaration of Human Rights, the International Covenant on Economic, Social and Cultural Rights and the International Covenant on Civil and Political Rights.
3. The index provided by these three authors is based on information given in David B. Barrett (ed.) (1992) *World Christian encyclopedia*, Nairobi: Oxford University Press.
4. Though dummy variables are at the interval level of measurement, they may still be regarded as continuous and used in correlation analyses to find out the effect of the presence versus the absence of a property. The problem with doing this is that the measure used to investigate association at the continuous level of measurement, Pearsons r (r_{xy}), is based on a logic that compares the unit's value to the mean value of all units. As dummy variables only have two values, 0 and 1, there is no meaningful mean value.
5. We have not counted right-wing parties arguing for a minimal state as constituting a problem of integration.

6. Terrorism and the West European Political Systems

In the preceding chapter we already found a positive association between the presence of problems of legitimacy in countries and the occurrence and extent of terrorism. Going into greater detail, we will now look closer into the countries and identify the problems of legitimacy facing them and follow up by discussing the terrorism that has faced them. We will do this by first discussing the problems of legitimacy that the West European countries may be said to have, or in other words see how the countries may be placed on the three variables: problems of continuity, problems of integration and problems of ethnicity. Then we will go on to see to what degree the West European countries have been faced with terrorism, through the position of these countries with respect to the occurrence and organized extent of terrorism. Following this we will go into detail on the political systems and see how they relate to terrorism.

PROBLEMS OF LEGITIMACY AND THE WEST EUROPEAN COUNTRIES

Combining the three variables we argue may contribute to producing problems of legitimacy we get a set of eight different combinations of values (see Table 6.1), granted we turn one of the variables into a measure of ethnic homogenous versus ethnic heterogenous countries. As a rule of thumb for the classification, a country in which the dominant group constitutes up to 96 per cent of the population has been considered ethnically heterogenous. This is a quite liberal measure, and ethnic diversity is in other words quite widely defined here. We expect differences in the occurrence and extent of terrorism between the countries in different groups.

The first group of countries is those that are ethnically homogenous and which do not experience problems of continuity or problems of integration (see Table 6.1). Five of the 18 countries included in this study belong in this category: Denmark, Iceland, Norway, Sweden and the Netherlands. These countries went through an unbroken and relatively untroubled process of democratization. Further, they have not experienced difficulties with large anti-

Table 6.1   Problems of legitimacy in West European countries

		Problems of		
	Ethnicity	*Continuity*	*Integration*	*Countries*
Group 1	*No*	*No*	*No*	Denmark, Iceland, Netherlands, Norway, Sweden
Group 2	*No*	*No*	*Yes*	Luxembourg
Group 3	*No*	*Yes*	*No*	Austria, Ireland
Group 4	*No*	*Yes*	*Yes*	Germany,* Greece, Portugal
Group 5	*Yes*	*No*	*No*	Belgium, Switzerland, United Kingdom
Group 6	*Yes*	*No*	*Yes*	–
Group 7	*Yes*	*Yes*	*No*	Finland
Group 8	*Yes*	*Yes*	*Yes*	France, Italy, Spain

Note:
* West Germany to October 1990 and united Germany after October 1990.

system parties. One of the large communist parties, the Icelandic one, was integrated through membership in government coalitions. Whereas all these five countries except Iceland have ethnic minorities, they make up only an insignificant part of the population. Combining, the relative homogenous population and the absence of troubling difficulties concerning the political history and the integration of political fringe groups, we find it unlikely that terrorism will occur and we do not expect whatever terrorist actions there may be to be channelled into organized campaigns.

Luxembourg is the sole ethnically homogenous country in our study to have experienced problems of integration without having had problems of continuity (see Table 6.1). It is thus the only country in the second group. The reason for arguing that Luxembourg has had problems of integration is the size of the country's communist party, traditionally loyal to Moscow. The country's problem of integration facilitates terrorism, whereas the ethnic homogeneousness and the absence of problems of continuity speak against the occurrence of terrorism.

Two countries are ethnically homogenous, but may be said to have had historical experiences that have produced problems of continuity, though they show no sign of going through problems of integration (see Table 6.1). These two countries, making up the third group, are Austria and the Republic of Ireland. Both countries experienced a civil war early in this century. Austria also went through a period of dictatorship. Nevertheless the countries have not experienced problems of integration, perhaps because of the need to display unity externally. In Ireland this need found an outlet through anti-British nationalism. In Austria, political forces united to defend and integrate into the new republic, culminating in the State Treaty of 1955. Nevertheless, though the position of these two countries on the ethnic diversity and problems of integration variables speaks against the occurrence of terrorism, the presence of problems of continuity may contribute to the occurrence of terrorism.

The fourth group of countries is ethnically homogenous but they have experienced both problems of continuity and problems of integration. Terrorism is more likely in these circumstances than in any of the three constellations of positions on the three variables producing problems of legitimacy discussed so far. Three countries fall into this group: Germany,[1] Greece and Portugal (see Table 6.1). Germany experienced both civil war and a long-lasting dictatorship. In the post-war period, West Germany faced problems of integration as a result of the experience with Nazism. The militant democracy of the Federal Republic formed in 1949 provided for a troubled relationship with the political fringes. In 1952 the Sozialistische Reichspartei (SRP), a neo-Nazi party, was banned. The communist party was prohibited in 1956, although it was only an insignificant party at the time. Later developments saw the exclusion of leftists from public positions. West Germany also experienced difficulties with extreme and radical right-wing parties, though none of these have been able to achieve lasting electoral support. Nevertheless such parties have also been banned. Naturally, the problems of continuity only became more difficult when the former German Democratic Republic was integrated into the Federal Republic in October 1990.

Through the experience with civil war, which lasted to 1949, and dictatorship in the years from 1967 to 1974, Greece finds itself in the same category as Germany. The legacy of the civil war and the strong anti-communism of the dictatorship provides Greece with difficulties in integrating the radical left. The communist party was banned even before the colonels took power, though it was legalized by the return of democracy.

Portugal went through a long-lasting authoritarian regime that was only overturned in the 1974 revolution. This regime was also strongly anti-communist and the democratic political system that appeared after the 1974 revolution had difficulties in handling the radical left. These are conditions that lay foundations for terrorism in all three countries.

Of the ethnically heterogenous states, terrorism is least to be expected in the countries that have not experienced problems of integration and continuity. There are three such countries among the 18 West European countries included in this study, making up the fifth group of countries (see Table 6.1). These are Belgium, Switzerland and the United Kingdom. All three countries are multi-ethnic countries, including the United Kingdom despite the dominance of the English language. In two of the countries, Switzerland and the United Kingdom, ethnic identities may also be founded on other dimensions than language, as religion and territoriality also play an important part in the formation of ethnic identities. All three countries have experienced a gradual development of democracy, without major setbacks or disruptions. Further, they have not been faced with difficulties integrating groups at the political extremes into the mainstream political process. Thus terrorism may be expected because of ethnic conflicts, but not as a result of problems of integration and continuity.

A sixth group of countries would consist of states that are ethnically heterogenous and which are faced with problems of integration but which do not experience problems of continuity. However, no case fitting into this category can be found among the countries making up this study (see Table 6.1).

Finland is the only country fitting into the seventh group, that is the constellation of a multi-ethnic country with problems of continuity but without problems of integration (see Table 6.1). The problems of continuity have their roots in the Finnish civil war of 1918–19. However the relationship of Finland to the Soviet Union provided for a need to display unity internally in face of the strong neighbouring power. Further, the close relationship between Finland and the Soviet Union in the post-war period provided for the inclusion of the strong Finnish communist party in the political system alongside other parties. For these reasons, it does not seem appropriate to place Finland in the category of countries experiencing problems of integration on the basis of the size of the communist party alone. Therefore an exception is made and Finland is placed in the category of multi-ethnic countries with problems of continuity but with no problems of integration. Nevertheless the presence of problems of continuity increases the likelihood of terrorism, though the two other variables speak against the possibility.

Group number eight has the highest likelihood of terrorism. These are the multi-ethnic countries with both problems of continuity and problems of integration. Three countries fit into this category: France, Italy and Spain (see Table 6.1). In terms of problems of continuity, France falls into this category because of the Vichy regime, which has to be counted as a regime internally produced. Further, the uneasy transition between the Fourth and Fifth Republics also contribute to the problems of continuity and integration in France. The Fifth Republic of de Gaulle met with opposition from both socialists and communists, and also from conservatives deep in nostalgia for the Vichy period. France also has one of Europe's larger communist parties, which gained substantial electoral support in both the Fourth and the Fifth Republic. In the Fourth Republic the right-wing radical Poujadists gained substantial support. Furthermore, the centralist French republic has several ethnic minority groups. Italy and Spain belong to the same category of countries as France does. Italy experienced a fascist dictatorship from 1921 to the end of the Second World War, providing for problems of continuity. Further, its communist party was Europe's strongest and Italy was also faced with a neo-fascist party that achieved representation in parliament. Both facts contribute to the problems of integration that Italy experienced. Finally, we have to mention that Italy has several ethnic minorities. The situation in Spain is much like that of Italy. The country is multi-ethnic. After a brutal civil war from 1936 to 1939 the country experienced a long-lasting dictatorship that continued for nearly 40 years. Both the Spanish and the Italian dictatorships pursued a centralist policy with repression of national minorities. In such circumstances conditions are favourably arranged for both ethnical and ideological terrorism.

Of the eight groups of countries, those in groups four and eight are expected to show the most serious hit by terrorism. Group four countries are those in which we find both problems of continuity and problems of integration. In group eight countries, problems of ethnicity are added to problems of continuity and problems of integration. We also expect terrorism to occur in countries within group five, the multi-ethnic countries that do not have any problems of continuity or integration. The countries in the groups mentioned are those in which conditions for the production of terrorism are present.

VARIATIONS IN TERRORISM BETWEEN WEST EUROPEAN COUNTRIES

Chapter 4 reminded us that terrorism is not always intensive outbursts of violence that leaves the place of impact strewn with casualties. This warns us to keep an eye on the organized extent of terrorism actions as well as on the intensity of violence. In this chapter we will turn our attention to the occurrence, intensity and extent of terrorism in Western Europe. We will first examine some general figures and compare the levels of terrorism in the countries before we turn to a more detailed treatment of each country. With our measures for the occurrence of terrorism we want to say something about whether a country has experienced terrorism or not, and if it has, how much terrorism the country has been exposed to. The measures for the intensity of terrorism indicate how violent the terrorism occurring in a country has been, by looking closer at the deaths and injuries caused by acts of terrorism. Finally, we also take a closer look at the organized extent of terrorism, so that we can distinguish the individual acts of violence from those acts of violence that originate with a common actor. For all measures of terrorism we have corrected the original figures to exclude firebombs that did not kill or injure or had no organizationally identified perpetrator (see Chapters 4 and 5).

The material available in the TWEED data set shows that four countries, Germany, Italy, Spain and the United Kingdom, have all experienced high levels of terrorism, in terms of both occurrence and extent. Terrorism is also a serious problem for France in terms of occurrence, but we note that the intensity of terrorism is low in this particular country. Greece and Portugal display intermediate levels of terrorism, while terrorism remains at a low or insignificant level in the remaining countries. Relating the figures to the eight groups of countries outlined above, this means that the countries in group eight, France, Italy and Spain, together account for 50 per cent of all terrorism in Western Europe in the post-war period. The countries in group five make up for 40 per cent of all acts of terrorism, but within this group the United Kingdom totally overshadows, Belgium and Switzerland, two countries with low levels of terrorist violence. The countries in group four, Germany, Greece and Portugal, make up the major part of the remaining 10 per cent. As we can see, the occurrence of terrorism is overwhelmingly concentrated in countries in the categories in which we expected terrorism to emerge. The pattern revealed is much the same as that found by Zimmermann (1989, pp. 182–5). Zimmermann found that political violence in Western Europe was concentrated in the countries having 'noisy-participatory' political systems, that is France, Italy, Portugal, Spain and the United Kingdom. In Zimmermann's view Greece and West Germany are placed in an intermediate position between these political systems and the peaceful democracies of the Nordic countries, the Benelux countries, Austria and Switzerland where there is no political violence of significance.

Variations in the Occurrence of Terrorism

Table 6.2 presents an overview of the occurrence of acts of terrorism in the West European countries for the period from 1950 to 1995. In Table 6.3 the total number of deaths caused by acts of terrorism has been tabulated for the countries so that we can see how the death tolls vary between them. It should be noted here that besides acts of terrorism actually taking place within the borders of a country, some countries also experience an import of terrorist acts from other countries in the West European region. As these acts are usually targeted against the terrorist's country of origin, such acts have been included with the country from which the acts were exported, that is the terrorist's country of origin. Although such imported acts of terrorism represent a security

Table 6.2   Acts of terrorism in West European countries according to TWEED, 1950–95

Country	Number of acts of terrorism	(Percent of total)
United Kingdom	2996	(38.7)
France	2573	(33.2)
Spain	754	(9.7)
Italy	555	(7.2)
Germany *	276	(3.6)
Greece	239	(3.1)
Portugal	206	(2.7)
Belgium	66	(0.9)
Switzerland	33	(0.4)
Netherlands	20	(0.3)
Austria	14	(0.3)
Ireland	6	(0.1)
Denmark	3	
Norway	1	
Sweden	1	
Finland	0	
Iceland	0	
Luxembourg	0	
Total (N)	7743	(100.2)

Note:
* West Germany to October 1990 and united Germany after October 1990.

problem for the importing country, they remain primarily a challenge to, indeed an embarrassment for, the exporting country. It should be emphasized that the number of exported acts is low, making up only 1.6 per cent of the total acts of terrorism recorded in the TWEED data set. The most important importer of acts of terrorism from other countries is France, which alone has a share of one-third of all exported acts of terrorism. France imports acts of terrorism from Spain, mainly due to the terrorist activities of actors from both sides in the Basque conflict. At an import volume of about half that of France, the other two major importers are Germany and the Republic of Ireland. The import of terrorism into the Republic of Ireland is due naturally to its closeness to the United Kingdom and the conflict in Northern Ireland. Germany has imported acts of terrorism from several countries. The Northern Ireland conflict has also led to acts of terrorism being carried out in Belgium, the Netherlands and Germany. Germany, or West Germany as it was, exported a small number of events to neighbouring countries such as Belgium, the Netherlands, Austria and Switzerland. In the following then, these exported acts, and their consequences such as deaths and injuries inflicted, have been counted together with the acts of the exporting country.

It should be further noted that some decisions relating to the coding of the data set may have influenced the extent to which the data set reflects export and import of terrorism. In the TWEED data set republican activities have been classified as having Northern Ireland and the United Kingdom as the home country, though an argument may be made for the possibility of republican terrorism in the United Kingdom having been imported from the Republic of Ireland. Similar arguments may also be presented for other West European conflict situations, most specifically the Basque conflict in Spain and France, and the South Tyrol conflict between Italy and Austria. In the case of Northern Ireland and South Tyrol, terrorist activities in the regions and in the country to which the regions belong have been recorded as happening in the United Kingdom and Italy respectively, and no import situation from neighbouring countries has been judged to occur. For the Basque conflict, activities by groups based in Spain have been classified as belonging to Spain, whether taking place inside or outside the borders of the country.

As we can see from Table 6.2, the United Kingdom stands out with a high occurrence of terrorism. After correcting for firebombs that did not kill or injure or had no organizationally identified perpetrator, the United Kingdom is left with nearly 3000 individual acts of terrorism. Its record of 2996 acts of terrorism is the highest figure in the group of countries investigated, representing 38.6 per cent of the total acts of terrorism in the West European countries. At 1489, the death toll is also the highest among the 18 countries covered by the investigation, and leaves United Kingdom terrorists alone responsible for over half the deaths recorded in the data set used for this investigation (see Table 6.3). France rivals the United Kingdom as to acts of terrorism, with 2573 recorded terrorist acts or about a third of the total number of acts. However when it comes to the death toll the situation in France differs dramatically from that in the United Kingdom. Whereas the United Kingdom has high volumes on both dimensions, France has a low death toll taking into account the high occurrence of terrorist acts. The more than 2500 acts of terrorism left 145 people dead (see Table 6.3), a fact that may be seen as somewhat surprising. Again we are reminded that terrorists are not necessarily out to kill as many people as possible.

From the top two countries there is a gap down to the next two countries, Spain and Italy, with 754 and 555 acts of terrorism respectively (that is 9.7 per cent and 7.1 per cent of the total) (see Table 6.3). In both cases these acts actually left more people dead than the many times higher figure for France. The

Table 6.3   Deaths caused by acts of terrorism in West European countries according to TWEED, 1950–95

Country	Number of deaths caused by terrorism	(Percent of total)
United Kingdom	1489	(53.6)
Spain	650	(23.4)
Italy	298	(10.7)
France	145	(5.2)
Germany *	97	(3.5)
Belgium	31	(1.1)
Portugal	28	(1.0)
Greece	27	(1.0)
Austria	4	(0.1)
Ireland	4	(0.1)
Netherlands	2	
Switzerland	1	
Sweden	1	
Denmark	0	
Norway	0	
Finland	0	
Iceland	0	
Luxembourg	0	
Total (N)	2777	99.5

Note:
* West Germany to October 1990 and united Germany after October 1990.

terrorist violence in Spain is especially intensive. In Spain 650 people lost their life as a result of the 754 acts of terrorism recorded in the TWEED data set, putting the Spanish death toll at 23.4 per cent of the total (see Table 6.3). The situation is somewhat less dramatic in Italy, where 298 people were killed as a result of terrorism in the years covered by the present investigation (10.7 per cent of the total death toll, see Table 6.3).

Germany, Greece and Portugal all have a considerable number of terrorist attacks recorded (see Table 6.2). Germany has the most recorded terrorist acts of the three, with 276 acts of terrorism for the period 1950 to 1995 (3.6 per cent of the total). Greece is recorded with 239 acts of terrorism (3.1 per cent of the total) and Portugal with 206 terrorist acts (2.7 per cent of the total). The difference between these three countries is greater when it comes to lives lost because of acts of terrorism. Here Germany, with a death toll of 97 (equalling 3.5 per cent of the total death toll), has three and a half times as many lives lost as the other two countries. The death toll of Greece is 28 and that of Portugal 27, both making up 1 per cent of the total death toll. We note with interest (see Tables 6.2 and 6.3) that the death toll in Belgium is in the same range as that of Greece and Portugal, only slightly higher, but that Belgium has a low figure for recorded acts of terrorism (66 acts, 0.9 per cent of the total).

In the remaining countries covered by this investigation, terrorism is only a minor problem. Granted, there are some differences. Switzerland for instance has recorded 33 acts of terrorism, but the death toll is only one death. The Netherlands has 20 acts recorded and Austria is at 14. The death toll is low in these two countries too, with the Netherlands at two recorded deaths and Austria at four. In terms of acts of terrorism, lower figures have been recorded for countries like Ireland, Denmark, Norway and Sweden. Not a single act of terrorism has been recorded for three countries, Finland, Iceland and Luxembourg. Ireland's death toll from terrorism stands at four in the TWEED data set, while Sweden's is at one death. No terrorist-inflicted deaths have been recorded for the rest of the countries, that is Denmark, Finland, Iceland, Luxembourg and Norway.

The material presented so far, by comparing Tables 6.2 and 6.3, gave an indication as to the differences in the intensity of violence in the different countries. In Table 6.4, this particular aspect is made more explicit. Countries are ranked according to their number of acts of terrorism, as in Table 6.2, and figures are presented for three measures of the intensity of violence. First, we present the percentage of the acts of terrorism inflicting injury or loss of life, followed by the percentage of acts causing loss of life. These two measures tell how common it is for acts of terrorism to overstep the threshold of inflicting personal injury and death, indicating the intensity of terrorism. Finally, we present in the third column figures for the average number of people killed in acts of terrorism. Here we have divided the total number of people killed because of terrorism by the total number of terrorist acts in the country. This may also say something about the intensity of the violence in the acts of terrorism in the countries.

As we can see from Table 6.4, the general pattern is that those countries that have experienced a high number of acts of terrorism also experience a high intensity of violence. However there are a number of interesting variations. We note for instance that intensity of violence is highest in countries with few terrorist acts, such as Sweden, Denmark or Ireland. That means that when terrorism strikes in those countries, which is not very often, the risk of injury or loss of life is high. Nevertheless, because of the infrequency of acts of terrorism in these countries, these figures are not that interesting. Noting the differences between countries that have experienced higher levels of terrorism is more

Table 6.4   *Intensity of terrorist violence in West European countries 1950–95 (N = 7743)*

Country	Percent of acts of terrorism leading to injury or loss of life	Percent of acts of terrorism leading to loss of life	Average number of people killed in acts of terrorism
United Kingdom	41.3	29.1	0.50
France	4.1	2.8	0.05
Spain	50.5	41.2	0.86
Italy	27.7	20.4	0.53
Germany *	31.9	14.1	0.35
Greece	19.7	9.6	0.11
Portugal	13.1	10.7	0.14
Belgium	28.8	19.7	0.47
Switzerland	6.1	3.0	0.03
Netherlands	10.0	10.0	0.10
Austria	35.7	7.1	0.29
Ireland	66.7	33.3	0.66
Denmark	66.7	0.0	–
Norway	0.0	0.0	–
Sweden	100.00	100.00	1.00
Finland	–	–	–
Iceland	–	–	–
Luxembourg	–	–	–

Note:

* West Germany to October 1990 and united Germany after October 1990.

interesting. We note for instance that Spain is the country in which acts of terrorism cause injury or death most frequently. About half the terrorist acts cause injury or death, with 41.2 per cent of all acts taking life. On average, 0.86 people died in each act of terrorism, the highest figure of all countries. The rate of injury is also high in the United Kingdom. Here 41.3 per cent of terrorist acts cause injury or death. The UK death intensity is somewhat lower though, with 29.1 per cent of acts of terrorism causing death. On average a terrorist incident in the United Kingdom causes the death of 0.50 people. In France, on the other hand, the intensity of acts of terrorism is much lower, with only 4.1 per cent of terrorist acts causing death or injury and only 2.8 per cent of the terrorist acts leading to the loss of life. An act of terrorism only causes, on average, the death of 0.05 people. Considering the high number of acts of terrorism overall in France, these facts are quite exceptional. In Italy 27.7 per cent of acts of terrorism cause injury or death, and at 20.4 per cent the death intensity is not much lower. Terrorism injures more frequently in Italy and Germany. In Germany 31.9 per cent of all acts of terrorism cause injury or death, but only 14.1 per cent of terrorist acts in Germany lead to the loss of life. The average loss of life in acts of terrorism in Germany is 0.35. In the case of Italy, 27.7 per cent of terrorist acts lead to injury or loss of life, while 20.4 per cent of terrorist acts cause death. The intensity of violence is nevertheless quite high, as acts of terrorism in Italy on average cause the death of 0.53 people. Finally, we may note the high intensity of terrorist violence in Belgium. The intensity levels are comparable to those of Italy or Germany. The intensity of acts of terrorism is lower in Greece and Portugal.

Variations in the Extent of Terrorism

Table 6.5 shows the degree to which the extent of terrorism varies in the West European countries. The table includes figures for the total number of groups registered within each country in the TWEED data set, followed by figures for the number of these groups registered as having killed people by their acts of terrorism. Finally, figures for the number of established terrorist groups in each country are presented. By established terrorist groups we mean, as in the previous chapter, terrorist groups that have survived for five years or more or which have killed five people or more.

In all countries investigated here we find that it is only a small number of organizations that are capable of carrying out large numbers of actions over a longer period. Nevertheless we find some interesting differences between countries. With a total of 41 registered terrorist groups, France stands out as the West European country with the most terrorist organizations in the post-war period. At the same time, only about a third of these groups are lethal groups and not more than four of them managed to establish themselves as serious challengers to the state. This indicates a high level of terrorist activity in France when it comes to organizing terrorist groups. However it seems these groups tend to avoid crossing the threshold represented by taking lives, and they are also weak when it comes to keeping up the campaign over time. Greece is rather like France in this respect. The country has a high number of registered terrorist groups, 26 in total, but only eight of these are registered as lethal groups. Further, only two Greek groups may be regarded as established terrorist organizations.

The other countries with larger numbers of terrorist groups have a relatively higher share of lethal groups. For instance Spain has 32 groups registered overall, of which 18 have taken lives and four may be regarded as established

Table 6.5   Extent of terrorism in West European countries, 1950–95

Country	Total number of terrorist groups	Number of lethal terrorist groups	Number of established terrorist groups
United Kingdom	20	13	8
France	41	14	4
Spain	32	18	4
Italy	24	15	4
Germany *	10	6	2
Greece	26	8	2
Portugal	14	6	1
Belgium	6	2	1
Switzerland	6	1	0
Netherlands	6	0	0
Austria	2	1	0
Ireland	0	0	0
Denmark	0	0	0
Norway	1	0	0
Sweden	0	0	0
Finland	0	0	0
Iceland	0	0	0
Luxembourg	0	0	0
Total	188	95	26

Note:
* West Germany to October 1990 and united Germany after October 1990.

groups. At 24, the number of registered terrorist groups is lower in Italy than in France, but as many as 15 of the Italian groups have killed people and four of them fall within our criteria of established groups. The same tendency for terrorist groups to be lethal, and in addition to be well established, is seen in the case of the United Kingdom. Of 20 registered terrorist organizations, 13 are responsible for the loss of life and eight of these fit our criteria for the established terrorist group. In other words, those groups that appear in the United Kingdom tend to be serious challengers. They may be expected to take life and to remain on the scene after appearing.

Of the countries with an intermediate occurrence of terrorism, Portugal and Germany stand out as having relatively few registered terrorist groups, at least when compared with Greece. In Portugal, 14 terrorist groups have been registered. Six of these are responsible for taking lives, but only one has managed to establish itself as a serious player. In Germany, a country that is frequently portrayed as having a serious terrorist problem, only ten terrorist groups have been registered for the post-war period, six of which were responsible for killing people. Two groups managed to establish themselves as serious contenders.

The impression left by this general comparison of terrorism in the West European countries is that the patterns generally fit well to what was expected. Terrorism may be a more serious problem for countries that have both problems of continuity and problems of integration, and some countries with problems of ethnicity also have experienced high levels of terrorism. We will now turn our attention to describing and interpreting terrorism in the countries under scrutiny. The aim is to specify the various aspects of problems of continuity, integration and ethnicity in each country that are relevant to understanding the absence or presence of terrorism and the levels of terrorism experienced by the countries. The countries will be dealt with in descending order according to the number of acts of terrorism they have experienced (see Table 6.2).

THE UNITED KINGDOM: THE DOMINANCE OF REGIONAL TERRORISM

The United Kingdom tops the list of countries as far as the number of acts of terrorism recorded is concerned. While not at the top of the list when it comes to the number of terrorist organizations, the country has a substantial number of terrorist groups, many of which have a high operational capacity. Terrorism in the United Kingdom is markedly intensive, in that acts of terrorism tend to leave people maimed or killed. These facts may be ascribed to the ethnic conflicts within the United Kingdom, deeply rooted in the political and historical development of that country.

Table 6.6 gives an overview of terrorism in the United Kingdom with respect to terrorist organizations and, by implication, important conflicts. Figures are given for the number of acts of terrorism the terrorist organization is responsible for and how many deaths these acts resulted in (as before, the firebombs that did not kill or injure or had no organizationally identified perpetrator were excluded). The period of activity of the terrorist organization is also given. This period is defined as the first and last years the terrorist organization in question was recorded with an act of terrorism in the TWEED data set. This does not exclude the possibility that the terrorist organization existed prior to the year given or continued its existence beyond the year noted in the table. Going through

Table 6.6 Terrorism in the United Kingdom, selected terrorist organizations

Region/Ideology Organization	Active period	Number of actions (% of total)		Number of people killed (% of total)	
Northern Ireland					
Republicans	1950–95	1369	(45.7)	602	(40.4)
Irish Republican Army/					
Provisional IRA	1971–72	11	(0.4)	14	(0.9)
Official Irish Republican Army	1975–92	24	(0.8)	37	(2.5)
Irish National Liberation Army	1986–92	3	(0.1)	2	(0.1)
Irish People's Liberation					
Organization	1974	1	(0.03)	12	(0.8)
Soar Eire					
Northern Ireland Loyalists	1966–94	17	(0.6)	32	(2.1)
Ulster Volunteer Force	1973–93	21	(0.7)	35	(2.4)
Ulster Freedom Fighters	1974	4	(0.1)	30	(2.0)
Red Hand Commando	1972–75	3	(0.1)	1	(0.1)
Ulster Defence Association					
Scotland	1973–75	3	(0.1)	0	–
Army of the Provisional					
Government of Scotland –					
Tartan Army					
Left-wing extremists	1967–71	26	(0.9)	0	–
Angry Brigade					
Total *		2996		1489	

Note:
* The total of all actions of terrorism and deaths caused by these actions in the country, not only those by the selected groups mentioned in the table.

periods of inactivity in terms of violent actions is not unusual for terrorist organizations.

Two interesting facts may be seen in Table 6.6. First, the overwhelming dominance of actors from the conflict in Northern Ireland, and second, the dominance of the Irish Republican Army. All together, 98.8 per cent of all acts of terrorism in the United Kingdom registered in the TWEED data set were carried out in the Northern Ireland context. Only two of the total of 1489 deaths resulting from terrorism in the United Kingdom were not related to the Northern Ireland conflict. Most, but by no means all, acts associated with Northern Ireland took place within the province itself, the rest being carried out by actors originating from Northern Ireland in other places in the United Kingdom (mostly in England). With one exception, all significant terrorist organizations in the United Kingdom are Northern Irish.

If we turn to ideological terrorism, we do not find any significant occurrence of terrorism in the United Kingdom, with one possible exception. This exception is the Angry Brigade, a small left-wing group active with low-intensity actions in the late 1960s and early 1970s (Carr 1975). Though it managed to carry out 26 acts altogether before it collapsed in 1971, the group did not take any lives. It is interesting to note that whereas similar groups originating within the radical student circles produced by the student risings of the late 1960s, most notably in Germany and Italy, were able sustain terrorist campaigns for decades, the Angry Brigade was not able to continue its struggles after police had apprehended the group's members. This may be explained with the United Kingdom's lack of problems of continuity and integration which left no significant community of support in which the Angry Brigade had the opportunity to recruit.

Terrorism in the United Kingdom is concentrated on the conflict between Irish nationalists and supporters of the union between Great Britain and Northern Ireland, which is a continuation of the Irish problem in British politics, a conflict that produced terrorist violence at an early date. As early as December 1867, Irish nationalists used explosives in an attempt to liberate imprisoned fellow partisans. The bomb, made with gunpowder, at Clerkenwell Prison killed 12 people. A bombing campaign of English cities was launched (Laqueur 1987, p. 104). However the present stage of the conflict has its roots in the partition of the island of Ireland by the British parliament's Government of Ireland Act of 1920.

When the Irish Free State was established in 1921, six of the counties in the province of Ulster, where the majority of people supported continued subjugation to the United Kingdom, were kept out of the new Irish state. The six counties were given measures of self-rule based on the British Westminster model, in what has been described as a 'pathological specimen of majoritarian "democracy "' (O'Leary 1989, pp. 562–3). The system provided for a virtual political, economic and social monopoly of power for the segment of society loyal to the British crown, that is the Protestant communities. From the introduction of provincial self-rule in 1920 to the introduction of direct rule from London in 1972, the unionist parties won every election and consequently held on to executive power in the province. The conflict over the partition of Ireland, and the internal relationship between Catholic nationalists and republicans on one side and Protestant unionists and loyalists on the other, explains why the United Kingdom is placed on the top of the list of countries afflicted by terrorism in Western Europe.

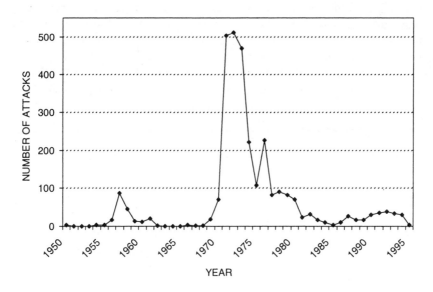

Figure 6.1 Number of terrorist attacks per year in the United Kingdom according to TWEED, 1950–95 (N = 2996), corrected for firebombs

The conflict in and about Northern Ireland early on laid the foundation for the rise of paramilitary organizations, as the terrorist groups are known in the Northern Ireland context. The Irish Republican Army (IRA) was formed as the National Volunteer Force (NVF) in 1916. In the Irish civil war 1922–3, fought between supporters and opponents of the agreement that partitioned the island of Ireland, the anti-partition NVF became known as the IRA. The position of the IRA in the south was however soon weakened and in 1939 the organization was banned in the south of Ireland after having conducted a bombing campaign against the political leadership of the Irish Free State.

In the time period under study here, the IRA has had its basis in Northern Ireland and directed its fight against British authorities. The group has been active throughout the post-war period, and was responsible for the occurrence of terrorism in the United Kingdom in the 1950s and 1960s, as can be seen in Figure 6.1. In 1969 the IRA was split over differences on ideology and strategy. Two factions emerged, the Official Irish Republican Army and the Provisional Irish Republican Army (PIRA) (Bruce 1992b; Moxon-Browne 1981).

The Official IRA is registered in TWEED with acts of terrorism in the years following the split, when it attempted to strengthen its position in the face of competition from the PIRA. According to the data set used here, the organization carried out 11 acts of terrorism in the years 1971 to 1972, killing a total of 14 people. The Official IRA later shifted its activities in the direction of political work rather than terrorist violence, causing another split leading to the establishment of the Irish National Liberation Army (INLA). Since 1975 this group has been responsible for a series of lethal attacks, killing a total of 37 people. The group is still active. Yet another split on the republican side resulted in the formation of the Irish People's Liberation Organization, a group that has carried out a small number of attacks.

Though the Official IRA continued to use violence for a couple of years, it was the PIRA that was to continue the violent traditions of the IRA. Thus, the PIRA may be seen as the continuation of the IRA. It is the PIRA that has been responsible for the main part of republican terrorism in the United Kingdom. The IRA/PIRA is alone responsible for 45.7 per cent of all acts of terrorism and 40.4 per cent of all terrorist killings registered for the United Kingdom in the TWEED data set. The organization attacks targets related to public authority (soldiers, police), reflecting its wish to be a national liberation front, but also the public in an attempt to influence the political attitudes of communities in both Northern Ireland and Britain. The PIRA may be said to be engaged in a struggle for the support and loyalties of the republican sympathizers based in Northern Ireland's Catholic community. The long existence and high level of activities of the organization is a sign that such support has not been lacking. At the same time, the PIRA aims at undermining the British will to keep Northern Ireland in the United Kingdom. To do this, the organization has carried out attacks outside Northern Ireland mainly directed at the general public in British cities.

On the Protestant side we find several small but lethal terrorist groups, none of which has managed to rise to the levels of activity of the IRA/PIRA. We also find a significant number of acts and killings, 79 acts and 80 killings, which may be attributed to loyalist actors but for which no group claimed responsibility or was being accused. One of the most important groups that do leave an imprint, the Ulster Volunteer Force (UVF), was formed in 1966 as a reconstitution of the mass movement of the same name formed in 1912 to fight against Irish home rule. At times, this early edition of the UVF had a semi-official character, participating in the First World War as the 36th Ulster Division, parts of which were later transformed and incorporated into the B-specials of Northern Ireland's provincial police force. This illustrates one reason for the weaker and more fragmented character of loyalist terrorism in Northern Ireland: loyalists wanting to fight republicanism can do this most effectively by supporting or joining the police or military. Loyalist terrorism finds itself challenging the authority and monopoly of violence of a state it wants to maintain (Bruce 1992a, pp. 11, 18; Bruce 1992c, pp. 268–90). The UVF, which is still active, is registered with 17 acts of terrorism in the 1966 to 1994 period and has been responsible for taking the lives of 32 people according to the TWEED data set.

A number of other small loyalist terrorist groups may also be found in the TWEED data set, the most important one being the Ulster Freedom Fighters (UFF). Through 21 acts of terrorism the UFF has killed 35 people. Other less significant groups are the Ulster Defence Association (UDA) and the Red Hand Commando, the latter a lethal group.

It is interesting to note that terrorism in the United Kingdom is marked by an upturn around 1970, as we can see from Figure 6.1. This applies to both republican and loyalist terrorism. By this point, the Northern Ireland provincial political system had gone through years of crisis. The unionist monopoly of power was challenged by a civil rights movement that wanted to see an end to political, social and economic discrimination of the Catholic minority. The Northern Irish provincial political system was unable to respond adequately to these demands and conflict gradually grew more violent. In this respect it is interesting to note that terrorism in Northern Ireland is also marked by a high number of terrorist acts with no identifiable terrorist organization responsible for carrying them out. Some of these may be related to the violent forms of political participation that is such a prominent feature of politics in Northern Ireland. Violence frequently erupts with street demonstrations, rallies and parades. This kind of violence runs parallel to and interacts with the activities of the terrorist organizations.

We should also note that at the same time as the violence from the paramilitary terrorist organizations grew, so did the actions of the state institutions. Military forces were sent to Northern Ireland in 1969, officially to keep the peace and the two rival communities apart. However, the military forces quickly became directly engaged in the conflict. With this engagement came loss of life, from then on an element in the Northern Ireland conflict that left people dead almost every year. Deaths resulting from the actions of the security forces are not only inflicted upon members of terrorist organizations. Also, civilians have been hit – such as the 14 people killed by British armed forces during Bloody Sunday in January 1972.

The terrorism in the Northern Ireland conflict is so dominant that it totally overshadows the activities of groups in other parts of the country, be they ethnically or ideologically motivated. As seen from Table 6.6 the Scottish terrorist group in the TWEED data set is a wholly insignificant group. The Army of the Provisional Government of Scotland – Tartan Army (APGS–TA), active from 1973 to 1975, is only recorded with three acts of terrorism, none of which led to loss of life. No terrorist activity is recorded for Wales. As we noted earlier in this chapter, the United Kingdom saw a left-wing terrorist group that did carry out a number of non-lethal acts of terrorism, but this group did not succeed in establishing itself in the way similar groups on the continent of Europe did. Further, the United Kingdom does not have terrorism from the extreme right. The conflicts leading to terrorism in the United Kingdom are thus limited to the ethnic conflict in Northern Ireland. The United Kingdom does not have problems of continuity or problems of integration and consequently no substantial terrorism related to these dimensions either.

FRANCE: TERRORISM, CENTRALISM AND THE REPUBLIC

France has a high frequency of terrorist acts in common with the United Kingdom, but whereas the United Kingdom also scores high on the dimension of intensity of violence, France has in general experienced much less intensive terrorist violence. Nevertheless it is important to note the diverse origins of terrorism in France. In the United Kingdom, as we have just seen, terrorism is concentrated around the conflict in Northern Ireland. In France, we may distinguish between three main waves of terrorism. The first wave (see Figure 6.2), starting in the late 1950s and extending into the early 1960s, originated from the extreme right. Then a second wave composed of ethnic terrorism followed in the wake of the nationalist awakening of the latter half of the 1960s. The occurrence of ethnic terrorism was also initiated in the late 1960s, but in the early 1970s we can see a dramatic increase. This wave of terrorism forcefully kept up its presence through the 1980s, bringing levels of terrorism in France to unprecedented heights, as can be seen in Figure 6.2. The third wave of terrorism in France, somewhat drowned graphically by the high number of acts of terrorism from extreme ethnic nationalists, is the campaign of terrorism from the extreme left that took place from the early 1980s. All three waves are related to central themes of French politics and the inheritance from the French Revolution, themes such as radicalism, republicanism and centralism.

The French Fourth Republic was founded on the ruins of the Third Republic that was crippled by l'Etat Français, the term the wartime Vichy regime applied to itself, and never restored after liberation. The Vichy regime, established in the parts of France not occupied by Hitler's troops, was based on the ideas of the strong man, clericalism and anti-republicanism. After the Second World War a new republic was formed, one that was to be characterized by weak and shifting governments, and a national assembly dominated by many parties with little discipline. The result was growing opposition to the Fourth Republic, from both the right and the left. As early as in 1951, nearly half the French electorate voted for parties that were against the political system existing at that time (Wright 1983, pp. 13–17). This opposition gradually eroded the legitimacy of the regime, finally undermining it. The crisis of legitimacy paved the way for Charles de Gaulle and the Fifth Republic set up under his sponsorship in 1958.

The right-wing terrorism that occurred in France from the late 1950s onwards

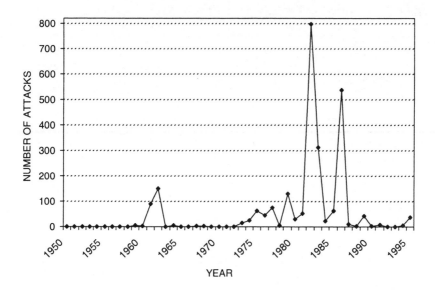

*Figure 6.2   Number of terrorist attacks per year in France according to
TWEED, 1950–95 (N = 2573), corrected for firebombs*

is closely related to the conflicts within the Fourth Republic and with the establishment of the Fifth Republic. The right-wing opposition to the Fourth Republic centred on two main questions: First, the struggle to maintain the French colonial possessions and in particular the French presence in Algeria, and second, the struggle to implement constitutional reforms in favour of a stronger executive.

The Algerian question became the rallying point for groups discontented with the Fourth Republic (Smith 1965, p. 117). These groups held the government to be too weak in face of the Algerian nationalists. Political initiative in the question was gradually shifted to the French in Algeria itself, where members of the French military forces achieved a prominent role (Wright 1983, p. 18). Members of the French military, in association with conservative nationalist Frenchmen, gained considerable room for manoeuvring in the Algeria question. It was an attempted *coup d'état* originating in Algeria in 1958 that led to the downfall of the Fourth Republic and paved the way for de Gaulle. The right-wing terrorism that hit France in the late 1950s and late 1960s also originated from the conservative and nationalist circles in favour of French Algeria.

The Algerian crisis started in 1954 and only a few years later groups emerged that fought Algerian nationalists and their allies in French political life. As we

Table 6.7   Terrorism in France, selected terrorist organizations

Ideology/Region Organization	Active period	Number of actions (% of total)		Number of people killed (% of total)	
Right-wing extremists					
Club Charles Martel	1973–86	2	(0.08)	4	(2.8)
La Main Rouge	1957–60	8	(0.3)	6	(4.1)
Résistance pour la démocratie et la liberté	1960	5	(0.2)	0	–
Organisation de l'Armée Secrète	1961–64	227	(8.8)	63	(43.4)
Left-wing extremists					
Action Directe	1980–86	40	(1.6)	5	(3.4)
Basque Provinces					
Iparretarrak	1983–87	12	(0.5)	3	(2.1)
Brittany					
Front de Libération de Bretagne	1968	33	(1.3)	0	–
Front de Libération de Bretagne – Armée Républicaine Bretonne	1973–79	24	(0.9)	1	(0.7)
Front de Libération de la Bretagne pour la Libération Nationale et Socialisme	1974	2	(0.1)	0	–
Corsica					
Action pour la Renaissance de la Corse	1975–76	5	(0.2)	3	(2.1)
Front de la Libération Nationale de la Corse	1976–91	1279	(49.7)	9	(6.2)
Frente Paesanu Corsu di Liberazione	1973–76	48	(1.9)	0	–
Ghijustizia Paolina	1974–82	8	(0.3)	0	–
Front d'Action Nouvelle Contre l'Independence et l'Autonomie	1977–79	18	(0.7)	0	–
Occitania					
Brigade Rouge d'Occitanie	1973–74	3	(0.1)	0	–
Farem Tot Petar	1975	16	(0.62)	0	–
Total [*]		2573		145	

Note:
[*] The total of all actions of terrorism and deaths caused by these actions in the country, not only those by the selected groups mentioned in the table.

can see from Table 6.7, there were two such early groups, la Main Rouge[2] and Résistance pour la démocratie et la liberté (RDL), neither of which were powerful enough to launch long-lasting intensive campaigns, but which nevertheless were important. The most violent of the two, the Main Rouge group, responsible for killing six people in eight acts of terrorism, was active for four years between 1957 and 1960. The group carried out its actions in several European countries, mainly selectively directed against the political allies of Algerian nationalists, as well as people the group suspected assisted Algerian rebels in acquiring guns. The RDL group carried out five actions, according to the TWEED data set, none of which resulted in the loss of life. The RDL was only active in 1960.

The Main Rouge and the RDL were only harbingers of what was to come. The main thrust of the extreme right's onslaught against the Fifth Republic came with the establishment of the Organisation de l'Armée Secrète (OAS) in 1961 (see Table 6.7). The OAS was originally formed by people that had been active in leading roles in the unsuccessful insurrection in Algeria in January 1960, many of whom were in exile in Spain (Henissart 1970). Later these were joined by people from the French military and these, under the leadership of General Raoul Salan, took over the OAS. At first, the activities of the OAS were concentrated on Algeria,[3] and directed against Algerian nationalists and Muslims. However the campaign quickly spread to metropolitan France, especially from the time when de Gaulle started preparing for the independence of Algeria. The OAS gained considerable support in France itself, and the organization was able to establish terrorist networks throughout the country. The OAS was in many ways a unique terrorist group because it was such a broad coalition. The organization consisted of both former and actively serving soldiers, many of them with experience from colonial wars, former resistance fighters as well as supporters of the Vichy regime, discontent Gaullists, Poujadists, neo-fascists and conservatives of various inclinations. The OAS enjoyed explicit and implicit support among the social and political elite (Challener 1967; Horne 1984, pp. 77–87). Compared with other West European terrorist groups, the OAS is unique in originating from what are usually the core groups in support of the state. Thus the OAS represented a particularly serious threat to the French state.

The broad coalition that made up the OAS was reflected in the organization's programme. Two main factions may be identified. On the one hand there was the faction that was mainly interested in keeping Algeria French. This was the political goal of General Salan and other conservatives within the OAS. On the other hand however, the OAS also contained a right-wing radical faction under the leadership of OAS leaders in Madrid. These wanted the OAS to spearhead a fascist revolution in France. These members held strongly anti-republican views and may be said to represent a continuation of the anti-republican policies of the Vichy regime. Though the faction under General Salan gained the upper hand in the internal struggle within the OAS, many of the OAS terror networks throughout France consisted of people that aimed at overthrowing the Fifth Republic in order to establish a new regime (Cerny 1981, pp. 97–103; Pickles 1973, pp. 47–51).

The expressed aim of the terrorist activities of the OAS, as formulated by General Salan, was threefold. It wanted to 'Attack everything and everybody representing the authority of the State.' First, the OAS aimed at creating a general insecurity in the French general public. Second, it aimed at paralysing France, and third, it aimed at paralysing the regime of Charles de Gaulle.[4] In other words, the OAS openly admitted that its aim was to strike at the state through the creation of fear amongst the public. The OAS attempted to achieve this by directing its attacks against the general public, in combination with attacks specifically aimed at the press and broadcasting, trade unions, political parties, state institutions and targets related to Algerian nationalism. In addition, the OAS made several attempts on the life of President de Gaulle. All together, the OAS was responsible for several hundred attacks. As we can see from Table 6.7, 227 OAS terrorist attacks have been registered in the TWEED data set. These acts varied in terms of intensity. On the one hand, some bombs were directed against material or symbolic targets, while other lethal actions were aimed at specific people. On the other hand, the OAS was also known to strike at the public randomly and with great intensity. One such act was the bomb that derailed the express train from Strasbourg to Paris on 18 July 1961. Twenty-eight people died and 107 were left injured. In total, the TWEED material shows (see Table 6.7) that the OAS killed 64 people in France, which is 43.4 per cent of the total number of people killed by domestic terrorism in France according to the TWEED data set. In other words, this means that the low intensity that we have previously noted is characteristic of terrorism in France, does not apply to the OAS.

Following the independence of Algeria in July 1962, the activities of the OAS fell dramatically. By the end of 1964 the organization had collapsed. The reason for the collapse of the OAS may be sought in the dilemma facing the proponents of French Algeria in general. These sections of the public were forced to choose between a reconstruction of the republic under de Gaulle and a continued French presence in Algeria. As early as 1958, the majority of the French people chose de Gaulle (Smith 1965). This left only a small intransigent minority supporting French Algeria above everything. When Algeria was granted independence in 1962, these people lost the country for which they fought at the same time as they faced the removal of the Algerian question from French politics. They had lost their case and their struggle in metropolitan France.

French right-wing terrorism never recovered from the collapse of the OAS. France has not since seen a strong and persistent terrorist organization on the extreme right. A few minor groups, partially associated with what was once the OAS, were active in the 1970s and 1980s. These groups mainly targeted North-

Africans or immigrants in general. This is the case with the Delta group, which takes its name from an OAS unit, Club Charles Martel (CCM), Faisceaux Nationalistes Européens (FNE), Honneur de la Police (HP), Mouvement Nationaliste Révolutionnaire (MNR), Ordre et Justice Nouvelle (OJN) and SOS–France. These terrorist groups have carried out a small number of acts of terrorism, one or two per group, and they are responsible for the loss of life. Right-wing terrorists are in total responsible for about one-tenth of the terrorist acts in France, but they are responsible for two-thirds of the killings.[5]

Centralism is one of the important values of the French republican tradition. Traditionally power in France has been concentrated in the supreme political institutions of the state in Paris. The state itself has been based upon French language and culture. Nevertheless France is far from being an ethnically homogenous country, though the official French policy was long to deny that France was a multi-ethnic country. Ethnic minorities of varying sizes live in most of the country's peripheries and in the 1960s a cultural and national revival set in among these communities, as was the case with ethnic groups across Western Europe. Ethnic minorities in France were strengthened in their cause by the fact that France gave up Algeria, a country that had been declared an integral part of France as early as 1848. By granting Algeria independence, France recognized the right of national groups to self-determination and admitted that even a French-speaking part of France was not automatically and forever an integral part of the country.

In the 1960s appeared national movements seeking an extension of the principle of right to self-determination, which was fought for by nationalists in Algeria, to regions within France, thereby challenging the right of the French state to exercise authority over the regions. It was argued that even regions within France had the right to self-determination, as many of them had been forcefully annexed to France in the course of the country's expansion over the centuries, and had subsequently been forced to adopt the French language (Beer 1977, p. 146). As a result of this process, ethnic nationalist movements appeared in Occitania of Southern France, among the Catalans of Roussillon (or North Catalonia), among the Corsicans, Basques, Bretons and Alsatians. From some of these movements emerged groups prepared to fight for their cause with violence. In Table 6.7, the most important of these are presented.

The ethnic nationalist terrorism in France displays three interesting patterns. First, four different ethnic groups gave origin to terrorism, most prominently the Corsicans, but also the Bretons and the Basques. Even Occitania saw two groups, the Brigade Rouge d'Occitanie and the more active Farem Tot Petar[6] (responsible for 16 acts of terrorism), in the years 1973–75 though they were both short lived. In contrast to the United Kingdom, where Northern Ireland dominates, many of the French ethnic movements produced terrorist groups. A second main pattern is that most registered ethnic terrorist groups in France were active for only a short period of time and carried out only a limited number of terrorist actions when they were active. Only two groups may be said to have succeeded in launching lasting campaigns against the French state, that of the Corsican Front de la Libération Nationale de la Corse (FLNC) and the Breton Front de Libération de Bretagne–Armée Républicaine Bretonne (FLB–ARB). The third pattern is the low number of people killed as seen in relation to the high number of acts of terrorism. Whereas ethnic groups were responsible for 86.7 per cent of all acts of terrorism in France, they were only responsible for about one-fifth of all the deaths resulting from domestic terrorism in the country.

Breton nationalism was for some time impeded by the reputation of some Breton autonomist groups for collaboration with the Nazis during the Second World War (Berger 1977, p. 168; Kuter 1985, p. 21; Rogers 1990, pp. 67–9). As regionalist groups managed to establish themselves, a spectrum of groups appeared. In contrast to the inclinations of Breton groups before and during the war, several of the new groups were leftist in orientation. Most prominent among the leftist national liberation fronts was the Front de Libération de Bretagne (FLB), a group that rose to prominence with a series of violent attacks in 1968. From this group emerged the Front de Libération de Bretagne–Armée Républicaine Bretonne (FLB–ARB), the main group fighting for independence for Brittany. FLB–ARB is registered in the TWEED data set with 24 acts of terrorism in the years 1973 to 1979. The group is responsible for killing one person. A third group, Front de Libération de la Bretagne pour la Libération Nationale et Socialisme (FLB–LNS), was the result of a split within the extreme Breton movement in 1972/73 (Berger 1977, pp. 170–1; Cerny 1981, pp. 107–8; Moxon-Browne 1983, pp. 7–10). The FLB–LNS collapsed after carrying out only a few acts of violence. Terrorism in conjunction with activities on the behalf of the Bretons largely ceased in the late 1970s.

Another low-intensity campaign of ethnic terrorism may be traced to the Basque region of France, that is in the country's south-west, north of the border with Spain. Long a retreat area for Basque activists from Spain, the region has its own terrorist organization, Iparretarrak,[7] that has made itself heard from time to time. The group's name means 'Those of ETA of the North', signalling the group's wish to take up the fight similar to that of the Basques in Spain. Though Iparretarrak emerged in the early 1970s, the group is registered in TWEED with 12 acts of terrorism in the 1983 to 1985 period. The group is registered as responsible for the death of three people. Compared with the intensive terrorist campaign of the Basques in Spain, Iparretarrak's struggle is rather insignificant. However, the group has managed to maintain its activities over a number of years.

France's only long-standing ethnic nationalist terrorist group is the Front de la Libération Nationale de la Corse (FLNC) (Savigear 1983, pp. 3–5; Moxon-Browne 1988, pp. 221–4; Moxon–Browne 1983, pp. 12–16). FLNC was formed in

1976 when two earlier groups, the Ghijustizia Paolina and the Frente Paesanu Corsu di Liberazione (FPLC), joined forces. The two groups had been fighting violently for the cause of Corsica since 1973, with the FPLC as the most active (48 registered acts of terrorism). Neither of the two groups claimed any casualties. Ghijustizia Paolina was named after Pasquali Paoli (1725–1807), the founder of Corsican nationalism. Paoli was at the head of an independent Corsican republic that lasted from 1755 to 1769. In 1729 the Corsicans had revolted against the Genoese, to which the island had belonged since the fourteenth century. A constitution established the republic of 1755. In 1769, Genova sold the island to France. The island was annexed by France and made into a French *department* in 1789.

The FLNC illustrates the difficulties of French ethnic terrorist organizations. They exist within a centralist political system that is very sensitive to demands for recognition of ethnic distinctiveness and regional autonomy. The political line of the FLNC was influenced by this. At times, the group has presented moderate demands for autonomy in the island of Corsica, by that recognizing French sovereignty. At other times however the group has demanded full independence. In conjunction with elections, FLNC is known to have declared ceasefires so that the elections could be held without the threats of violence influencing voters. This shows the somewhat hesitant approach of the FLNC towards the French state. When it comes to carrying out acts of violence however, the group is not moderate in terms of the number of explosive devices it sets off. The group is known to carry out large numbers of coordinated bomb attacks, often directed against material targets within the Corsican tourist industry or symbolic targets of the French state. For the 1976 to 1991 period the group is registered as responsible for 1291 acts of terrorism, which is nearly half of all acts of terrorism in France. Nevertheless the group is mostly careful to avoid inflicting personal injury in its attacks, and in all its actions the group is responsible for killing nine people. In other words it is the operational pattern of the FLNC that explains so much of the low intensity of French terrorism in general.

As we have seen, the continuity problems of France gave themselves expression mainly in right-wing terrorism. It is interesting to note that the OAS emerged at a time when the political right gained a victory in the French political system. A similar trait may be seen later on, when the integration problems France had with its communists, and to some extent its socialists, were about to be solved. From the start, the Fifth Republic had a troubled relationship with the political left, which had expressed opposition·to the establishment of de Gaulle's republic. However, the stance of the Parti Communiste Français became increasingly moderate as the 1970s drew to a close. A socialist, Mitterrand, conquered the presidency in 1981 and appointed a cabinet based on a coalition between the socialists and the communists. In this situation France experienced terrorism from the extreme left.

No left-wing organization (apart from the ethnic organizations also inspired by socialism) is identified with terrorism in France before 1978. In 1979 Action Directe (AD) appeared, a group inspired by the left-wing terrorist campaigns of Germany and Italy (Dartnell 1994). Its first registered act of terrorism in the TWEED data set took place in 1980. As we can see from Table 6.7, the activities of AD are relatively few compared with those of the FLNC or the OAS. Through the years 1980 to 1986, the group is registered with 40 acts of terrorism, which in all took the life of five people, mostly belonging to the state apparatus.

Terrorism in France has been related to questions concerning the centralist unitary state and the republican ideology. In France, republicanism has been a contentious issue which has left its imprint on the relations between the state authorities in Paris and the ethnic minorities in the regions, as well as on the relationship between the political left and right. Thus terrorism in France grew out of the ethnic conflicts produced by the centralist state's attempt at dominating national minorities. Further, the conflicts over the republican ideological tradition have been severe at times, and have left France with both problems of continuity and problems of integration. Out of this grew ideological terrorism, primarily from the extreme right, but with a smaller element of terrorism from the extreme left.

SPAIN: TERRORISM IN THE DEMOCRATIC TRANSITION

The civil war in Spain led to the downfall of the Republic. In its place was established an authoritarian regime, formally a monarchy, under the leadership of General Franco. This regime was characterized by strong anti-communism and a strongly Catholic conservatism. The state was organized along centralist lines in opposition to the willingness of the Republic to devolve powers to the regions. The political expressions of the national minorities were oppressed, along with those of the political opposition in general. These are traits that, on a later date, set the tone for terrorism in Spain.

We may say that there are three main kinds of terrorism in Spain. The most important kind of terrorism originates from the nationalist movements of Spain's ethnic minorities, and fights for the liberation of those minorities from the centralism and nationalism of Castilian Spain. Around 80 per cent of the acts of terrorism have a regional background, with terrorism in the Basque conflict dominating. In total, and including the attacks exported to other countries (mainly, but not exclusively, to France), the Basque conflict accounts for 62.7 per cent of all acts of terrorism in Spain. The conflict produced terrorism from the 1960s onwards. Nevertheless, Spain follows the French pattern of having

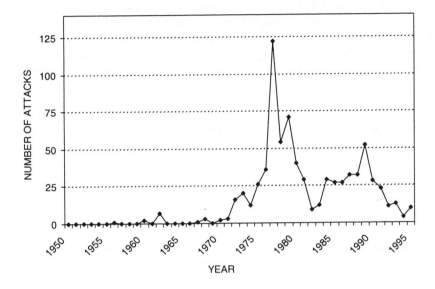

*Figure 6.3   Number of terrorist attacks per year in Spain according to
TWEED, 1950–95 (N = 754), corrected for firebombs*

experienced terrorism in conjunction with the struggles of several minorities,
rather than the pattern of the United Kingdom (as we have already seen) or Italy
(as we shall see below) where terrorism is concentrated mostly around one
conflict. The second kind of terrorism in Spain is the right-wing terrorism
characterized by a strong anti-communism and a perhaps even stronger
sentiment opposing the nationalism of the Basques. This type of terrorism has
its strongest period in the early 1970s. The third type of Spanish terrorism is that
associated with the extreme left. This tendency emerged from the mid-1970s and
has been active until recently. In general, terrorism in Spain went through an
upsurge in the years of transition to democracy, as can be seen from Figure 6.3.

The transition to democracy in Spain was a gradual process under which old
and new institutions and elites coexisted for a long time. The first free election
in Spain took place nearly two years after the death of Franco in November 1975.
Three years went by before a new constitution was adopted. In this period of
transition, the repressive measures of the Franco regime were relaxed. The
political mobilization and high level of political activity did not easily fit with the
repressive traditions of the authorities. The years until 1981 are characterized by
several civilian deaths in conjunction with demonstrations and strikes, often met
with brutal police action. The political transition was in many ways open-ended

in Spain, which laid Spain bare to those attempting to influence the direction of developments, not only by peaceful means but also with violence.

From late 1973 it was clear that the regime of Franco was drawing to a close. The general himself was getting old, but it was an act of terrorism that was to become the symbol of the regime's lack of a future. In December 1973 a bomb set off by the Basque group Euskadi ta Askatasuna (ETA)[8] killed the man Franco had appointed to succeed him, the Spanish prime Minister Admiral Luis Carrero Blanco (Clark 1984, pp. 70–81). This was the 'detonator which precipitated the change of the political system in Spain from authoritarianism towards a liberal democracy', in one opinion (Reinares 1987, p. 121). While the regime seems to have understood this and adapted to new circumstances, the extreme right also took up the challenge in its own way. The years from 1973 until the failed coup attempt in 1981 are the years of right-wing terrorism in Spain, a reaction to the liberalization and development towards democracy.

Overall, right-wing terrorism accounts for only a small percentage of the acts of terrorism in Spain (4.6 per cent of those acts for which we know the ideological identity of the actor), and as we can see from Table 6.8 the right-wing groups are rather small (but occasionally quite deadly). The low occurrence of this type of terrorism in Spain may be explained by the fact that the values of the radical right were, to a large degree, institutionalized in the military and police apparatuses, state administration, and so on of the Franco regime. Breaking the loyalty to those institutions and to the regime by taking up illegal means of action would not be immediately appealing. Nevertheless two groups that did emerge show some interesting features. Two of the more important right-wing terrorist groups in Table 6.8 are the Guerrilleros de Cristo Rey (GCR) and the Alianza Apostólica Anticomunista (AAA). The names of these groups are expressions of their ideological connection with the nationalist, Catholic and authoritarian conservatism of the Franco regime, and show that the aim of these groups was to launch a crusade to save Spain from communism. In the view of these groups, democracy brought with it institutions that lay the country open to a communist attempt to take power. Not only did the groups react to liberalization from within the Franco regime itself, they also objected to more liberal views in the church, and the increased recognition of the national minorities. The terrorist activities of the extreme right-wing groups were directed against targets that symbolized the liberalization. These were activists on the political left, the liberal press and Basque nationalists, but also members of the Spanish government.

A third interesting right-wing terrorist group is the Fuerza Nueva (FN), an attempt to establish a political mass movement in defence of Francoist ideas and for the protection of the authoritarian regime. The group especially sought the support of officers in the military and in the Guardia Civil. FN fielded candidates for election and won representatives to the Spanish parliament. It was opposed

Table 6.8   Terrorism in Spain, selected terrorist organizations

Region/Ideology Organization	Active period	Number of actions (% of total)		Number of people killed (% of total)	
Right-wing extremists					
Alianza Apostólica Anticommunista	1977-78	3	(0.4)	8	(1.2)
Batallón Vasco Español	1976-82	3	(0.4)	6	(0.9)
Fuerza Nueva	1980	2	(0.3)	2	(0.3)
Guerrilleros de Cristo Rey	1973-77	10	(1.3)	1	(0.2)
Left-wing extremists					
Frente Revolucionario Antifascista y Patriótico	1975-77	4	(0.5)	3	(0.5)
Grupo de Resistencia Antifascista Primero de Octubre	1976-93	62	(8.2)	50	(7.7)
Grupos de Acción Revolucionaria Internacionalista	1974	3	(0.4)	0	(-)
Basque Provinces					
Euskadi ta Askatasuna/Euskadi ta Askatasuna-militar	1967-95	374	(49.6)	447	(68.8)
Euskadi ta Askatasuna-polimilis	1978-84	40	(5.3)	7	(1.1)
Grupo Antiterrorista de Liberación	1980-89	25	(3.3)	27	(4.2)
Canary Islands					

Movimiento para la Auto-
  determinación e Independencia
  del Archipiélago de las Canarias
	1977-78	85	(11.3)	1	(0.2)

Catalonia					
Milicia Catalana	1986	3	(0.4)	0	(-)
Tierra Lliure	1986-88	13	(1.7)	2	(0.3)
Galicia					
Ejército Guirrilleiro do Pobo Galego Ceibe	1987-90	22	(2.9)	4	(0.6)
Total *		754		650	

Note:
* The total of all actions of terrorism and deaths caused by these actions in the country,
not only those by the selected groups mentioned in the table.

to the democratic constitution of 1978 and was involved in street demonstrations and attacks on political opponents. FN is registered in TWEED with two acts of terrorism, claiming the lives of two people (see Table 6.8). Members of FN were heavily involved in other right-wing terrorist groups, especially the AAA (Lodenius and Larsson 1994, p. 256; Degenhardt 1983, p. 468; Janke 1983, p. 85).

Terrorism from the extreme right gradually transforms into organizations opposing regional autonomy, especially for the Basque provinces and Catalonia. These two regions attained temporary regional autonomy in 1977, within three years replaced by permanent autonomous regional institutions.[9] These developments were regarded by the extreme right as a threat to the unity of the Spanish state. The TWEED material registers only one anti-Catalan group, the Milicia Catalana (MC), a comparatively insignificant group compared with those active within the Basque conflict. Three anti-Basque terrorist groups are mentioned in Table 6.8. The Batallón Vasco Español (BVE) was active in the early years of the transition to democracy and into the early 1980s at which point was introduced the terrorist activities of the Grupos Armados Españoles (GAE). The most important group however was the Grupo Antiterrorista de Liberación (GAL) which was active in Spain and southern France throughout the 1980s. The latter group's activities in targeting supposed ETA members caused a public scandal in Spain when it became known that the group was sponsored by the Interior Ministry. As noted, the right-wing groups are only responsible for a small number of the terrorist acts in Spain. However their significance lies not so much in the pure numbers of their acts of terrorism, as in the lethality of their actions. The BVE and GAE together killed ten people, though they only carried out four acts of terrorism. Even more murderous was the GAL, killing 27 people in 25 acts of terrorism.

During Franco's reign, all parties but the Phalangist party were banned and there were few channels of legal expression of dissent within Spain. Political parties were only allowed to organize early in 1977 and free elections were held for the first time since 1936. Banned from Spain, the parties, especially those on the left, organized themselves in exile. In this situation a few anti-regime groups that used violent means arose, some of them continuing the Spanish anarchist political tradition. These groups, with names such as Grupos de Acción Revolucionaria Internacionalista (GARI) (see Table 6.8), Movimiento Ibérico de Liberación (MIL), Iberian Revolutionary Liberation Directorate (IRLD) and Libertarian Youth (LY), were active from an early date and until the death of Franco (Reinares 1987, p. 124).[10] However the number of acts carried out is rather insignificant and the groups did not kill anyone.

The main thrust of terrorist violence from the extreme left came as the transition to democracy took off, in the important years following 1975. The terrorist groups that made themselves known in these years originated in small left-wing political groupings and parties that found the situation favourable for initiating a political revolution. The Frente Revolucionario Antifascista y Patriótico (FRAP) was formed in 1973 by members of the small Spanish Maoist communist party, the Partido Comunista de España – Marxist–Leninista

(PCE–ML), starting its brief violent campaign in 1975. It left three people dead. As we can see from Table 6.8, the main left-wing terrorist group in Spain is the Grupo de Resistencia Antifascista Primero de Octubre (GRAPO). This organization was originally founded as the armed wing of the Partido Comunista Español Reconstitudo (PCE–R) (Degenhardt 1983, pp. 464–5; Janke 1983, pp. 78–9). It took its name from the date, 1 October 1975, on which the PCE–R retaliated against the execution of left-wing radicals by the Franco regime. Two members of FRAP were executed in 1975. The activity of GRAPO is founded on a notion that Spain never went through a democratic transformation process. The PCE–R leadership decided that starting an armed campaign to fulfill the revolutionary expectations it thought the people held was necessary. GRAPO's first act of terrorism came immediately before the 1977 election, the first democratic election in Spain since before the civil war. All together, the TWEED data set registers 62 acts of terrorism from GRAPO, claiming a total of 50 lives. GRAPO has been active until recently, targeting mostly people connected with the state, be it police officers, military personnel, or members of the judiciary. However the group has also targeted the public at large. The violent activities of GRAPO came at a decisive moment in the transition to democracy in Spain, raising the level of tension and contributing to making the process of liberalization more difficult (Reinares 1987, p. 126).

As already noted, terrorism in Spain is to a large degree ethnic terrorism, and within this category, the Basque conflict dominates. The Basque conflict has provided the origin for the most important challenger group to the Spanish state, that of ETA. However other Spanish regions have experienced terrorism as well, as noted in Table 6.8. More specifically, those regions are the Canary Islands, Catalonia and Galicia. Terrorism in these three regions makes up for a total of 17.1 per cent of the total number of acts of terrorism in Spain. Most numerous are the acts of terrorism in the Canary Islands, but the occurrence of terrorism there was concentrated in two years (1977 and 1978). The group Movimiento para la Autodeterminación e Independencia del Archipiélago de las Canarias (MPAIAC), once recognized as a national liberation organization by the Organization of African Unity,[11] was responsible for most acts of terrorism in the Canary Islands. Most of its acts were directed against the tourist industry in the islands. MPAIAC's operational pattern is much like that of the Corsican FLNC: a high number of low-intensity acts of terrorism. The group is booked with 85 acts of terrorism. One policeman died as a result of the explosion of an MPAIAC bomb he was trying to disarm. In March 1977 MPAIAC set off a bomb at Las Palmas airport. Traffic was diverted to Tenerife where two of the rerouted planes collided on the airstrip; 585 people died in the accident (Degenhardt 1983, p. 476).[12]

The occurrence of terrorism is considerably lower in Catalonia and Galicia than in the Canary Islands. However the intensity of violence has been somewhat greater. Terrorism in these two regions mostly occurred after the regions had been granted autonomy. The terrorist groups active in these regions are separatist, that is they consider the autonomy granted to be inadequate. In Galicia, the Ejército Guirrilleiro do Pobo Galego Ceibe (EGPGC, meaning the 'Guerilla Army of the Free Galician People') was active from 1988, carrying out 22 acts of terrorism and killing four people. In Catalonia the group Tierra Lliure (TL, meaning 'Free Land') was active with 13 acts of terrorism from 1986 to 1988, killing two people.

The dominant kind of ethnic terrorism in Spain is that associated with the Basque conflict. In its present phase, the Basque conflict was shaped by the Franco regime's abolition of the traditional rights of the historical regions of Spain and its repression of their languages and cultures. After the end of the civil war in 1939, the traditional rights of the Basque provinces were abolished, national and cultural symbols prohibited and the Basque language banned from public life (Clark 1984, pp. 15–16; Clark 1989, p. 23).[13] Political activists were jailed, executed or driven into exile (Shubert 1990, p. 246; Pollack and Hunter 1988, pp.121–2). The Basque opposition to Franco's regime was headed by the Basque government in exile in Paris, with the resistance struggle coordinated by a Junta de Resistencia. Activities among the exiles remained at a minimum until after 1945, when activities were stepped up. One important development was the rebuilding of the Basque nationalist party, the Partido Nacionalista Vasco (PNV). General strikes were called in 1947 and again in 1951 but the Franco regime could not be moved. The frustration and discontent caused by this situation contributed to the establishment of the Euskadi ta Askatasuna (ETA).

In 1959 radical members of the PNV and its youth wing joined forces with the nationalist group *Ekin*[14] to form ETA (Clark 1984). The group was characterized by internal disagreement and rivalries right from the start. The disagreement had its roots in the conflict over class and ethnicity and which of the two was to have the more prominent position, and caused several splits within the organization. One main position emphasized class struggle and wanted cooperation with other radical groups in opposition to Franco, including other Spanish groups. As opposed to this, another faction wanted to emphasize the ethnic character of the struggle, which discouraged involvement in Spanish affairs. The most important split caused by these disagreements occurred in 1974 when ETA split into two separate groups, the Euskadi ta Askatasuna–militar (ETA–m) and the Euskadi ta Askatasuna–polimilis (ETA–pm) (Clark 1984, pp. 28–119; Heiberg 1988, pp. 11–22). Though ETA–pm continued the armed struggle for some time – it is registered in TWEED with 40 acts of terrorism and seven killings – it stressed political work over the violent struggle. It was ETA–m that took the violent line and continued the fight that ETA had started (a development resembling that of the IRA's split into the Officials and the Provisionals).

ETA started its violent campaign at a time when the Franco regime was safe in its position. The first acts of terrorism, as registered in TWEED, took place in 1967. In the early years, ETA carried out relatively few actions, but nevertheless its activities were met with heavy repression from the government. In the years from 1962 and until the death of Franco, states of emergency were declared repeatedly, either for all of Spain or limited to the Basque provinces (Clark 1984). During these states of emergency police were granted increased powers and these periods are therefore marked by the internment and imprisonment of opposition activists, in particular Basque nationalists. ETA's activities increased in the early 1970s, in terms of both terrorist acts and people killed. With some variations, its activities remained more or less at the same level well until 1977, the year of the first free election in Spain. The great upsurge in ETA/ETA–m activities followed parallel to the process leading to the implementation of autonomy for the Basque provinces.

In December 1977 the Basque provinces were granted symbolic, preliminary, measures of autonomy. This was followed by the constitution of 1978 that recognized the right of autonomy for the regions. However this process lacked legitimacy in the Basque provinces. The nationalist party, PNV, urged voters to boycott the referendum on the constitution held in December 1978. This resulted in the absence of more than half the voters in the Basque provinces (Reinares 1987, p. 128). Further, the negotiations on autonomy proved to be difficult. Though 94.6 per cent of the voters supported the autonomy statute in the October 1979 referendum, the result was marred by a low turnout (Reinares 1987, p. 128; Clark 1984, pp. 103–4). In the first election to the Basque assembly in March 1980 (Clark 1984, pp. 116–17), the large but moderate Basque nationalist party PNV, achieved 40.6 per cent of the vote. Herri Batasuna, the radical nationalist party close to ETA, got 17.6 per cent of the vote, while another radical Basque nationalist party, Euskadiko Eskerra, got 10.4 per cent.

It was in this situation, in the times when the future of the Basque provinces was in the process of being moulded, that ETA started its most violent campaign ever. The peak was reached in 1980, when 76 people were killed because of ETA activity. The explanation for ETA's intensified campaign at this point lies in its rejection of the Spanish state regardless of its authoritarian or democratic regime. It did not matter to ETA that Franco was dead and his regime gone, the goal was still Basque independence from Spain. ETA's campaign to achieve this goal has continued until the present. In total (see Table 6.8), the group is responsible for 374 acts of terrorism, according to the TWEED data set, an activity that has left 447 people dead. While the group is known to have targeted people associated with the Spanish state apparatus, especially soldiers and police officers, the group is also known to attack politicians and the public at large.

Spain's prolonged transition to democracy implied a gradual replacement of old authoritarian institutions with democratic ones. Parallel processes of liberalization, democratization and regionalization took place in a situation characterized by a high degree of political mobilization. Actors on all sides wanted to influence the outcome of the transition process, including those ready to use violence. Thus terrorism in Spain is closely associated with the problems of continuity and integration created by Spain's long Francoist dictatorship, a dictatorship that through its centralism and promotion of the Castilian language also aggravated the ethnic conflicts of Spain, particularly that concerning the Basque provinces.

ITALY: TERRORISM RIGHT, LEFT AND PERIPHERY

With the attention devoted to the terrorism of the 'red brigades', one might think that terrorism in Italy is easily accounted for. However, as we can see from Table 6.9, terrorism in Italy is more complex than that. Only about 20 per cent of terrorist acts in Italy are attributable to left-wing extremists. Left-wing terrorists were responsible for 24.5 per cent of the terrorist killings. The bulk of activity, 50.6 per cent of all Italian acts of terrorism, is due to ethnic nationalists. However ethnic activists were only responsible for 4.7 per cent of the killings resulting from acts of terrorism in Italy. This leaves us with right-wing extremists that are responsible for 15.5 per cent of the acts of terrorism but as much as 54.4 per cent of all terrorist killings. In other words, terrorism in Italy is made up of serious threats from both the left and right and also from ethnic nationalist terrorists. Moreover, as can be seen from Figure 6.4, terrorism has been a more or less permanent phenomenon in Italy since the latter half of the 1950s.

Italy's problems of continuity starts with the fascist regime introduced in 1922, finally ending only with the defeat of the Axis powers in 1945. The re-establishment of democracy, culminating with the constitution of 1947, fostered ideas about a betrayed revolution. No leading member of the anti-fascist resistance movement got any leading position in the new democratic Italy. The attempt at clearing the country of fascist influences was largely a failure (Di Palma 1982). The old administrative and economic elite kept the positions they had held previously. Neo-fascists soon appeared on the political scene, and the neo-fascist party became represented in parliament through the vote. In the reconstituted political system, the Democrazia Christiana (CD) managed to hold on to a majority that secured it a near monopoly of power. The Catholic and conservative DC dominated every government after 1948, right until the crisis of the Italian republic heralded its fall from power. This implied that the communist party, Partito Comunista Italiano (PCI), which was among Western Europe's largest communist parties, gaining up to 36 per cent of the vote, was left to permanent opposition. The dominating position of the DC, and its identification

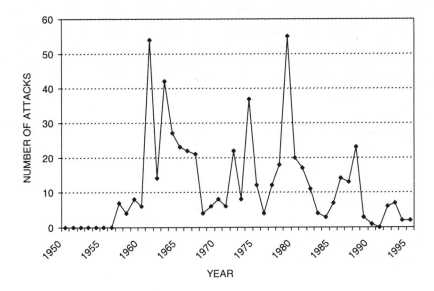

Figure 6.4   Number of terrorist attacks per year in Italy according to TWEED, 1950–95 (N = 555), corrected for firebombs

with the Italian state, created opposition and challenges to the legitimacy of the state from both the left and the right wings of Italian politics. Thus ideological terrorism in Italy is closely related to a double set of fears originating in the reciprocal suspicion between the left and right in Italian politics.

In theory, the 1947 constitution of Italy prohibited the reconstitution of the fascist party, Mussolini's Partido Nazionale Fascista (PNF). Nevertheless the nostalgic right did not hesitate long before organizing politically. In 1946, the Movimento Sociale Italiana (MSI)[15] was founded, which officially had to renounce the PNF as this was required by the constitution. Nevertheless the party drew heavily on the platform of the PNF (Caciagli 1988, p. 23). In 1948 the party won six seats in the first election to the Italian parliament, maintaining representation ever since, gaining up to 8.7 per cent of the vote in its record election.[16] The party has oscillated between the wish to be a respectable party and a position as an anti-system party (Furlong 1981, pp. 68–9). This ambiguity has made itself felt in the party's attitude to violent actions. On the one hand the party participates in the regular parliamentary channels and is officially against the use of violence. Thus the party portrays itself as a party of law and order. On the other hand, MSI has treated people involved in violence with leniency. And this is why MSI is also known to challenge the legitimacy of the Italian state

Table 6.9　Terrorism in Italy, selected terrorist organizations

Ideology/Region/Other Organization	Active period	Number of actions (% of total)		Number of people killed (% of total)	
Right-wing extremists					
Falange armata	1993	5	(0.9)	5	(1.7)
Ordine Nero	1974-83	12	(2.2)	23	(7.7)
Nuclei Armati Rivoluzionari	1980-85	8	(1.4)	90	(30.2)
Movimiente Sociale Italiano	1971-76	2	(0.4)	2	(0.7)
Left-wing extremists					
Brigate Rosse	1972-88	59	(10.6)	48	(16.1)
Gruppi d'Azione Partigiana	1972	1	(0.2)	1	(0.3)
Nuclei Armati Proletari	1974-77	3	(0.5)	0	(-)
Potere Operaio	1973	1	(0.2)	2	(0.7)
Primea Linea	1978-80	7	(1.3)	9	(3.0)
South Tyrol					
Befreiungsausschuss Südtirol	1957-69	231	(41.6)	14	(4.7)
One Tyrol [a]	1986-88	41	(7.4)	0	(-)
Criminals					
Organized criminal groups ('Mafia')	1979-93	24	(4.3)	40	(13.4)
Total [b]		555		298	

Notes:
[a] No indigenous name was found for this group.
[b] The total of all actions of terrorism and deaths caused by these actions in the country, not only those by the selected groups mentioned in the table.

openly. This explains why MSI is registered with acts of terrorism in the TWEED data set. MSI is registered with two acts of terrorism, one in 1971 and the other in 1976, and two killings (see Table 6.9).

Besides the MSI, Italy has seen a range of extreme right-wing organizations and groupings of varying militancy. Right-wing attitudes and hostility to the Italian political system were found even among members of the state's own police and military forces. This resulted in a complex mix of activities, including acts of terrorism, some acts of provocation intended to smear political opponents (typically the radical left), coup plans and other conspiracies (Furlong 1981, pp. 77–9; Middelthon 1975; Lodenius and Larsson 1994, pp. 124–38; Bjørgo and Heradstveit 1993, pp. 77–80).[17] This 'strategy of tension', a term coined by a British newspaper,[18] aimed at preparing the ground for a fascist takeover of Italy. The coup plans mainly centred around a group called Rosa dei

Venti (RdV), consisting mainly of extreme right-wing military officers and members of the military security service, Servizio Informazioni Difensa (SID) (Lodenius and Larsson 1994, p. 130). The RdV leader, who was the SID's commander, later gained parliamentary immunity as a member of parliament for the MSI. These circles are thought to have cooperated with terrorist groups on the extreme right.

The TWEED material records seven right-wing terrorist groups in Italy. However the organizational pattern of Italian right-wing terrorism is quite loose, and as a result a large number of the acts of terrorism from the extreme right in Italy cannot be attributed to a specific organization though the ideological tendencies of the perpetrators were known. One such action was the bomb set off in Piazza Fontana in Milan in December 1969, an act that was to set an example for Italian right-wing terrorism: the action in a public place, hitting the public randomly. In Milan, 16 people were left dead and 87 people were injured. At first, responsibility for the action was placed with the extreme left. The investigation was frustrated by right-wing sympathizers in the police and security service.[19]

Of the several terrorist groups on the Italian extreme right, two groups stand out as particularly violent. These are (see Table 6.9) the Ordine Nero (ON), heir to the Ordine Nuevo group, and the Nuclei Armati Rivoluzionari (NAR) (Degenhardt 1983, pp. 445–6; Seton–Watson 1988, pp. 92–3; Lodenius and Larsson 1994, pp. 124–8, 130–38). The actions of the ON were expressions of the extreme anti-communist attitude of this group. This struggle against communism came to include the governments of the christian democrats, as the ON regarded the DC to be much too indulgent towards the Marxists. In 1974 the ON organized a bombing campaign against the Italian public. The first of these, which left eight people dead and 95 injured, was directed against an anti-fascist demonstration in Brescia. Another bomb was placed onboard the Italikus express train between Rome and Munich. Twelve people died and 48 were injured in the blast. This kind of highly violent action was continued by the NAR in the early 1980s. On 2 August 1980 the group set off a bomb that was to be the most devastating act of domestic terrorism in post-war Western Europe. The bomb, placed in the railway station of Bologna, killed 85 people and injured about 200. Such acts of terrorism directed against the public, killing and injuring at random, aims at creating a chaotic situation in which the fascists can claim power.

While the Italian right feared the communists, the communists themselves looked with suspicion on the freedom with which the radical right were allowed to move in Italian society. The discontent of the communists with the Italian political system was further maintained by the monopolization of cabinet power by the DC. The PCI's relationship with the Italian political system was a central issue in Italian post-war politics. Questions were raised about the loyalty of the party to the system, and the possibility of forming a government with PCI participation was discussed. The PCI was in a strong position right after the war. Communists had played a prominent role in the resistance movement and enjoyed considerable support. At first, the party appeared as moderate and the PCI was willing to cooperate with other parties. Until 1947 the party formed a coalition with the DC and the socialist party Partito Socialista Italiano (PSI). However in 1947 the anti-communist DC blocked the PCI from further government participation, indicating the suspicion with which the party has been met since.

In the latter half of the 1960s Italy went through a period of radicalization, closely followed by a wave of political protest. One aspect of this process was the development of a number of small left-wing radical groups, more radical and activist than the PCI. These groups were strongly opposed to the DC-dominated political system and rejected what they saw as the DC state. Several of these groups were militantly active in workplaces and in the streets, fighting the extreme right. The PCI however went for the option of national cooperation in the face of the threat from the extreme right, and was gradually accepted by the DC as a party loyal to the political system. The process of integrating the PCI culminated with the historical compromise that prepared for PCI's participation in the parliamentary support for the cabinets of 1977–79. Radicals within the party and on the left saw this as a betrayal of the working class and the revolution. This is the political situation that gave rise to left-wing terrorism in Italy (Drake 1982, pp. 105–6; Seton–Watson 1988, pp. 90–91).

The material used here covers several small groups on the extreme left, registered with a few, nonetheless occasionally lethal, acts of terrorism, such as the Gruppi d'Azione Partigiana (GAP) or the Potere Operaio (PO) often seen as forerunner of the Brigate Rosse (see Table 6.9). These are groups that grew out of the revolutionary, anti-fascist movement of the late 1960s mentioned above. They were largely pursuing a conventional political path, but were militantly anti-fascist. Their acts of terrorism were usually targeted against neo-fascists. In addition to such groups we find those that are more usually profiled as terrorist groups (see Table 6.9). One such group was Primea Linea (PL) which was active in the mid– to late-1970s. It carried out a small number of attacks – seven are registered in the TWEED data set – but their acts were highly lethal. Nine people were killed in PL attacks. Another extreme left-wing terrorist group is the Nuclei Armati Proletari (NAP) which was also active in the mid-1970s. This group did not carry out more than three attacks according to TWEED, and the group's activities did not claim casualties.

The most persistent challenge against the Italian state from the extreme left came from the Brigate Rosse (BR) (Drake 1982; Jamieson 1989; Seton-Watson 1988, pp. 95–101, Furlong 1981, pp. 70–76; Degenhardt 1983, pp. 450–54). The BR was formed in 1970 by radical students and discontented former members of the PCI. The founders had been active in smaller groups engaged in students' and workers' protests in the years following 1967, groups that were gradually radicalized as the PCI became more moderate and as the political system turned out to be as unshakeable as ever before. Their activities were also influenced by the apparent success of the fascists, and their position was hardened by the severity of the police in controlling demonstrations in the streets.

The pronounced goal of the BR was to provoke a fascist takeover of power in Italy that in turn would bring Italian communism back to its revolutionary stance betrayed by the historical compromise. Initially the BR sought to achieve this by armed propaganda, that is activity directed against capitalists and the MSI. Later the BR increasingly targeted state institutions and representatives of the state by attacking politicians, judges and police officers. Striking against the heart of the state became the aim of the BR, which the group did most forcefully by kidnapping and later killing the DC politician Aldo Moro in spring 1978. In the view of the BR, the act represented a blow to the stagnated, conservative political system dominated by the DC, as well as a strike against the cooperative line of the PCI.

Following a similar line of reasoning, in attempts to attack both the DC and the PCI, several actions of the BR took place in times of election campaigns or cabinet crises (Furlong 1981, p. 74; Jamieson 1989, pp. 41–41, 81, 92, 114–15, 119–24). In April 1974 BR kidnapped a public prosecutor three weeks before the referendum on divorce, that is in a situation in which the DC was staunchly pitched against its coalition partners and the PCI. The public prosecutor was subsequently released. Two weeks before the elections of July 1976, at which the PCI was expected to gain, the BR killed another public prosecutor. The kidnapping and killing of Aldo Moro came after a prolonged cabinet crisis that was only solved when Moro succeeded in securing PCI support for a new cabinet under the DC's Andreotti. Moro was abducted on the day Andreotti presented the new cabinet's platform to parliament.

As we can see from Table 6.9, the BR is registered with 59 acts of terrorism, claiming a total of 48 lives. BR activities lasted from 1972 until 1988 since which the group has not carried out any acts of terrorism. The group's organization into independent cells of active terrorists, supported by a group of people performing auxiliary functions and with a wider segment of supporters,[20] made the BR into a serious challenge to the Italian state. The group of sympathizers was quite large and was maintained by ideological tracts supporting the BR produced by intellectuals supporting its cause (Drake 1982, pp. 112–7). The BR attempted to maintain a link with workers at factories and was never as isolated from society as their colleagues in the German RAF. In other words the BR was able to draw a certain amount of support from the population. The terrorist violence of the BR appealed both to the widespread discontent with the DC power hegemony and the historical role of the left in the struggle against social injustice and fascism.

So far we have been dealing with the terrorism that struck Italy from the late 1960s and through the following decades. Still, as we can see from Figure 6.4, Italy also experienced high levels of terrorism in the years leading up to the struggles between the extreme right and extreme left. That terrorism came from a different conflict, that over the province of South Tyrol, known in Italian as Alto Adige, with a German-speaking population. South Tyrol was awarded to Italy following the collapse of the Austro-Hungarian empire in the First World War. The incorporation of the province in Italy was followed by a policy of assimilation that was only reinforced when the fascists gained power. The Italian constitution of 1948 granted internal autonomy to various areas inhabited by national minorities. However, South Tyrol was made part of an autonomous region of Trentino-Alto Adige, which gave an overall Italian-speaking population. Implementation of autonomy was long delayed, a fact that was seen by the German population as a continuation of the repressive policies undertaken by Mussolini.

The mobilization on the part of the German-speaking population is irredentist, that is it seeks to reunite South-Tyrol with Austria. From the late 1950s the discontent in South Tyrol made itself violently felt in the appearance of the Befreiungsausschuss Südtirol (BAS) (see Table 6.9). From 1957 onwards this organization launched a campaign of terrorist attacks, mainly directed at material targets and targets symbolic of South Tyrol's position as a part of Italy, that is a type of campaign reminiscent of that later fought by the FLNC in Corsica (see above). The aim of this campaign was to force through a political solution to the South Tyrol conflict based on the principle of self-determination that the BAS hoped would reunite the province with Austria. The conflict was thus raised to the bilateral Italian–Austrian level and in 1964 a tentative agreement was reached that met a number of the demands advocated by the South Tyrolese. However the most important political party among the German-speaking population, the Südtiroler Volkspartei (SVP), did not trust the promises of the Italian government, and the party declined to support the agreement. Continued negotiations followed and finally, in 1969, a deal was struck that was supported by the SVP.

As negotiations gave promise of a solution to the conflict, the BAS turned in the extreme right direction, partly under Austrian influences. The organization continued its attacks against targets representing the Italian state, such as border and customs posts, and their actions started to claim lives. A total of 14 people were killed by the BAS in the course of the campaign that lasted until 1969. Following the implementation of the 1969 agreement between Italy and Austria, which gave South Tyrol autonomy, the actions from the BAS ceased. However the conflict is still latent and has from time to time burst out in violence. One example is the actions of the group One Tyrol, which carried out a number of low-intensity terrorist acts from 1986 to 1988 (see Table 6.9).

The use of terrorism by organized criminals is a final prominent type of terrorism, in many ways peculiar to Italy. In the present work it has been maintained that terrorism is a way to influence bonds of loyalty and allegiance between groups in society. The terrorist acts of organized criminals, whether targeting selected individuals or the public at large, may be said to attempt just that. According to one student of the organized crime in Italy (Duggan 1987), the mafia may be seen as local resistance to the state's attempt to control administratively and judicially the southern parts of Italy following the unification of Italy in 1860. An alternative, private system for the resolution of conflict emerged, that still exists, and it is within this system that the mafia operates. In its competition with the state's system for the administration of justice, the mafia has taken up terrorism as one way to defend its autonomy.

While the material available does not allow sharp distinctions as to the various criminal groups behind the acts of violence,[21] collectively organized criminal terrorism is responsible for 13.4 per cent of the deaths resulting from terrorism in Italy (although in terms of the number of acts it is not that significant; only 24 acts of criminal terrorism are registered in TWEED, see Table 6.9). Criminal terrorism is known in the TWEED data set from 1979 and acts have been registered until 1993.These acts are attacks levelled by organized crime, mainly against representatives of the state such as judges or police investigators, especially those involved in persecuting mafia crimes. Nevertheless some terrorist acts perpetrated by criminals have been directed against the public. A series of attacks against cultural institutions in 1993, five attacks leaving five people dead, was claimed by what appeared to be a right-wing group, the Armed Phalange (see Table 6.9). It is suspected that mafia groups may have been involved in these attacks.

Italy has experienced terrorism from the extreme right, the extreme left, and from the periphery. The country's experience of fascist dictatorship was central in shaping both terrorism from the extreme left and the extreme right. The policies of the fascist dictatorship towards the German-speaking minority in Northern Italy also helped aggravating this conflict. However the ethnic terrorism and the terrorism from organized crime may also be seen as originating in the territorial problem complex of Italian state-building. In relation to ethnic terrorism, this relates to the drawing of the borders of Italy against German-speaking Europe. In relation to the terrorism launched by organized crime it is a case of the state attempting to pacify and gain control over an internal territory.

GERMANY: TERRORISM AND MILITANT DEMOCRACY

One might say that Germany's most recent problem of continuity and integration comes from the incorporation of East Germany, previously under a communist dictatorship for more than 40 years. Of course the country's problems of continuity and integration go further back than that, to the collapse of the Weimar republic at the hands of Nazism. Following the Allied victory in 1945, a de-Nazification programme was initiated in the Western zones of occupation (Herz 1982). Though the programme of de-Nazification filed cases against 3.6 million people, only a relatively small number of people were classified as serious offenders. Faced with the task of keeping the occupational zones running administratively, the de-Nazification programme soon petered out and civil servants returned to their positions. Throughout the post-war era the question of continuity was kept alive by revelations, scandals and court cases involving public figures, politicians and civil servants (Stöss 1991, pp. 101–2). This is the background for the question of continuity of personnel between Nazi Germany and the democratic Federal Republic set up in 1949, a question that has appeared recurrently and which still appears. The issue has contributed to challenging the legitimacy of the Federal Republic, despite the efforts of the government and the courts in limiting the activities of the right-wing though measures such as the prohibition of right-wing extremist groups and political parties.

The existence of political groups on the extreme right represented another side of Germany's problems of continuity. Though the Nazi regime was defeated at war, and the Nazi party abolished and banned, there continued to exist a potential number of right-wing radical voters. In the early years of the Federal Republic, this segment was maintained by former members of the Nazi party and by refugees from the East. However the voters on the outer right were largely absorbed by the large conservative parties, though extreme parties such as the Deutsche Rechtspartei and the Deutsche Gemeinschaft did experience some success at the regional level (Stöss 1991, p. 114). A split-off from the Deutsche Rechtspartei, the neo-Nazi Sozialistische Reichspartei, founded in 1949, was declared unconstitutional and prohibited in 1952.

From about 1965 a new generation of right-wing extremists emerged and this time an extreme right-wing party was successfully set up. The Nationaldemokratische Partei Deutschlands (NPD) gained representation in seven *Landestage* and in 1969 the party received 4.3 per cent of the vote in the Federal election. The electoral fortunes of the party since declined (Stöss 1991, p. 146).

Table 6.10 offers an overview of selected terrorist groups in Germany. Compared with other countries, there are relatively few major terrorist groups in Germany. Of the ten groups registered in the TWEED data set, three are groups

Table 6.10   Terrorism in Germany, selected terrorist organizations (West Germany to October 1990, united Germany after that date)

Ideology Organization	Active period	Number of actions (% of total)		Number of people killed (% of total)	
Right-wing extremists					
Deutsche Aktionsgruppen	1980	4	(1.4)	0	–
Volkssozialistische Bewegung Deutschlands/Partei der Arbeit	1980	2	(0.7)	3	(3.1)
Wehrsportgruppe Hoffmann	1977–80	4	(1.4)	15	(15.5)
Left-wing extremists					
Bewegung 2. Juni	1974–75	2	(0.72)	1	(1.0)
Revolutionäre Zellen	1982–87	24	(8.7)	1	(1.0)
Rote Armée Fraktion	1968–93	106	(38.4)	31	(32.0)
Total *		276		97	

Note:
* The total of all actions of terrorism and deaths caused by these actions in the country, not only those by the selected groups mentioned in the table.

ideologically at home on the extreme right, and the rest are extreme leftist groups. Right-wing terrorists are responsible for 43.8 per cent of the acts of terrorism in which the ideological tendency of the actor could be determined. However the registered right-wing terrorist groups are only responsible for less than a tenth of the right-wing acts of terrorism. Looking at the figures for killings, we find that right-wing extremists are responsible for 57.5 per cent of the terrorist killings in Germany. However the right-wing terrorist groups are responsible for 20.6 per cent of the total number of terrorist killings in Germany. In other words, most of the right-wing terrorism in Germany lacks a firm organizational basis, and this is especially evident in the developments after unification. Germany then experienced an upsurge in attacks from the extreme right, mainly directed against immigrants, refugees and asylum seekers, bringing terrorist violence in Germany to unprecedented levels, as can be seen from Figure 6.5. However no single organization appeared to coordinate the spate of attacks, which according to the TWEED data set left 27 people dead in the course of three years (with 1991 leading up to 1992, the peak year).[22]

The organized right-wing terror occurred earlier than the spate of attacks following unification, that is in the late 1970s and early 1980s (see Table 6.10). Responsible for the organized terror were groups such as the Deutsche Aktionsgruppen (DA), the Wehrsportgruppe Hoffmann (WGH) and the

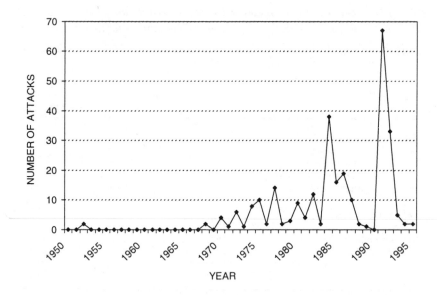

Figure 6.5　Number of terrorist attacks per year in Germany according to TWEED, 1950–95 (N = 276), corrected for firebombs (West Germany to October 1990, united Germany after that date)

Volkssozialistische Bewegung Deutschlands/Partei der Arbeit (VSBD/PdA) (Degenhardt 1983, pp. 428–9; Lodenius and Larsson 1994, pp. 210–14). Though together they only carried out ten attacks, they killed a total of 18 people. Of the three groups, the WGH and the VSBD/PdA proved to be the most lethal. The WGH is responsible for one of the worst attacks of domestic terrorism in Germany. In September 1980 the group set off a bomb during the Oktoberfest in Munich, killing 13 and injuring 200 people.

Despite allegations of continuity with the undemocratic past, since the set-up of the Federal Republic, Germany has been characterized constitutionally by a militant democracy (*streitbare Demokratie*). In the Weimar republic, enemies of democracy on both the right and the left had exploited the freedoms offered by the democratic system to fight democracy itself, ultimately using elections and the parliamentary channel to abolish democracy altogether. This worried the founders of the Federal Republic, and the right of the democratic constitutional system to defend itself against enemies of democracy was therefore enshrined in the constitution of 1949. The federal constitutional court was granted the right to declare political parties unconstitutional, should they be found to represent a danger to the democratic constitutional order. Following these provisions, parties and groups on both extremes have been banned as unconstitutional.

Problems concerning the integration of left-wing radicals in the political system became particularly pronounced in the years leading up to and following the student revolt of the 1960s (Braunthal 1989, pp. 309–10; Niclauss 1982, p. 46ff; Dyson 1975, p. 306). The Federal Republic of Germany, set up in 1949, found itself in a political situation in which Nazism had been defeated, but with a new enemy, communism, taking roots in the part of Germany occupied by the Soviet Union. As the Cold War emerged, communism was then regarded as the main challenger to democratic Germany and the radical left was seen as the main potential enemy of democracy. Although the German communist party, Kommunistische Partei Deutschlands (KPD), was small and insignificant – it won only 2.2 per cent of the vote in the 1953 election (Waller and Fennema 1988, p. 262) – the party was declared unconstitutional and prohibited in 1956. KDP members were arrested and brought to court (Blanke 1981, p. 398–399). For 20 years the Christlich Demokratische Union (CDU) held on to power. The strong position of the CDU caused accusations that the authoritarian and undemocratic style of leadership had continued in what was labelled the CDU state. Originally radical in profile, the Sozialdemokratische Partei Deutschlands (SPD) moderated its platform following the 1959 Bad Godesberg convention. In 1966 the SPD went into a grand coalition with the CDU, only to become the dominant cabinet party in the coalition with the Freie Demokratische Partei (FDP) in 1969. In parallel with the SPD's rise to power, the militant German democracy proved unable to integrate the radical opposition on the left that appeared with the radicalization of students.

West German left-wing terrorism emerged in a political system torn by two sets of fears (Dyson 1975, p. 306). On the one hand, the political right dominated by the CDU and its Bavarian allies, the Christlich Soziale Union (CSU), saw the Federal Republic as a fighting democracy and consequently feared the radicalization among students (Braunthal 1989, p. 310). The parties opposed democratization of universities and were opposed to the social democrats' liberalization of legislation concerning public demonstrations. The parties supported surveillance of radical groups. On the other hand, the radical left feared the strong anti-communism and intolerance they felt was produced by the militant democracy. Especially strong feelings were stirred up by the 1972 decree on radicals, the Radikalenerlass (Blanke 1981; Dyson 1975, pp. 308–9; and Kolinsky 1984, pp. 239–43), issued by the SPD government under pressure to demonstrate a strong stance against communism. The decree aimed at keeping left-wing radicals out of positions in public administration (*Berufsverbot*) (Blanke 1981, pp. 401–402), and was seen by the radical left as an attempt to crush it.

In this situation, German left-wing terrorism appears. As we can see from Table 6.10, even German left-wing terrorism is restricted to a couple of major actors, the Rote Armée Fraktion (RAF)[23] and the Revolutionäre Zellen (RZ), of which the former is the most important challenger to the (West) German state. The origins of the RAF may be traced to a faction within the Sozialistischer Deutscher Studentenbund (SDS), originally associated with the SPD but expelled from the party in 1961 because the organization did not accept the moderate line of the social democrats after the Bad Godesberg manifesto. The SDS kept a radical and revolutionary Marxist line and constituted one of the core groups within the Außerparlamentarische Opposition (APO). Because of its pronounced revolutionary aim and its participation in violent demonstrations, the SDS was declared a threat to the constitution in December 1967. This leading to internal rivalries, the SDS dissolved itself. The first action of the RAF came in 1968, that is at a time at which the group was still a faction within the SDS. Other groups that were to join the RAF – such as the Bewegung 2. Juni (B2W) which operated independently for a couple of years (see Table 6.10) before being gradually absorbed by the RAF – or that constitute the organization's apparatus of support, also originated from the radical student movement (Kolinsky 1984, pp. 205–43; Degenhardt 1983, pp. 436–7; Janke 1983, pp. 21–2). The B2W took its name from the date on which the student Benno Ohnesorg was killed by Berlin police during demonstrations against the visit of the Shah of Iran to Germany, an event that influenced student radicals (Aust 1990, pp. 41–4). To left-wing radicals the event, and the date, became a symbol of the repressive actions of the police and authorities.

The RAF is registered in the TWEED data set with 106 acts of terrorism, the most voluminous terrorist campaign from a terrorist group in Germany, and 31 killings, within a period of activity stretching from 1968 to 1993.[24] Several of the group's actions drew much attention, being directed at leading people in politics, the civil service or business. Among the first these actions we find the killing of the president of the Supreme Court of (West) Berlin, Günter von Drenkmann, in November 1974. In 1977 the RAF killed chief federal prosecutor Siegfried Bruback, banker Jürgen Ponto and, most prominently, the head of the West German Industries Federation Hanns-Martin Schleyer. RAF's last victim was Detlev Rohwedder, the director of Treuhandanstalt, the agency responsible for the privatization of industry in the former East Germany, killed in April 1991.

The Revolutionäre Zellen (RZ) also developed from the extreme left, but chose a different organizational form and line of action and was in opposition to the RAF. As the name indicates, the RZ organized revolutionary cells that were independent of each other, unlike the hierarchical structure of the RAF. The RZ is far less violent than the RAF: it generally carries out acts of terrorism that do not claim lives. It appears that the one person killed by the RZ died unintentionally (Degenhardt 1983, p. 440. For the duration of its period of activity, from 1982 to 1987, the group killed one person in a campaign consisting of 24 acts of terrorism, mostly bomb attacks. This reflects the wish of the RZ to appeal for support among broad groups of the public and to demonstrate that maintaining revolutionary activity is possible (Degenhardt 1983, p. 440; Janke 1983, p. 21).

Summing up, we may say that the main thrust of terrorism in Germany is, in one way or another, related to the problems of continuity and integration created by Germany's experience with Nazism. This applies both to the organizationally stronger terrorism from the extreme left and the organizationally weaker, but still highly lethal, terrorism from the extreme right. In other words, the situation is much like that found in Italy, except that Italy has also faced ethnic terrorism.

GREECE: TERRORISM AFTER THE TRANSITION

Table 6.11 gives an overview of selected terrorist groups in Greece while Figure 6.6 shows the distribution of acts of terrorism in Greece over time. As we can see from Figure 6.6, most of the occurrence of terrorism in Greece is concentrated in the years following the return of democracy to the country, and especially the decade from the early 1980s to the early 1990s. Though the list of terrorist organizations in Table 6.11 is fairly short, Greece has seen a large number of terrorist groups, 26 in all. This is a larger number than for countries such as Italy, Germany, Portugal or even the United Kingdom (see Table 6.5 above). However most of the Greek groups are short lived and displayed only a weak capacity for carrying out acts of terrorism. Moreover, 22 of the 26 terrorist groups registered for Greece in the TWEED data set are left-wing groups, while only four are ideologically right-wing. This fact illustrates well the main source of terrorism in Greece: the problem of integrating the political left after the loss of the communists in the Greek civil war.

The civil war ended in 1949 with victory for the Greek army and the supporters of the monarchy. The Kommunistikon Komma Ellados (KKE), Greece's communist party, had been banned in 1947 and the years following the end of the civil war were characterized by strong anti-communist sentiments and legal persecutions of people involved with the losing side.[25] The political system was dominated by the political right, in alliance with the king and military officers. The Greek military was the guarantor for the system. However Greek society went through a process of modernization and from the late 1960s the new middle class presented demands for increased participation. The role of the king and the military in politics started to be questioned. At the 1963 elections, the liberal centre union, Enosis Kentrou (EK), won and George Papandreou became prime minister. Despite the EK's anti-communist attitudes, military officers considered the party as too weak towards the left and thus unreliable. This view was only reinforced as the son of the prime minister, the radical Andreas Papandreou, was elected to parliament in 1964. Prime Minister Papandreou's government soon

Table 6.11   Terrorism in Greece, selected terrorist organizations

Ideology *Organization*	Active period	Number of actions (% of total)		Number of people killed (% of total)	
Right-wing extremists					
Organismos Ethnikis Anorthosoos	1978	40	(16.7)	0	–
Left-wing extremists					
Democratic Defence	1969	1	(0.4)	0	–
Democratic Resistance Committees	1968	2	(0.8)	0	–
Epanastatiki Organosi 17. Noemvri	1975–94	49	(20.5)	18	(66.7)
Epanastatikos Laikos Agonas	1978–94	26	(10.9)	1	(3.7)
Pan-Hellenic Liberation Movement	1970	1	(0.4)	0	–
Popular Resistance Sabotage Groups	1968	1	(0.4)	0	–
Social Responsibility	1988–90	13	(5.4)	0	–
Total *		239		27	

Note:
* The total of all actions of terrorism and deaths caused by these actions in the country, not only those by the selected groups mentioned in the table.

found itself in dispute with the king and one month ahead of the 1967 elections, a military coup ended all attempts at achieving greater civilian influence and more democracy in Greece (Psomaides 1982, pp. 252, 268; Kourvetaris and Dobratz 1987, pp. 58–9; Diamandouros 1991, p. 16). A military junta was established.

The opposition to the junta's rule mainly came from the left, and some of the opposition groups are registered with a few acts of terrorism, a situation somewhat similar to that in Spain and Portugal during the dictatorships in those countries. These are groups such as the Pan-Hellenic Liberation Movement (PAK) headed by Andreas Papandreou, the Popular Resistance Sabotage Groups (LAOS), the Democratic Defence (DD) and the Democratic Resistance Committees (DRC) (see Table 6.11).[26] The groups are only registered with one (or in one case two) acts and no killings.

Following the Cyprus crisis, the military junta surrendered power to civilians in July 1974 and a multi-party democracy was established under the constitution of 1975. It is after the transition to democracy that terrorism emerges as a significant problem in Greece. Three groups are worth mentioning. Two of them,

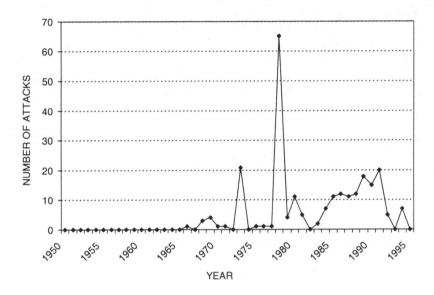

Figure 6.6   *Number of terrorist attacks per year in Greece according to*
TWEED, 1950–95 (N = 239), corrected for firebombs

the Epanastatikos Laikos Agonas (ELA, meaning 'People's Revolutionary Struggle') and Social Responsibility (SR),[27] continue the low-intensity type of action mainly against symbolic targets of capitalism and the state. While the SR was active in the 1988–90 period, the ELA has been active longer, from 1978 until 1994. One of the ELA's terrorist actions left one person dead. However the most serious challenge to the Greek state comes from a group known as the November 17 Revolutionary Organization, or properly Epanastatiki Organosi 17. Noemvri (EO17N) (Corsun 1991). The group takes its name from the date in 1973 when the military junta brutally suppressed a student occupation of the Athens polytechnic, leaving several people dead.[28] The EO17N has a wide range of targets. The first EO17N attack was directed at a convicted torturer from the days of the military dictatorship. However the group has also attacked representatives of the police and military of democratic Greece, as well as representatives from the country's political and judiciary systems. The group is also known to attack foreign targets, chiefly associated with United States military personnel. A final category of targets is made up of those symbolic of industrialist enterprises and the upper class. In total, with its 49 attacks, EO17N is responsible for one-fifth of all terrorism in Greece. It is responsible for 18 killings, which is two-thirds of all terrorist deaths in Greece. The group has been active from 1975 until the present.

Many left-wing terrorist groups in Greece were active in the early 1980s, that is in a time when the political left in Greece experienced a success. The communist party, KKE, had been made legal again in 1974, together with any party willing to accept parliamentary democracy. At the first democratic election after the fall of the military dictatorship, which was also the first election contested by the party since 1936, the KKK – in alliance with other leftist groups – achieved about 10 per cent of the vote (Waller and Fennema 1988, p. 263). The socialist party, Panhellinio Sosialistiko Kinema (PASOK), which in the first years after its foundation in 1974 appeared as a radical socialist party, gained in support in both the 1974 and 1977 elections. Moderating its ideology and rhetoric, the party polled 48.1 per cent in the 1981 election and PASOK then formed the government. The party managed to integrate the left into Greek politics, primarily by making a party of the left acceptable as the party of government, but also by offering an alternative for groups of voters that had previously been excluded from the political system. PASOK managed to reconcile socialism with nationalism, two ideological tendencies that had previously been opposed to each other. By doing this, PASOK managed to increase the legitimacy of the new Greek political system (Diamandouros 1991, pp. 23–8; Kourvetaris and Dobratz 1987, pp. 73–4). It is, in other words, in a situation where the left has positioned itself as a part of the establishment, that left-wing terrorism appears in Greek politics. The situation is similar to that of Italy and France, where the integration of the communist parties and a socialist rise to power happened at the same time as left-wing terrorism started to make an impression.

Greece has a strong conservative and anti-communist political tradition, for a long time well established within the ranks of the Greek military. However the views of the radical right were discredited by the repressive military regime. After the re-establishment of democracy, purges were carried out in the military. Abortive coup plans and conspiracies further discredited the radical right (Psomaides 1982, p. 263; Lodenius and Larsson 1994, p. 254). Nevertheless after the fall of the military junta in 1974 the extreme right made itself felt in terms of terrorism. It is a striking feature however that although Greek right-wing terrorism accounts for just over a quarter of all acts of terrorism in Greece, right-wing terrorism in Greece is weak organizationally. Only three Greek right-wing terrorist organizations are registered in TWEED and only one of these carried out a significant number of terrorist acts. This is the Organismos Ethnikis Anorthosoos (OEA, 'the Organization of National Revival'), which carried out 40 bomb attacks in Athens during 1978, all of them detonated on the second anniversary of the killing of a junta torturer by the EO17N (see Table 6.11). No one was killed in the attacks and the group has not been heard from since.

Unlike Spain in which, as we have seen, experienced terrorism in the transition process, terrorism in Greece emerged as an organizational challenge *after* transition to democracy. The transition was rapid as the authoritarian regime collapsed from within. The problems of continuity and integration facing Greece are mainly related to the situation of the political left. Not surprisingly, the organized terrorist challenge in Greece has mainly come from the extreme left and while the extreme left-wing terrorist groups in other West European countries more or less disappeared towards the end of the 1980s, the organizational expression of left-wing terrorism in Greece actually managed to sustain its low-intensity campaign into the twenty-first century.

PORTUGAL: TERRORISM AS A REVOLUTION PROLONGED

On 25 April 1974, officers from Portugal's armed forced carried out a coup that toppled the country's ailing regime. The officers, most of whom were low ranking and veterans of the colonial wars in Africa, were organized in the Movimento das Forças Armadas (MFA). This body took power without resistance and overthrew the Estado Novo, the authoritarian, corporatist dictatorship founded by Salazar in the early 1930s.[29] The *coup d'état*, also known as the Revolution of the Carnations, marked the start of the transition to democracy in Portugal, while at the same time signalling an active role for the military forces in politics. This was also to set its mark on the terrorism that Portugal experienced after going through a successful transition to democracy.

Portugal, like Spain and, as we have see above, Greece, saw some groups fighting the authoritarian regime with violence. These groups were active from the mid-1960s until the time before the coup, but mainly carried out only low-intensity acts. The most important of these groups was the Acção Revolucionária Armada (ARA), the resistance movement of the Portugese communist party. As we can see from Table 6.12, the ARA was active from 1970 to 1972, with a fair number of actions. However, the group did not kill anyone. A second group in the resistance category was the Popular Action Force (PAF), which was active earlier than the ARA, in the years 1964–65. The PAF is only registered in TWEED with two acts of terrorism, but with one killing. These are examples of the terrorism that occurred in Portugal prior to the transition to democracy. Most of the terrorism Portugal has experienced is concentrated in the years after the introduction of democracy.

As we can see from the overview in Table 6.12, few groups were active in the time when the MFA carried out its coup and revolution. The terrorism that did occur at the time of the revolution is spread among several actors. Most of the acts of terrorism in the year following the coup were reactions to the political development among the coup makers. The MFA originated as a pressure group

Table 6.12   Terrorism in Portugal, selected terrorist organizations

Ideology/Region Organization	Active period	Number of actions (% of total)		Number of people killed (% of total)	
Left-wing extremists					
Acçào Revolucionária Armada	1970–72	10	(4.9)	0	–
Armed Revolutionary Organization	1986	4	(1.9)	0	–
Forças Populares do 25. Abril	1982–86	135	(65.5)	7	(25.9)
Movimento Reorganizativo do Partido Proletariado	1974–75	3	(1.5)	1	(3.7)
Popular Action Force	1964–65	2	(1.0)	1	(3.7)
Right-wing extremists					
Exército de Libertação Português	1975	4	(1.9)	2	(7.4)
Azores					
Frente da Libertação das Açores	1978	3	(1.5)	0	–
Madeira					
Frente da Libertação do Arquipélago de Madeira	1975	2	(1.0)	0	–
Total *		206		28	

Note:
* The total of all actions of terrorism and deaths caused by these actions in the country, not only those by the selected groups mentioned in the table.

without defined political goals for Portugal (Opello 1985, pp. 65–80). Senior officers, politically moderate or conservative, occupied the leading positions of the new regime from the coup in April to the autumn of 1974. In September 1974 these moderates were replaced by a radical faction within the MFA. A prominent personality of this faction was Otelo Saraiva do Carvalho, later to become associated with discontent radical opposition to the political developments in Portugal. The radicals strengthened their position following a failed counter-coup in March 1975. At this point the MFA appeared as a left-wing radical national liberation front that envisaged a permanent role for itself in Portugese politics. The MFA appealed to industrial and agricultural workers for support and nationalized industrial companies and businesses. Support was received from the Partido Comunista Portugûes (PCP). Officers were known to make contact with extreme left-wing groups that aimed at instigating revolt among soldiers and workers in industry and agriculture.

These developments lay the foundations for 'the hot summer of 1975', a situation characterized by clashes between leftist groups and their opponents on the political right, attacks against the offices of the PCP and other left-wing groups, demonstrations, occupations of large estates and so on. The unrest also involved the police and the military, and life was lost in the attempt by these institutions to control the unrest. Table 6.12 contains two kinds of expressions of the violent conflicts in the radicalization process. On the one hand, we find groups on the extreme left that tried to influence the developments of 1974–75. On the other hand we find a reaction to the development of Portugal in a socialist direction from the political right. One can also include the regionalist movements in the Azores and Madeira in this reaction from the right.

The extreme left-wing groups are represented by organizations such as the Movimento Reorganizativo do Partido Proletariado (MRPP) (see Table 6.12). This Maoist group was formed before the coup took place, but was especially active in the activities following the shift of power to the officers. The MRPP was involved in clashes with conservative opponents and the police and is registered with three acts of terrorism in the TWEED data set, leading to the loss of one life. In March 1975 the MRPP was banned by the authorities because of its engagement in street disorders (Opello 1985, p. 107; Janke 1983, p. 68). In addition to the activities of the MRPP, the TWEED material also shows a number of acts of terrorism in which no organized perpetrator was identified. These are of the same nature as those committed by the MRPP, that is in conjunction with clashes between political opponents and with the police.

The right-wing reaction to the radicalization of the MFA and the new regime made itself felt violently through groups such as the Exército de Libertação Português (ELP) (see Table 6.12). In 1975 this group carried out a few acts of terrorism (four) and killed two people. The group drew its support from traditionally conservative parts of Portugal, mainly in the north of continental Portugal and in the islands of the Azores and Madeira (Janke 1983, pp. 67–8). The two latter regions, while ethnically no different from mainland Portugal, reacted to the increased socialist influences in the new regime by forming right-wing radical regionalist groups or 'liberation movements' (Degenhardt 1983, pp. 461–2; Janke 1983, pp. 64–5). The Frente da Libertação do Arquipélago de Madeira (FLAMA) was active in 1975, mainly directing its activities against opponents on the political left. Its activities ceased following the introduction of regional autonomy for Madeira. The Frente da Libertação das Açores (FLA), active from 1975, was originally formed as a reaction to the influence of the PFP and the attempt by the new regime to introduce its administration to the islands. The activities of the FLA dropped when the Azores were granted regional autonomy, guaranteed by the Portugese constitution of 1976. However the FLA activities registered in TWEED took place in 1978, the year when the FLA attacked a socialist cabinet minister visiting the islands. Both FLAMA and FLA carried out a limited number of acts of terrorism (two and three respectively) and neither of the groups killed anyone.

The main part of the occurrence of terrorism in Portugal is due to the activities of a group that emerged some time after the transition had settled and Portugal was established as a democracy. This group was the Forças Populares do 25. Abril (FP–25), a group that took its name from the date of the Revolution of Carnations. Otelo Saraiva do Carvalho was one of the officers involved in the planning and implementation of the 1974 coup. Later he became a central figure in putting down a coup attempted by moderates. Otelo Saraiva do Carvalho came to support a radical revolutionary ideology inspired by socialist countries in the Third World. Standing as a candidate for the presidency in the 1976 election, at 16.5 per cent of the vote he was resoundingly defeated by the moderate Ramalho Eanes. Trying his luck again in the 1980 presidential election, Otelo Saraiva do Carvalho only polled 1.5 per cent of the vote (Lewis and Williams 1984, p. 121).

The declining fortune of a candidate like Otelo Saraiva do Carvalho demonstrates the direction the political development in Portugal took. Following an attempted coup by radical officers in November 1975, radicals were removed from positions of influence. Moderates that supported democracy and socialism took power and managed to hold on to it. The MFA was given a subordinate role, but with the power to monitor political institutions. Nationalization of industry and expropriation of agricultural estates was on the agenda. The constitution of 1976 contained articles proclaiming socialism as the goal and made the Revolutionary Council, originally appointed by radical officers following the March 1975 moderate coup attempt, responsible for supervising the development towards socialism. While the Revolutionary Council was formally an advisory body to the president, it had the power to review legislation. The Revolutionary Council used this power to veto conservative attempts to privatize public companies.

The constitution of 1976 could not be revised until 1981 (Maxwell 1982, p. 243; Bruneau 1984, pp. 74–5). As soon as legally possible, the conservative party Aliança Democráica (AD) initiated the process of revising the constitution. Breaking with its own president, the Partido Socialista Português supported the moves by AD. President Eanes, who was one of the officers behind the 1974 coup, wanted to preserve the constitution and its socialist aims. The constitutional revision strengthened the powers of the national assembly at the expense of the presidency. The tool of the radical officers, the Revolutionary Council, was abolished. Nevertheless, the socialist aims were kept, mainly because of the need to secure PSP support for the constitutional changes (Bruneau 1984, pp. 74–5; Opello 1985, pp. 151–6). Following the constitutional changes, the non-socialist government started dismantling state control of the economy. These developments were clearly contrary to the socialist aims of the 1976 constitution.

In this situation, marked by setbacks for the radical socialists, the FP–25 was

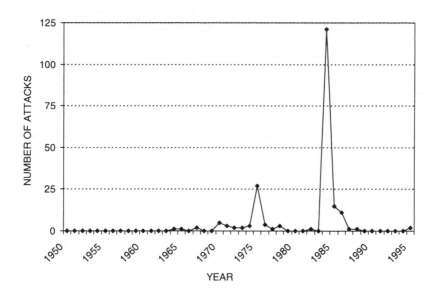

Figure 6.7   Number of terrorist attacks per year in Portugal according to
TWEED, 1950–95 (N = 206), corrected for firebombs

formed. The group was founded in 1980 as an attempt to continue the revolutionary socialist line established by some of the officers in the 1974 revolution. Though he denied being involved, Otelo Saraiva do Carvalho was suspected of playing a crucial role in the group.[30] The first registered activity on part of the FP–25 is from 1982 (see Table 6.12). The main thrust of its campaign took place in the following year however, when the group carried out 120 of its 135 acts of terrorism. Its activities then declined in the following two years, until the group disappeared from the scene. Seven people were left dead because of the FP–25 campaign. Portugese and foreign capital were among the main targets of FP–25 attacks, as were targets associated with Portugal's participation in the NATO alliance.

Terrorism in Portugal, then, appeared in two waves, as we can clearly see from Figure 6.7. The first wave was associated with the turbulent times in the year following the revolution in April 1974 and the first year of transition into democracy. No particular group dominated the first wave of activities, which was anyway characterized by low-intensity actions. The violent activities subsided when the responsibility for shaping Portugal's future was left to the voters and the political parties. Then after nearly a decade, terrorism reappears. This second wave of terrorism was directed by an organized challenge. It was associated with the struggle over the constitution and may be seen as an attempt to counter the growing moderate and conservative direction of Portugese politics and to revert to the radical political goals held by some of the officers staging the Revolution of Carnations.

BELGIUM: THE ODD MAN OUT

Belgium appears to be in a category by itself. The country has experienced 66 acts of terrorism, that is, well below countries such as Germany, Greece or Portugal, and 31 killings, that is, more terrorist killings than Greece or Portugal. Belgium is a multilingual country, divided into two large communities, the Flemish- or Dutch-speaking Flanders and French-speaking Wallonia, with a smaller German-speaking community close to the border with Germany. Somewhat surprisingly however, the language conflict, which has been a dominant political cleavage in Belgium, has not been the root of the country's exposition to terrorism (Laufer 1988, pp. 179–83; Covell 1981). Only a couple of actions from Flemish activists have been recorded in the early 1960s. This near absence of terrorism originating from the country's most difficult issue may be due to the way the language issue has been handled within the political system. The Belgian political system is known for its negotiated settlements and compromises between elites. An electoral system based on proportional representation secured representation for both language groups and made cooperation in coalition governments necessary. The political system has adapted to the challenges raised by the language issue, by reorganizing the setup of the political system according to language lines. This has been done to the territorial-administrative system and even to the party system. Power has been transferred to the linguistically defined regions.

About a quarter of the surprisingly high occurrence of terrorism in Belgium happened in conjunction with the conflict over the position of Leopold III, king of the Belgians, after the Second World War (Fitzmaurice 1988, pp. 43, 46). As the supreme commander of the Belgian armed forces, Leopold capitulated on his own initiative only two weeks after Nazi Germany attacked the country. The Belgian government denounced the action and fled into exile, but the king remained in Belgium under German occupation. As the Allies liberated Belgium towards the end of the war, the Germans took Leopold with them as they retreated. The accusations of collaboration were especially raised by leftists in the resistance movement. Similar accusations were levelled against Flemish nationalists for their doings during the war. After the war, King Leopold's brother was made prince regent because the communists, socialists and some liberals did not want the return of Leopold. The question of the king's return was put to a referendum, in which 57.6 per cent of voters favoured the return of Leopold. However a majority of voters in Wallonia, 58 per cent, were against the king's return. Flanders was strongly for the king, with 72 per cent supporting his return (Fitzmaurice 1988, p. 47).[31] The result of the referendum caused unrest, protests and demonstrations, especially among communists and socialists in Wallonia. The events also led to acts of terrorism, 19 in all registered in the TWEED data set. No one was killed as a result of these acts. The unrest led to the king's abdication in favour of his son Baudouin in August 1950.

The left-wing group Cellules Communistes Combattantes (CCC) is a second large contributor to terrorism in Belgium (Jenkins 1990, pp. 304–6; Laufer 1988, pp. 186–91). The CCC, inspired by leftist terrorist groups in other European countries, was active in 1984 and 1985, with 19 acts of terrorism and three killings. The group attacked targets related to the NATO alliance as well as targets representing the banking system. Though the group got much attention, it did not manage to survive. The high number of terrorist killings in Belgium is due to the activities of a criminal group that was set in a political context. This was the Bende van Nijvel (BvN), a group that carried out a series of violent robberies in the years 1983 to 1985. Four such actions are registered in the TWEED data set, claiming the lives of 17 people. The political dimension of these acts is the suspicion that elements within the police were involved in the activities of the BvN in an attempt to destabilize the Belgian government, a Belgian equivalent of the strategy of tension (see the section on Italy above) (Jenkins 1990, pp. 300–303).[32]

The earliest incidents of terrorism in Belgium were associated with a national issue related to the Second World War, but did not develop into an organized campaign capable of sustaining a terrorist organization. Belgium's more recent exposure to terrorist violence consisted of a short and unsuccessful attempt to launch a left-wing campaign mirroring those of Germany, Italy and France, and a short and deadly spate of armed attacks possibly carried out under a false flag. In other words, terrorism in Belgium is a series of exceptions to what would be expected: terrorism in conjunction with the language conflict.

THE PEACEFUL DEMOCRACIES

The remaining 11 countries in the sample of countries investigated here have not experienced levels of terrorism similar those the countries discussed above have been exposed to. Nevertheless some interesting differences appear within this group of countries too. While a few countries have not experienced acts of terrorism at all (Finland, Iceland, Luxembourg), there are a couple of countries that have occasionally been exposed to terrorist violence, though in low levels and never through sustained campaigns.

The Defusion of Ethnic Conflict

Initially in this chapter, three countries were grouped together as having problems of ethnicity but neither problems of continuity nor problems of integration. These countries are the United Kingdom, Belgium and Switzerland. As we have already seen, these countries have experienced vastly different levels of terrorism, with the United Kingdom outranking all other countries under investigation here. However the political and historical situation that is the source of terrorism in the United Kingdom has an interesting parallel in Switzerland. This parallel is the Jura conflict. While the cantonal structure in Switzerland largely follows linguistic lines, the predominantly French-speaking Jura had for a long time until recently been a part of the German-speaking canton of Bern. This canton is organized along the lines of a unitary state.

The movement for a secession of Francophone Jura from Bern renewed its efforts from the 1950s, and it is on the fringes of this movement that we find a small amount of ethnic terrorism in Switzerland. The occurrence is small, 14 acts of mostly non-lethal terrorism in total, and not continuous. Nevertheless the conflict did produce a terrorist group, the Front de libération jurassien (FLJ), but even this group only carried our four acts of terrorism between 1964 and 1972 according to the TWEED data set. It is likely that the Swiss system of solving conflict may have contributed to the low level of terrorism in the Jura conflict. In the case of the Jura conflict, mobilization sought to take advantage of the opportunities for citizens' initiative and referendums. Referendums on how to solve the conflict were held on the communal, cantonal and federal levels, no less than seven times altogether (Thompson 1989). By an amendment to the constitution of Bern in 1950, Jura was guaranteed representation in the cantonal council (Jenkins 1986, p. 100).

Leading the conflict into constitutionally acceptable forms, its violent potential was defused. This is a sharp contrast to the majoritarian system of government that set its imprint on Northern Ireland, with no options for minority representation or power sharing. In the long run, this caused violent conflict and Western Europe's longest-running terrorist campaigns. In the case of Jura mobilization for separation from Bern, the conflict ended in 1979 in a peaceful split by which a part of the Jura region was constituted as a new canton in the Swiss confederation.[33]

Countries with Settled Problems of Continuity

Based on the theoretical expectations, countries such as Austria, Finland and Ireland, all of which have had problems of continuity (Finland also problems of ethnicity) were expected to have experienced terrorism. This is not the case. Terrorism has been occurring only sporadically and at a low level of intensity in Austria and Ireland, and not at all in Finland. The reason for this may be sought in the ability of these countries to incorporate fringe groups, especially the losing side from the conflict that produced the problems of continuity. Thus the three countries have not found themselves faced with substantial political groups that use problems of continuity to challenge the state.

In terms of problems of continuity, Austria has a double experience of dictatorship (Engelmann 1982, pp. 135–7). The first dictatorship originated from internal Austrian conflicts in the First Republic, those between the conservative Catholic camp and the social democratic camp. From 1933 the fascist Dolfuss cabinet governed by authority of emergency legislation. In 1934 the social democratic party was banned. An authoritarian, corporativist regime inspired by Italian fascism was set up. In March 1938 this was defeated by the incorporation of Austria into Nazi Germany, a state of affairs that lasted until Nazi Germany was defeated at the hands of the Allies in 1945. This double exposure to dictatorship laid the foundations for a settlement of the sharp conflicts between the different political parties from the First Republic (Mommesen-Reindl 1980, p. 282; Engelmann 1982, pp. 135–7).

Under dictatorship, the opposing political camps found themselves in the same political situation and their common experience from concentration camps and the illegal opposition drew them closer together. This led to the development of a shared understanding that cooperation and compromise were necessary should it be possible to re-establish the Austrian republic. With the defeat of Nazi Germany and the re-emergence of Austria as a separate entity, though under Allied occupation, a coalition government was formed. Though the conservatives, the Österreichische Volkspartei (ÖVP) won the 1945 elections and had the possibility of forming a cabinet on their own. However, wanting a national government that could reconcile former opponents and present a united national view in relation to the occupation powers, the party chose to enter into grand coalition with the social democrats, the Sozialistische Partei Österreichs (SPÖ) (Mommesen-Reindl 1980, pp. 282–3). The ÖVP and SPÖ shared power until 1966 when the conservatives formed the government alone. The social democrats returned to power in a one-party cabinet formed in 1970. This experience of one-party government from both camps demonstrated the gap of confidence had been bridged and that the polarization that had destroyed the First Republic was no longer a danger.

The re-established Austrian republic has not been met with challenges from the political extremes either (Engelmann 1982). The political left was dominated by the social democrats, and with a communist party, the Kommunistische Partei Österreichs (KPÖ), that saw its fortunes gradually dwindle from a not too impressive poll of 5 per cent in 1945 (Waller and Fennema 1988, pp. 262–3). A stronger anti-system potential has existed on the extreme right. After the Allied victory over Nazi Germany and re-establishment of the Austrian republic, more than a half million people were denied the right to vote because of their membership of the Nazi party. These voters were however gradually incorporated into the two larger parties, and also into the third party, the Freiheitliche Partei Österreichs (FPÖ). Originally a liberal party, the FPÖ has recently been transformed into more of a radical right-wing party under the leadership of Jörg Haider who rose to power in the party in 1986. Simultaneously with the nationalist and right-wing turn of the FPÖ, Austria has experienced a spate of terrorist attacks from the extreme right. Whereas the extreme right in Austria previously did not produce significant terrorist groups, from 1993 two right-wing extremist terrorist groups appeared, the Volkstreue Ausserparlamentarische Opposition (VAO) and the Bayuvarische Befreiungs Armée (BBA). The two groups are together responsible for seven terrorist attacks in the years from 1993 to 1995 according to the TWEED data set, and the BBA is responsible for four killings. Nevertheless, right-wing terrorism has not been able to maintain a sustained high level campaign in Austria.

In the Republic of Ireland, the civil war between supporters and opponents of the treaty that established the Irish Free State and partitioned the island of Ireland led to strong polarization between parties in the political system (Coakley 1986, pp. 40–47; Chubb 1982, pp. 7–47). Still, although the treaty opponents lost the civil war, the chief proponent of the anti-treaty sentiment, the Fianna Fáil (FF) party, pursued a pragmatic course under its leader Eamon de Valera. The FF displaced the strongly republican and anti-treaty party Sinn Féin, which did not recognize the new state. Thus within a decade of the civil war and partition, the FF leader managed to lead his party to power and the most prominent anti-treaty party was to become the party that led the Irish Free State onwards to full independence from the United Kingdom. This was finally and formally achieved in 1949 when the Republic of Ireland was proclaimed.

The Irish constitution of 1937 reflects the ambivalent Irish position. On the one hand, in Article 2 it claims sovereignty over the entire island of Ireland, but on the other hand, in Article 3 it recognizes *de facto* that Northern Ireland is a part of the United Kingdom.[34] The question of partition and of Northern Ireland has been prominent in Irish politics, but has been subject to national consensus. Thus the issue has not successfully been a rallying point for parties that rejected the existence of the Republic of Ireland, as does Sinn Féin.

The fact that the Northern Ireland conflict has produced so little violence in the Republic, especially as compared to the levels of violence in the United Kingdom part of the island, may also be due to the fact that militant republicans do not want to fight a war on two fronts. They may prefer to keep the Republic as a retreat area and base from which they can operate. Nevertheless it remains a fact that the fundamental questions over the position of the state have been a territorial question in relation to another state, the United Kingdom, and not a question of how to organize the Irish state internally. Thus the conflict over Northern Ireland has not provided a basis for a sustained campaign of terror against the Irish state.

Similar traits of national consensus may be seen in Finland. From the formation of independent Finland in 1917, attempts were made to settle the ethnic conflict between the Finnish-speaking majority and the Swedish-speaking minority (Allardt and Starck 1981). Swedish was declared an official national language by the constitution. The political party advocating the interests of the Swedish speakers gained representation in the national parliament, and has participated in coalition governments. Separatist mobilization in the Åland archipelago following the declaration of Finnish independence in 1917 was soon met with offers of regional autonomy (Högman 1986; Norman 1986). Consequently this has not been a source of irreconcilable conflict in Finland.

The potentially most dangerous conflict concerns the continuity problems of Finland. The civil war between white and red forces that erupted following Finnish independence in December 1917 led to victory for the white side. The atrocities of the civil war and the persecution of reds that followed left deep impressions on Finnish society and made their mark on Finnish politics until the Second World War. The Finnish communist party was banned. The victorious whites took over the state apparatus. However, the social democrats formed a minority government in 1926 and the party's acknowledgement of executive responsibilities was to initiate a certain integration of the left into Finnish politics. National unity was created by the Winter War (1939–40), initiated by the aggression of the Soviet Union. Though Finland lost both the Winter War and the Continuation War (1941–44), the struggle for national independence led to national unity in the post-war period. The official line of the communist party, which was now legal,[35] was that open confrontation with the Finnish state would lead to another civil war with a subsequent Soviet invasion, which was to be avoided. The communists participated in the government from 1945 to 1948. The moderate line of the communists was parallelled by a new official line towards the Soviet Union. With the aim of securing Finnish independence, the Finnish government agreed in 1948 to the Treaty of Friendship, Cooperation and Mutual Assistance with the Soviet Union.[36] The communist party found itself in the legitimizing shadow of the treaty. Consequently one may say that Finland's problems of continuity were settled after the end of the Second World War.

Countries that have experienced both problems of continuity and problems of integration have also experienced terrorism as a political problem. It may seem that problems of integration, by providing people and ideas, are necessary for problems of continuity to transform into a terrorist problem. As we have seen, countries such as Austria, Finland and Ireland have managed to avoid problems of integration and seem to have settled their problems of continuity. One reason for this may be the international political situation in which these countries found themselves, and the national unity in face of external pressure that favoured integrating former enemies. In these situations internal conflict and terrorism may have contributed to weakening the countries in the face of powerful and expansionist neighbours, thus threatening the independence or territorial integrity of the country (see Chapter 2).

The Absence of Terrorism

Table 6.2 shows that in addition to Austria, Finland and Ireland, which have already been mentioned, some additional countries are entirely without terrorism or have been exposed to only sporadic, mostly isolated terrorist attacks. These countries are Denmark, Iceland, Luxembourg, the Netherlands, Norway and Sweden. With the exception of Luxembourg, they belong in group one, that is countries without problems of ethnicity, continuity or integration (see Table 6.1). As an ethnically homogenous country without problems of continuity, but with problems of integration, Luxembourg is placed in group one (see Table 6.1).

Of the countries just mentioned, the Netherlands has the most actions registered in the TWEED data set (20 in total).[37] The Netherlands has had a large and active non-parliamentary opposition, working on issues such as peace, the environment and anti-racism. This activity has not transformed into sustained campaigns of terrorism, but these activities do find their way into the TWEED material. Most of these acts are low intensity (the number of terrorist killings in the Netherlands is two). Schmid points out that the tolerant attitude and policies of the Dutch government may explain the absence of terrorism in the country (Schmid 1988, pp. 147–53). Firstly the Dutch authorities have been careful not to stigmatize opposition activities outside the parliamentary channel as terrorist, out of the fear that stigmatization might indeed lead the activities into unwanted directions. Thus the Dutch authorities talk about 'politically motivated violence' and not 'terrorism' in cases of extreme behaviour. Secondly the authorities have actively sought to co-opt opposition activities outside the parliamentary channel. Opposition groups, even those on the extremes, have been integrated into mainstream political life, through participation in committees, working groups, and so on. In some cases groups have been supported financially through public subsidies. In addition to this, the authorities themselves have largely not engaged in activities that lack legitimacy in the eyes of the public, or sections of it. This overall tolerance has the effect of creating public space for diverse political activity, even that which may lie beyond what is normally tolerated in the parliamentary channel of political participation. In turn this makes the threshold activists must step over before entering into terrorism quite high. We may say that the Dutch attitude is the opposite of that produced by the militant democracy ideology prevalent in Germany.

The other countries without terrorism may share some of the traits described for the Netherlands, though probably not to the same degree. Schmid mentions Denmark as a country that is close to the Dutch case in terms of toleration towards extra-parliamentary participation (Schmid 1988), and Bjørgo and Heradstveit argue that the same principles of toleration apply to the Nordic countries and Switzerland (Bjørgo and Heradstveit 1993, p. 114; Heradstveit 1992, pp. 112–6, 127). The lack of problems of continuity and integration in these countries, combined with the open and tolerant attitudes prevalent in these political systems, makes it difficult for fringe groups to challenge the state by terrorist violence without excluding themselves totally from any source of support in the public. In countries that do experience problems of legitimacy, extreme fringe groups find groups and segments of the public that they share a political platform with and that they may appeal to. Though this does not guarantee a positive response from this segment in cases of acts of terrorism, the chances for a favourable response are present and such a response is what terrorists need to keep up a sustained campaign of terrorism in challenge to the state. It is this political constellation that is unevenly distributed among the West European countries, and that rewards the countries lacking problems of legitimacy and punishes those with such problems.

THE POLITICS OF TERRORISM IN WESTERN EUROPE

One main aim of the present investigation is to describe and explain differences in the occurrence and extent of terrorism in the West European countries in the post-war period. In this chapter we have seen how closely related the occurrence and extent of terrorism are to issues and conflicts in the political systems of the West European countries. It is a widely accepted view that party politics and party systems originate in conflict structures that have deep historical roots and which manifest themselves in the political attitudes and loyalties of citizens. In this chapter it has been argued that terrorism too may be traced to similar political structures. Furthermore the discussion has revealed that terrorism is frequently associated with constitutional crises and regime transition. The discussion has demonstrated the importance of taking into account the problems of legitimacy countries face when explaining why some countries are heavily exposed to terrorism while other countries more or less avoid the problem. The presence of problems of legitimacy works to integrate terrorist challengers with segments of the public, making it more likely that a terrorist campaign might be successfully launched and sustained.

Drawing on the series of figures from Chapter 2, the arguments set out here imply the possible existence of several target groups among the public.

Terrorists may want to appeal to or influence these groups in different ways. In relation to one particular group, those faithful to the state authorities, it may be a question for the terrorist of showing strength and proving that there is a powerful challenger to the established authorities. Over time the aim might be to weaken the bonds of loyalty and allegiance between the particular group of citizens and the state. In relationship to another group, that which is composed of people critical of the state, it may be a question of appealing for the establishment of a new set of loyalties and allegiances to replace that currently supporting the state authorities.

Conditions for the occurrence of terrorism are most favourable in cases where the public is fragmented into several antagonistic sections, one of which is the segment critical of the state. It has been argued here that problems of legitimacy, that is problems of ethnicity, problems of continuity and problems of integration, contribute to making these conditions. Where these problems do not appear, a terrorist challenge to the state will only exclude the perpetrator from the public because there is no pre-existing segment of the public to which the terrorist can successfully appeal for support. Thus in these countries we will only see sporadic terrorist attacks that do not develop into sustained campaigns.

NOTES

1. The country was informally known as West Germany for most of the time period covered in this study, but is properly known as the Federal Republic of Germany (FRG). From October 1990, the FRG includes the *Länder* of the former German Democratic Republic, or East Germany.
2. The similarity in name with the Northern Irish Red Hand Commandos is no doubt coincidental.
3. Only acts of terrorism carried out in metropolitan France are registered in TWEED.
4. For a more detailed account of the OAS manifesto, see *Keesing's* p. 20955.
5. See Lodenius and Larsson (1994, pp. 189–99) for an overview of the French extreme right and also Moxon-Browne (1983, pp. 20–22) for a discussion of anti-Semitic terrorism in France.
6. Schmid et al. (1988, p. 550) translate the name as 'We Shall Blow Everything Up'.
7. Often the name is incorrectly translated as 'Those from the North'. See the discussion of the name question in Jacob (1994, p. 231).
8. The name, which means 'Basque Homeland and Freedom,' is sometimes also spelt Euzkadi ta Azkatasuna.
9. Later the entire country was divided into autonomous regions, with wider powers for the Basque Provinces, Catalonia and Galicia than for the others. For a discussion of the negotiating process leading to the introduction of regional autonomy, see Clark (1989).
10. No Spanish names were found for the IRDL or the LY.
11. MPAIAC was recognized as such by the OAS's committee for colonial liberation in July 1968, see Janke (1983, p. 84).

12. In the data set used here, MPAIAC has not been recorded as responsible for the accident and the deaths resulting from the collision between the airliners.

13. These measures were especially directed at the two Basque provinces that had supported the republican side in the civil war, that is Guipúzcoa and Vizcaya. The provinces of Alava and Navarra had supported Franco and were allowed to retain certain economic privileges.

14. Ekin was originally the name of a newspaper, the name means 'to make' or 'to do'.

15. The name refers to Mussolini's Italian Social Republic also known as the Sàlo Republic after its seat.

16. Typically the party polled around 5 per cent. In 1972 MSI joined the Royalist Partito Nazionale Monarchio to become the Movimento Sociale Italiana–Destra Nazionale (MSI–DN) (Caciagli 1988).

17. See also *Keesing's* pp. 26410–11, 26821, 28494, 29057 and 29224.

18. According to Lodenius and Larsson (1994, p. 129) the term was coined by the British newspaper the *Observer*.

19. See *Keesing's* p. 29057 for allegations of SID involvement in the Piazza Fontana bomb and the attempt to frustrate the investigation. According to *Keesing's*, the allegations were made in 1974 by the minister of defence Giulio Andreotti. Two SID officers were later sentenced to jail because of their involvement in the case. The SID was reorganized.

20. In Degenhardt (1983, p. 454) the number of BR activists is estimated at 500 while the number of sympathizers is put at 10 000.

21. Though some generic names for regional criminal groups may be found in the source, *Keesing's*, most acts are just attributed to organized crime or 'the mafia'.

22. For more detailed statistics, see the annual reports of the Federal Office for the Protection of the Constitution, for instance Bundesamt für Verfassungsschutz (1997, pp. 91–9).

23. According to Aust (1990, p. 120) the name Rote Armée Fraktion was only adopted in 1971 though the group emerged in 1968. From 1968 until 1971 the group was known as the Baader–Meinhof Group after its two founders.

24. In April 1998 a declaration sent to Reuters news agency in Cologne declared that the RAF had decided to disband.

25. According to *Keesing's* pp. 12431, 13086, 19974, about 21 000 people were imprisoned by reason of war crimes following the end of the civil war. In 1952 about 20 000 people were pardoned, but as late as 1963 1100–1200 people were still in jail because of their activities in the civil war. In the early 1950s, death sentences were handed down to members of the communist party.

26. The Greek names of these groups are not known to this author.

27. No Greek name has been found for this group.

28. The number of people killed is still not certain. According to official figures released immediately after the event (and reported in *Keesing's*) 13 people were killed. However an investigation performed after the fall of the junta put the number at 34.

29. António de Oliveira Salazar established the Estado Novo in the years from 1930 to 1933, with himself as prime minister with dictatorial powers until 1968 when power was transferred to Marcello Caetano (Opello 1985, pp. 49–61).

30. Otelo Saraiva do Carvalho denied involvement with the FP–25, though in 1986 he was sentenced to jail for heading the organization, see Manuel (1996, pp. 56–57).

31. Fitzmaurice (1988, p. 47) and *Keesing's* pp. 10597, 10881f.

32. See Jenkins (1990, pp. 300–303) and *Keesing's* pp. 37680–37681.
33. The southern part of Jura is predominantly Protestant, like the canton Bern, whereas the northern parts of Jura are overwhelmingly Catholic. The southern parts chose to stay within Bern and did not form part of the new canton (Campbell 1982, p. 279; Thompson 1989, pp. 194, 204ff).
34. The constitution was changed following the referendum that approved the measures agreed to by the government of the Republic of Ireland in the Good Friday Agreement on the future of Northern Ireland, signed by the British and Irish governments, and representatives of political parties in Northern Ireland, in Belfast 10 April 1998. The constitutional amendments were approved in a referendum on 22 May 1998. For a constitutional history of Ireland before these developments, see Chubb (1982, pp. 41–46).
35. During the Winter and Continuation Wars a provisional communist government, or puppet government, of Finland was formed by communists in Soviet Carelia. Following the war, rumours of a communist takeover circulated (Arter 1987, pp. 17–19).
36. Following the collapse of the Soviet Union, the treaty was terminated in 1991.
37. Acts of terrorism by actors from the former Dutch colonies have been excluded from the TWEED data set as they originate from outside Western Europe. From 1975 to 1978 the Netherlands experienced a spate of terrorist acts from South Moluccan activists (Herman and van der Laan Bouma 1981).

Conclusion

PATTERNS OF TERRORISM IN WESTERN EUROPE

We chose as our theoretical point of departure a definition that sees terrorism as violence employed in a relationship of communication. This allowed us to develop a perspective that integrates terrorism into a wider understanding and explains the phenomenon of terrorism as political. The perspective presented emphasizes that terrorism aims at influencing bonds of loyalty and allegiance between groups in a society. In turn, that discussion was furthered to relate terrorism to the concepts of the state and legitimacy. Building on the definition that sees terrorism as communicative violence, we found that in addition to the various audiences terrorists may seek to influence, the state is always one of the groups with which terrorists communicate. This enabled us to look for characteristics of the state that might be thought to play a part in the appearance of terrorism within the state's territory. While general characteristics as freedom and democracy have been launched as explanatory factors, we also saw that socio-economic factors have been used to explain the outbreak of terrorism in modern societies. However we also argued that problems of legitimacy affecting a state may contribute to the emergence of terrorism.

The research question raised required us to look for characteristics of the West European states that might help explain the appearance of terrorism, or the lack of terrorism. The analysis produced several important empirical findings. One first pattern discerned is that terrorism became a more important feature of West European politics over the period investigated. Over time, terrorism increased in frequency and terrorism spread to more countries. Whereas the 1950s and 1960s showed some occurrence of terrorism, with terrorist campaigns limited to three countries, the levels of terrorism virtually exploded from the early 1970s onwards. Terrorism affected more countries, and more countries were exposed to sustained campaigns of terrorism. From the early 1970s, the frequency of terrorist attacks rose. Especially dramatic was the rise in the death toll that followed from the increased number of terrorist attacks. In other words terrorism seems to have grown in importance after 1970. However it should also be noted that after 1990 levels of terrorism fell back to what they were before 1970. Still, in the first part of the 1990s the number of countries affected by terrorism did not drop. This suggests that terrorism as a political means gained popularity from the 1970s onwards, and it remains a political means that actors anywhere might consider.

We also briefly noted that domestic terrorism has been more widespread in Western Europe than international terrorism, defined as terrorist attacks originating from outside the region. While international attacks tend to strike hard when they hit European countries, producing a death toll that is frequently as high as the death toll of domestic terrorism, in the period investigated here the domestic levels of terrorist attacks have always been higher than the annual international attack rate. In other words, in terms of frequency and death toll, terrorism in Western Europe has primarily, though not exclusively, been a home-grown problem.

It is important to note though that most attempts at instigating terrorist campaigns are short lived. Most of the terrorist groups investigated have a low capacity for action and are short lived. Most terrorist groups only carry out one, or just a few, acts of terrorism before disappearing. More than half of the terrorist groups do not kill anyone. Nearly two-thirds of the groups disappear in their first year of terrorist activity. This means that the sustained organized terrorist campaigns are limited to relatively few cases. We find these few cases in a certain number of countries, in which conditions are favourable for prolonged terrorist campaigns.

One conclusion from this study is that terrorism is related to high levels of freedom and democracy. The analysis showed terrorism to be systematically related to measures of freedom and democracy, with a tendency for low levels of freedom, human rights and democracy to be associated with high levels of terrorism. It should be noted that this pattern is particularly strong for ideological terrorism, and that this may suggest a less important role for political factors like freedom, human rights and democracy in producing ethnic terrorism. Further, we also noted that the countries that were dictatorships in the period of time studied were exposed to terrorism only after the transition to democracy. Nevertheless it remains the case that some of the countries with the highest score on the freedom and democracy dimensions are countries that have only sporadically been hit by terrorist attacks. This makes it somewhat unclear whether it is democracy and freedom that stimulate terrorism directly, or whether these are just factors that make terrorism possible but do not directly act as motivational factors for terrorists.

Further, the analysis also showed that terrorism is related to economic modernization and inequality. Economic modernization, measured as growth in real GDP, is especially associated with ideological terrorism. On this point the results of the analysis were not as unambiguous as for ethnic terrorism. Relationship between economic modernization and ethnic terrorism overall were weaker. Nevertheless we conclude that ideological terrorism seems to be more strongly associated with countries that have experienced stronger economic growth. When turning our attention to the importance of income distribution, we found a tendency for higher levels of terrorism in those countries in which income is most unevenly distributed. Again, the relationship was found to be strongest for ideological terrorism. This indicates a tendency for terrorism to appear in countries in which injustices may be perceived as greater than in other countries. The impact of the third socio-economic dimension, that of the post-industrial society, was less clearly discernable. The analysis suggested that a high degree of unionization in a country works against the occurrence and extent of terrorism, but at the same time we found that terrorism is not associated with societies in which the tertiary sector is strong. In our view, this does not support the suggestion that terrorism is related to the post-industrial type of society. We may conclude that rapid economic growth, and political and social injustices, have all played a part in producing terrorism in the West European countries. Despite the varying results of the analysis, terrorism, and particularly ideological terrorism, shows signs of being associated with both political and socio-economic factors. However the impact of socio-economic variables can only be felt through political motivational factors, which, it has been argued, are to be found in the varying severity of problems of legitimacy facing West European countries.

The study also demonstrated that terrorism is related to problems of legitimacy. Looking closer at the relationship between the problems of legitimacy and the occurrence and extent of terrorism, we found a strong association between ethnic diversity, a measure of the ethnic problems of countries, and ethnic terrorism. As expected, ideological terrorism turned out to be unrelated to ethnic diversity. In other words countries that are ethnically heterogenous tend to have more terrorism than countries that are ethnically homogenous. The analysis further found strong positive associations between problems of continuity and ideological terrorism. This means that terrorism, again in particular ideological terrorism, tends to appear in the countries that went through a difficult development to democracy. Further, we found a similar strong association between problems of integration and ideological terrorism. As we see it, this may be an indication that terrorism, particularly ideological terrorism, tends to appear at its highest levels in the countries that experience difficulties in integrating groups on the political fringes.

The result of the analysis suggests that rapid economic growth, as well as social and political injustices, may play a part in causing terrorism. When going into further detail on the relationships between problems of legitimacy and the occurrence and extent of terrorism in the countries analysed here, we are able to see more specifically what political issues and conflicts terrorist groups operate within. Thus a more detailed analysis was able to relate terrorism to the political systems in the states of Western Europe. We found that rather than being unrelated to conventional politics and operating on the outside of politics, terrorism originates from the same political issues and controversies that keep the other actors of a political system going. Furthermore the analysis revealed that terrorism frequently appears in times of constitutional crisis and transitions from one regime to another.

The discussion has demonstrated that when explaining why some countries are heavily exposed to terrorism while others essentially avoid the problem, it is important to take into account the variations in the problems of legitimacy the countries face. When problems of legitimacy are present, this contributes to integrating the challenges of terrorists with political segments in the public. This increases the chances of a terrorist campaign succeeding. By using acts of terrorism, terrorists may attempt to influence various political groups in society. Terrorists may want to violently demonstrate to those loyal to the state that there is a powerful contender against the state, and hope that the loyalty of this particular group to the state will be weakened by continued acts of terrorism. In relationship to the group of people critical of the state, terrorists may try to appeal for the establishment of a new set of loyalties and allegiances to replace that currently supporting the state authorities.

The conditions for the emergence of terrorism are most favourable in countries where the public is fragmented into several opposing groups, polarized on a dimension ranging from acceptance to rejection of the state. It has been argued in this work that the presence of problems of legitimacy affecting a state, that is problems of ethnicity, of continuity and of integration, contribute to making the conditions favourable for the appearance of terrorism. In countries where these problems of legitimacy do not appear, there is no segment of the public to which the terrorists can successfully appeal for support, and terrorist attacks challenging the state work to exclude the terrorist from the public. Consequently, terrorism appears only as individual sporadic attacks in these countries and the terrorists have little chance of developing their attacks into a sustained campaign.

TERRORISM IN WESTERN EUROPE SINCE 1995: IS AN AGE OF TERRORISM OVER?

What has happened to Western Europe's terrorism since 1995? In light of the ongoing War on Terror, with its intensified focus on terrorism as a major political challenge, the developments in Western Europe may stand out as somewhat surprising. The general trend in West European terrorism since 1995 demonstrates lower levels of terrorism, a reduction in number of countries hit, and the disappearance of a number of long-standing terrorist groups. In terms of the occurrence of terrorism, it seems the situation has returned to the levels of the early 1960s. It is as if an age of terrorism draws towards its end.

One first important development is the continued weakening and gradual disappearance of the organized challenge from left-wing terrorism in Western Europe. Despite the names of some of the old groups appearing sporadically with attempts of revival, most notably the Red Brigades in Italy, all the long-standing terrorist groups of the extreme left originating in the 1970s have now vanished from the scene. Though characterized by low frequency of attacks, the most persistent group in the category has been the November 17 Revolutionary Organization (EO17N) in Greece. However with the series of arrests of group members starting in late June 2002, even this group has been struck a severe blow, putting an end to a campaign lasting two and a half decades. With the arrest and trial of the EO17N in Greece, the last of the old left-wing groups with roots in the 1970s was removed from the scene of West European terrorism.

Secondly, it is worth noting the developments on the extreme right. Though there were warnings of rising levels of right-wing extremism, developments since 1995 have not shown a stronger organized terrorist challenge from the extreme right, though there have been important occurrences of right-wing violence in some countries, most notably Germany and Sweden, a country previously not hit by terrorist violence. However it should be noted that no organized terrorist challenge has emerged from the extreme right in any of the countries under study here.

A lower frequency of internal terrorist attacks goes parallel with a reduction in the number of countries experiencing internal terrorist attacks. This means the terrorism that remains is concentrated in a small group of countries. Given the patterns of terrorism that were found in the present analysis, it should come as no surprise that higher levels of terrorist violence after 1995 are found in countries like France, Spain and the United Kingdom. In these three countries terrorism is fuelled by ethnic conflicts in the regions of Corsica, the Basque country and Northern Ireland. It should be noted however that even in these three countries, important developments have occurred that might further weaken terrorism and produce lower levels of it rather than keeping terrorism at persistently higher levels, especially in France and the United Kingdom.

In France internal terrorism since 1995 is still connected with the conflict in Corsica and the sporadic outburst of terrorist violence characteristic of that conflict, despite moves towards increased autonomy for the island. The most notable persistence of internal terrorist violence however is the continued campaign by the established ethnic terrorist groups, most notably by ETA against the Spanish state. Though periodically on a self-declared ceasefire, ETA has continued its campaign against the Spanish state, killing both representatives of the state's institutions of force, political opponents and members of the general public. In view of developments elsewhere, the continued terrorism associated with the conflict over the status of the Basque country stands out as a particularly persistent source of terrorist violence in Western Europe.

In the United Kingdom, the peace process in Northern Ireland has produced some interesting patterns concerning the occurrence of terrorism. First of all, it is important to note that terrorism did not disappear with the signing of the peace agreement. Rather, the political developments in Northern Ireland demonstrate the difficulties in ending terrorism through a negotiated peace agreement. In Northern Ireland the peace process and the 1998 peace agreement, known alternatively as the Belfast Agreement or Good Friday Agreement, did not initially end terrorism, though cessation of violence by one of the most prominent terrorist groups, the Provisional IRA, played an important part in the process. The most immediate effect of the peace process was twofold: splintering and reaction. Both splintering and reaction produced the same effect, at least in the short term: the continuation of terrorist violence. Reaction from previously less-dominant actors initially produced continued loyalist terrorism by groups disaffected with the peace process. Similarly, splits in the republican movement also contributed to the continuation of terrorism. Though the split in the Provisional IRA goes back to the late 1980s, the ceasefire and the peace process brought the Continuity IRA to the forefront in 1996, followed by another splinter group, the Real IRA, a year later. Both groups were opposed to the peace process and continued the struggle by violent means. Dissident republicans of the Real IRA were responsible for the worst incident of terrorist violence ever recorded in Northern Ireland, the car bomb detonated in Omagh on 15 August 1998 leaving 29 people dead. Thus developments in Northern Ireland demonstrate the difficulties involved in getting armed groups to stop using violence and to embrace action through conventional political channels as the sole way of action, and the dilemma produced by the evidence that peace processes and peace agreements may in fact initially lead to continued, and even worse, terrorist violence than experienced earlier.

The decline of internal terrorism in Western Europe started long before the attacks of September 11 2001 and the War on Terror that followed. Nevertheless the current worldwide focus on combating terrorism may reinforce the pressure contributing to the decline of West European terrorism through two factors: first, through the increased need for terrorists and their political allies to avoid association with the terrorist activities and terrorist groups currently highlighted as the main threat in the War on Terror; and second through the increased cooperation between governments in fighting terrorism and the resulting international solidarity in working against it which makes it more difficult for those suspected of involvement in terrorism to be able to find refuge in other countries and avoid extradition.

Though Western Europe's own terrorism is in sharp decline, we are reminded daily that the fear of terrorism is still very much with us, though from the West

European perspective, and compared to the situation of recent decades activities now seem to take place outside the region. It should be remembered however that terrorism is about political issues and conflicts, and consequently we must expect terrorism to always be with us. Though internal terrorism is now in decline, it is unlikely that terrorism is a problem that will disappear, even from democratic and highly advanced societies. Terrorism is a flexible means, largely independent of political ideologies, and can be employed by almost any actor. The patterns of terrorism in Western Europe since 1950 tells us that through the post-war decades terrorism appeared in many guises. Most impressive perhaps is the ideological transformation from extreme right to extreme left that provided a continued justification for terrorism from national liberation groups. Such a transformation may happen again. Though the home-grown terrorism of Western Europe currently appears to have subsided, this situation is not guaranteed to last. Even in the countries of Western Europe we may expect new circumstances, different issues and conflicts, to produce campaigns of internal terrorism different from those seen before.

Appendix

TERRORIST ORGANIZATIONS REGISTERED IN THE TWEED DATA SET

In the tables in this appendix information is given for the 188 West European terrorist organizations identified in the TWEED data set. Groups are ranked alphabetically according to country. The names of the terrorist groups appear in the original language of the group as far as this is known. In the column labelled 'orientation' groups have been classified according to their ideological tendencies or platform into broad categories of leftist (L), rightist (R), ethnic or regionalist (E) or other (O). Note that some groups labelled as ethnic or regionalist may be siding with the state centre and defend the integrity of the state. These are nevertheless judged to be parties to an ethnic conflict. The column 'active period' indicates the group's dates of activity, defined as year of first registered act of terrorism and year of last recorded act of terrorism in the TWEED data set. Note that between the first and last years of recorded activity, a group may have had years of inactivity, and that activity may have continued after the 1995 cut-off date. In the two last columns, information is given for the total number of acts committed by the terrorist organization and the total number of deaths caused by these actions as recorded in the TWEED data set. Note that substantial volumes of activities in the data set are unattributable to specific groups, appearing instead under various generic labels.

Country/ Organization	Orientation	Active period	Number of: Attacks	Killings
Austria				
Bayuvarische Befreiungs Armée	R	1993–95	5	4
Volkstreue Ausserparlamentarische Opposition	R	1994	2	0
Belgium				
Bende van Nijvel	O	1983–85	4	17
Brigades socialistes revolutionnaires	L	1989	1	0
Cellules Communistes Combattantes	L	1984–85	19	3
Front de la Jeunesse	R	1980	1	0
Revolutionary Front for Proletarian Action	L	1985	3	0
Vredesveroveraars	O	1985	1	0
France				
Action Directe	L	1980–86	40	5
Action pour la Corse Francaise	E	1976	1	0
Action pour la Renaissance de la Corse	E	1975–76	5	3
Action Révolutionnaire Corse	E	1976	1	0
Armée Corse de la Liberation Nationale	E	1983	2	0
Autonomous Fighters Against Capitalism	L	1979	1	0
Autonomous Group for Radical Action against Capital	L	1979	4	0
Autonomous January 22 Movement	L	1979	1	0
Black War	L	1988	1	0
Brigade Rouge d'Occitanie	E	1973–74	3	0
Club Charles Martel	R	1973–86	2	4
Collective of Autonomous Groupings	L	1979	8	0
Commando de Souvenir	L	1978	1	1
Commandos révolutionnaires Corses	E	1975	1	0
Delta	R	1975–80	2	1
Faisceaux Nationalistes Européens	R	1980	2	0
Farem Tot Petar	E	1975	16	0
Francs-Tireurs et Partisans Corses	E	1981	2	0
Frente Paesanu Corsu di Liberazione	E	1973–76	48	0
Front d'Action Nouvelle Contre l'Independence et l'Autonomie	E	1977–79	18	0
Front de la Libération Nationale de la Corse	E	1976–91	1279	9
Front de la Libération Nationale de la Corse – Historical Channel	E	1994	2	0
Front de Libération de Bretagne	E	1968	33	0
Front de Libération de Bretagne – Armée Républicaine Bretonne	E	1973–79	24	1
Front de Libération de la Bretgne pour la Libération Nationale et Socialisme	E	1974	2	0
Ghjuistizia Paolina	E	1974–82	8	0

Country/ Organization	Orientation	Active period	Number of: Attacks	Number of: Killings
Honneur de la Police	R	1979	2	1
International Revolutionary Solidarity	L	1988	1	0
Iparretarrak	E	1983–87	12	3
Jewish Brigades	L	1980	1	0
Justizia et Libertà	E	1975	1	0
M-5	O	1984	2	0
Main Rouge	R	1957–60	8	6
Mouvement M-10	L	1986	1	1
Mouvement Nationaliste Révolutionnaire	R	1980	1	1
Ordre et Justice Nouvelle	R	1980	1	0
Organisation de l'Armée Secrète	R	1961–64	227	63
Résistance pour la démocratie et la Liberté	R	1960	5	0
Revolutionary Coordination Group	L	1979	2	0
SOS-France/Commandos of France	R	1985	1	4
Union du Peuple Corse	E	1980	1	0
Germany				
Anti-Fascist Struggle	L	1977	1	0
Anti-Imperialist Cells	L	1995	1	0
Bewegung 2. Juni	L	1974–75	2	1
Deutsche Aktionsgruppen	R	1980	4	0
March 6. Group	L	1975	1	0
Revolutionäre Zellen	L	1982–87	24	1
Rote Armée Fraktion	L	1968–93	106	31
Roter Morgen	L	1977	1	1
Volkssozialistische Bewegung Deutschlands/ Partei der Arbeit	R	1980	2	3
Wehrsportgruppe Hoffmann	R	1977–80	4	15
Greece				
Aftonomos Antistasi	L	1981	1	0
Anarchist Action	L	1986	2	0
Antistratiotiki Pali	L	1983	1	1
Democratic Defence	L	1969	1	0
Democratic Resistance Committees	L	1968	2	0
Epanastatiki Organosi 17 Noemvri	L	1975–94	49	18
Epanastatikos Lairos Agonas	L	1978–94	26	1
Epanastratiki Organosi 80 Oktovri	L	1980	3	0
June 1978 Movement	L	1979	1	1
Khristos Tsoutsouris Revolutionary Organization	L	1987	2	0

Country/ Organization	Orientation	Active period	Number of: Attacks	Number of: Killings
League of Fighters and Victims of National Resistance in Northern Greece	R	1966	1	1
May 1 Revolutionary Organization	L	1987–89	3	1
National Front	R	1985	1	0
November 12 Group	L	1984	4	0
Organisation for the Struggle Against the State	L	1985–87	3	1
Organismos Ethnikis Anorthosoos	R	1978	40	0
Pan-Hellenic Liberation Movement	L	1970	1	0
People's Revolutionary Solidarity	L	1988	1	0
Popular Front Action	L	1980	1	2
Popular Resistance Sabotage Groups	L	1968	1	0
Revolutionary Anti-Capitalist Initiative	L	1981	1	0
Revolutionary Group of International Solidarity - Christos Kassimis	L	1985–86	5	0
Revolutionary Left	L	1980	4	0
Revolutionary Solidarity	L	1989	1	0
Secret Yellow Organisation of Air Force Officers	R	1984	1	0
Social Responsibility	L	1988–90	13	0
Italy				
Avangardia Nazionale	R	1973–76	3	1
Avanguardia Operaia	R	1995	2	0
Befreiiungsausschuss Südtirol	E	1957–69	231	14
Brigate Operaie	L	1981	5	1
Brigate Rosse	L	1972–88	59	48
Brigate Rosse-Partito Communista Combattente	L	1987–88	2	3
Communist Group for Proletarian Internationalism	L	1981–85	6	0
Falange armata	H	1993	5	5
Gruppi d'Azione Partigiana	L	1972	1	1
Movimiente Sociale Italiano	R	1971–76	2	2
Nuclei Armati Proletari	L	1974–77	3	0
Nuclei Armati Rivoluzionari	R	1980–85	8	90
Nucleo Communista	L	1982	1	0
One Tirol	E	1986–88	41	0
Ordine Nero	R	1974–83	12	23
Popular Brigade – New Order	R	1974	1	0
Potere Communista	L	1984	1	1
Potere Operaio	L	1973	1	2
Prima Linea	L	1978–80	7	9
Prima Posizione	L	1981	1	1

Country/ Organization	Orientation	Active period	Number of: Attacks	Killings
Reggio for capital	R	1970	3	0
Revolutionary Communist Nuclei	L	1974	1	0
Squadre d'Azione Mussolini	R	1971–74	4	0
Unione dei Communisti Combattente	L	1986–87	2	2
Netherlands				
Action Group Against Nuclear War	O	1985	3	0
Lubbers Commando Half-Mast	O	1986	2	0
Nordelijk Terreurfront	R	1985	1	0
Revolutionaire Anti Rasistische Actie	L	1990–91	5	0
Revolutionaire Cellen, Ins Blaue Meinein	O	1986	2	0
Rood Revolutionair Front	L	1986	1	0
Norway				
Nasjonalt Folkeparti	R	1985	1	0
Portugal				
Acção Revolucionaria Armada	L	1970–72	10	0
Anti-capitalist and anti-militarist Organization	L	1985	1	0
Anti-Capitalist Brigades	L	1988	1	1
Armed Revolutionary Organization	L	1986	4	0
Grupos Autónomos Revolucionarios	L	1985	3	0
Autonomous Revolutionary Workers' Commando	L	1984	1	1
Exército de Libertação Portugês	R	1975	4	2
Forças Populares do 25 Abril	L	1982–86	135	7
Frente da Libertação do Arquipélago de Madeira	E	1975	2	0
Frente de Libertação Açores	E	1978	3	0
Liga de União e Acção Revoluciária	L	1967	2	0
Movimento Reorganizativo do Partido de Proletariado	L	1974–75	3	1
Popular Action Front	L	1964–65	2	1
Revolutionary Brigades	L	1973	2	0
Spain				
Acción Nacional Española	E	1979	2	1
Alianza Apostolólica Anticommunista	R	1977–78	3	8
Antiterrorismo ETA	E	1976	2	0
Autonomous Anarchist Groups	L	1979	1	0
Batallón Vasco Espanõl	E	1976–82	3	6
Catalan Red Liberation Army	E	1987	2	0
Comandos Autónomos Anticapitalistas	E	1984	1	2
Ejército Guirrilleiro do Pobo Galego Ceibe	E	1987–90	22	4

Country/ Organization	Orientation	Active period	Number of: Attacks	Killings
Euskadi ta Askatasuna/Euskadi ta Askatasuna-Militar	E	1967–95	374	447
Euskadi ta Askatasuna-Polimilis	E	1978–84	40	7
Fifth Adolf Hitler Commando	R	1973	1	0
Frente Revolucionario Antifascista y Patriótico	L	1975–77	4	3
Fuerza Nueva	R	1980	2	2
Gatazka	E	1984	1	1
Grupo Antiterrorista de Liberación	E	1980–89	25	27
Grupo de Resistencia Antifascista Primero de Octubre	L	1976–93	62	50
Grupos Armados Españoles	E	1980	1	4
Grupos de Acción Revolucionara Internacionalista	L	1974	3	0
Guerilleros Rojos	L	1977	2	0
Guirrilleros de Cristo Rey	R	1973–77	10	1
Hammer and Sickle Co-operative	E	1972	1	1
Iberian Revolutionary Liberation Directorate	L	1960	2	0
Jauzibia	E	1984	1	1
Libertarian Youth	L	1962	2	0
Liga Armada Gallega	E	1978	1	1
Milicia Catalana	E	1986	3	0
Moviemiento Iberico de Liberacion	L	1973	1	0
Movimiento para la Autodeterminación e Independencia del Archipiélago de las Canarias	E	1977–78	85	1
Revolutionary Organization of Anti-Fascist Spain	L	1977	1	1
Spanish National Socialist Party	R	1973	1	0
Terra Lliure	E	1986–88	13	2
United International Secret and Revolutionary Cells	O	1976	1	0
Switzerland				
Autonome Zellen – AZ – Cellules autonomes	L	1985	7	0
Béliers	E	1993	2	1
Front de la liberation jurasien	E	1964–72	4	0
Second revolutionary faction of the Béliers	E	1985	1	0
Socialist-Nationalist movement	R	1988	1	0
Valais Group against Hydro-Rhône	O	1985	1	0
United Kingdom				
Alliance	E	1983	1	0
Angry Brigade	L	1967–71	26	0
Army of the Provisional Government of Scotland – Tartan Army	E	1973–75	3	0
British Nationalist Party	R	1962	1	0
Catholic Reaction Power	E	1983	1	3

Country/ Organization	Orientation	Active period	Number of: Attacks	Killings
Freedom Fighters for All	E	1973	1	0
Irish National Liberation Army	E	1975–92	24	37
Irish People's Liberation Organization	E	1986–92	3	2
Irish Republican Army (Official)	E	1971–72	11	14
Irish Republican Army/Provisional IRA	E	1950–95	1369	602
Loyalist Prisoners' Action Force	E	1980	1	1
Protestant Action Force	E	1991	1	3
Red Hand Commando	E	1974	4	30
Scottish National Liberation Front	E	1983	1	0
Soar Eire	E	1974	1	12
Soar Uladh	E	1955–73	3	0
South Armagh Republican Force	E	1975	2	2
Ulster Defence Association	E	1972–75	3	1
Ulster Freedom Fighters	E	1973–93	21	35
Ulster Volunteer Force	E	1966–94	17	32

References

Allardt, Erik (1979), 'Implications of the ethnic revival in modern industrialized society: a comparative study of the linguistic minorities in Western Europe', *Commentationes Scientiarum Socialium*, Helsinki, (**12**), 1–81.

Allardt, Erik and Christian Starck (1981), *Språkgränser och samhällsstruktur: Finlands svenskarna i ett jämförande perspektiv*, Stockholm: AWE/Gebers.

Andriole, Stephen J. and Gerald W. Hopple (1984), 'The rise and fall of event data: from basic research to applied use in the U.S. Department of Defense', *International Interactions*, **10** (3–4), 293–309.

Arter, David (1987), *Politics and Policy-Making in Finland*, Brighton: Wheatsheaf Books.

Aust, Stefan (1990), *Baader-Meinhof: sju år som förändrade Förbundsrepubliken*, Stockholm: Symposium.

Azar, Edward E. (1980), 'The Conflict and Peace Data Bank (COPDAB) Project', *Journal of Conflict Resolution*, **24** (1), 143–52.

Azar, Edward E., Stanley H. Cohen, Thomas O. Jukam and James M. McCormick (1972), 'The problem of source coverage in the use of event data', *International Studies Quarterly*, **16** (3), 373–88.

Beer, William R. (1977), 'The social class of ethnic activists in contemporary France', in Milton J. Esman (ed.), *Ethnic Conflict in the Western World*, (Conference on Ethnic Pluralism and Conflict in Contemporary Europe and Canada), Ithaca, NY: Cornell University Press, pp. 143–58.

Benard, Cheryl (1994), 'Rape as terror: the case of Bosnia', *Terrorism and Political Violence*, **6** (1), 29–43.

Bendix, Reinhard (1962), *Max Weber: An Intellectual Portrait*, New York, NY: Doubleday.

Berger, Suzanne (1977), 'Bretons and Jacobins: reflections on French regional ethnicity', in Milton J. Esman (ed.), *Ethnic Conflict in the Western World*, (Conference on Ethnic Pluralism and Conflict in Contemporary Europe and Canada), Ithaca, NY: Cornell University Press, pp. 159–78.

Bjørgo, Tore (1989), 'Vold mot innvandrere og asylsøkere', *NUPI-rapport*, **136**, 1–72.

Bjørgo, Tore and Daniel Heradstveit (1987), *Politisk kommunikasjon: Introduksjon til semiotikk og retorikk*, Oslo: Tano.

Bjørgo, Tore and Daniel Heradstveit (1993), *Politisk terrorisme*, Oslo: Tano.

Blanke, Thomas (1981), '*Berufsverbote* and political repression in the Federal Republic of Germany', *International Journal of the Sociology of Law*, **9**, 397–406.

Bollen, Kenneth A. (1980), 'Issues in the comparative measurement of political democracy', *American Sociological Review*, **45** (June), 370–90.

Bonante, Luigi (1979), 'Some unanticipated consequences of terrorism', *Journal of Peace*

Research, **16** (3), 197–211.

Braunthal, Gerard (1989), 'Public order and civil liberties', in Gordon Smith, William E. Paterson and Peter H. Merkl (eds) (1989), *Developments in West German Politics,* Basingstoke: Macmillan, pp. 308–22.

Brosius, Hans-Bernd and Gabriel Weimann (1991), 'The contagiousness of mass-mediated terrorism', *European Journal of Communication,* **6** (1), 63–75.

Bruce, Steve (1992a), 'Northern Ireland: reappraising loyalist violence', *Conflict Studies,* **249**, 1–21.

Bruce, Steve (1992b), 'Northern Ireland: reappraising republican violence', *Conflict Studies,* **246**, 1–29.

Bruce, Steve (1992c), *The Red Hand: Protestant Paramilitaries in Northern Ireland,* Oxford: Oxford University Press.

Bruneau, Thomas C. (1984), 'Continuity and change in Portugese politics: ten years after the revolution of 25 April 1974', *West European Politics,* **7** (2), 72–83.

Bundesamt für Verfassungsschutz (1997), *Verfassungsschutzbericht 1996,* Bonn: Bundesministerium des Innern.

Byrne, Brendan T. (1987), 'Foreword', in Marius H. Livingston, Lee Bruce Kress and Marie G. Wanek (eds), *International Terrorism in the Contemporary World,* (Contributions in Political Science: 3), Westport, CT: Greenwood Press, pp. xv–xvi.

Caciagli, Mario (1988), 'The Movimento Sociale Italiano-Destra Nazionale and neo-fascism in Italy', *West European Politics,* **11** (2), 19–33.

Campbell, David B. (1982), 'Nationalism, religion and the social bases of conflict in the Swiss Jura', in Stein Rokkan and Derek W. Urwin (eds), *The Politics of Territorial Identity: Studies in European Regionalism,* London: Sage, pp. 279–307.

Carr, Caleb (1996), 'Terrorism as warfare: the lessons of military history', *World Policy Journal,* **13** (4), 1–12.

Carr, Gordon (1975), *The Angry Brigade: The Cause and the Case,* London: Victor Gollancz.

Cerny, Philip G. (1981), 'France: Non-terrorism and the politics of repressive tolerance', in Juliet Lodge (ed.), *Terrorism: A Challenge to the State,* Oxford: Martin Robertson, pp. 91–118.

Challener, Richard D. (1967), 'The French Army: from obedience to insurrection', *World Politics,* **19** (4), 678–91.

Chomsky, Noam (1991), 'International terrorism: image and reality', in Alexander George (ed.), *Western State Terrorism,* Cambridge: Polity Press, pp. 12–38.

Chomsky, Noam and Edward S. Herman (1979), *The Washington Connection and Third World Fascism: The Political Economy of Human Rights – Volume I,* Nottingham: Spokesman.

Chubb, Basil (1982), *The Government and Politics of Ireland,* 2nd edn, London: Longman.

Clark, Robert P. (1984), *The Basque Insurgents: Eta, 1952–1980,* Madison, WI: University of Wisconsin Press.

Clark, Robert P. (1989), 'Spanish democracy and regional autonomy: the autonomous community system and self-government for ethnic homelands', in Joseph R. Rudolph Jr. and Robert J. Thompson (eds) (1989), *Ethnoterritorial Politics, Policy, and the Western World,* Boulder, CO: Lynne Rienner Publishers, pp. 15–44.

Coakley, John (1986), 'The evolution of Irish party politics', in Brian Girvin and Roland

Sturm (eds), *Politics and Society in Contemporary Ireland*, Aldershot: Gower, pp. 29–54.

Connor, Walker (1978), 'A nation is a nation, is a state, is an ethnic group, is a ...', *Ethnic and Racial Studies*, **1** (4), 377–400.

Corsun, Andrew (1991), 'Group Profile: The Revolutionary Organization 17 November in Greece', *Terrorism: An International Journal*, 14 (2), 77–104.

Covell, Maureen (1981), 'Ethnic conflict and elite bargaining: the case of Belgium', *West European Politics*, **4** (3), 199–218.

Crelinsten, Ronald D. (1987a), 'Terrorism as political communication: the relationship between the controller and the controlled', in Paul Wilkinson and Alasdair M. Stewart (eds), *Contemporary Research on Terrorism*, Aberdeen: Aberdeen University Press, pp. 3–23.

Crelinsten, Ronald D. (1987b), 'Power and meaning: terrorism as a struggle over access to the communication structure', in Paul Wilkinson and Alasdair M. Stewart (eds), *Contemporary Research on Terrorism*, Aberdeen: Aberdeen University Press, pp. 419–50.

Crenshaw, Martha (1981), 'The causes of terrorism', *Comparative Politics*, **13** (4), 379–99.

Crenshaw, Martha (1988), 'Theories of terrorism: instrumental and organizational approaches', in David C. Rapoport (ed.), *Inside Terrorist Organizations*, New York, NY: Columbia University Press, pp. 13–31.

Crenshaw, Martha (1992), 'Current research on terrorism: the academic perspective', *Studies in Conflict and Terrorism*, **15** (1), 1–11.

Dartnell, Michael (1994), 'France's *Action Directe*: Terrorists in search of a revolution', in Edward Moxon-Browne (ed.), *European Terrorism*, (International Library of Terrorism: 3), New York, NY: G.K. Hall, pp. 187–218.

Davies, John L. and Chad K. McDaniel (1993), 'The global event-data system', in Richard L. Merritt, Robert G. Muncaster, and Dina A. Zinnes (eds), *International Event-Data Developments: DDIR Phase II*, Ann Arbor, MI: University of Michigan Press, pp. 19–44.

Degenhardt, Henry W. (ed.) (1983), *Political Dissent: An International Guide to Dissent, Extra-Parliamentary, Guerilla and Illegal Political Movements*, Harlow: Longman.

Di Palma, Guiseppe (1982), 'Italy: Is there a legacy and is it fascist?', in John H. Herz (ed.), *From Dictatorship to Democracy: Coping with the Legacies of Authoritarianism and Totalitarianism*, (Contributions in Political Science No. 92: Global Perspectives in History and Politics), Westport, CT: Greenwood Press, pp. 107–34.

Diamandouros, Nikiphoros (1991), 'PASOK and state–society relations in post-authoritarian Greece (1974–1988)', in Speros Vryonis (ed.), *Greece on the Road to Democracy: From the Junta to PASOK 1974–1986*, New Rochelle, NY: Aristide D. Caratzas, pp. 15–35.

Drake, Richard (1982), 'The Red Brigades and the Italian political tradition', in Yonah Alexander and Kenneth A. Myers (eds), *Terrorism in Europe*, London: Croom Helm, pp. 102–40.

Drake, C.J.M. (1996), 'The Phenomenon of conservative terrorism', *Terrorism and Political Violence*, **8** (3), 29–46.

Duggan, Christopher (1987), 'The Sicilian origins of the mafia', *Conflict Studies*, **203**, 1–21.

Dyson, Kenneth H.F. (1975), 'Left-wing political extremism and the problem of tolerance in Western Germany', *Government and Opposition*, **10** (3), 306–31.

Engelmann, Frederick C. (1982), 'How Austria has coped with two dictatorial legacies', in John H. Herz (ed.), *From Dictatorship to Democracy: Coping with the Legacies of Authoritarianism and Totalitarianism,* (Contributions in Political Science No. 92: Global Perspectives in History and Politics), Westport, CT: Greenwood Press, pp. 135–60.

Engene, Jan Oskar (1994), *Europeisk terrorisme: Vold, stat og legitimitet,* Oslo: Tano.

Fentress, James and Chris Wickham (1992), *Social Memory,* (New Perspectives on the Past), Oxford: Blackwell.

Fitzmaurice, John (1988), *The Politics of Belgium: Crisis and Compromise in a Plural Society,* 2nd edn, London: C. Hurst & Co.

Flora, Peter (1983), *State, Economy and Society in Western Europe 1815–1975: A Data Handbook. Volume I: The Growth of Mass Democracies and Welfare States,* Frankfurt: Campus.

Franzosi, Roberto (1989), 'One hundred years of strike statistics: methodological and theoretical issues in quantitative strike research', *Industrial and Labor Relations Review,* **42** (3), 348–62.

Furlong, Paul (1981), 'Political terrorism in Italy: responses, reactions and immobilism', in Juliet Lodge (ed.), *Terrorism: A Challenge to the State,* Oxford: Martin Robertson, pp. 57–90.

George, Alexander (1991), 'The discipline of terrorology', in George, Alexander (ed.), *Western State Terrorism,* Cambridge: Polity Press, pp. 76–101.

Guelke, Adrian (1995), *The Age of Terrorism and the International Political System,* (Library of International Relations: 2), London: Tauris Academic Studies.

Gurr, Ted Robert (1986), 'The political origins of state violence and terror: a theoretical analysis', in Michael Stohl and George A. Lopez (eds), *Government Violence and Repression,* New York, NY: Greenwood Press, pp. 45–71.

Gurr, Ted Robert (1988), 'Empirical research on political terrorism: the state of the art and how it might be improved', in Robert Slater and Michael Stohl (eds), *Current Perspectives on International Terrorism,* Basingstoke: Macmillan, pp. 115–54.

Hardman, J.B.S. (1949), 'Terrorism', in Edwin R.A. Seligman (ed.), *International Encyclopaedia of the Social Sciences,* Volume 13, New York, NY: Macmillan Company, pp. 575–80.

Harff, Barbara (1986), 'Genocide as state terrorism', in Michael Stohl and George A. Lopez (eds), *Government Violence and Repression,* New York, NY: Greenwood Press, pp. 165–87.

Hazlewood, Leo A. and Gerald T. West (1974), 'Bivariate associations, factor structures, and substantive impact: the source coverage problem revisited', *International Studies Quarterly,* **18** (3), 317–37.

Heiberg, Marianne (1988), 'Saint and sinners: an analysis of the political violence of ETA', *NUPI-notat,* **394,** 1–30.

Henissart, Paul (1970), *Wolves in the City: The Death of French Algeria,* New York, NY: Simon and Schuster.

Heradstveit, Daniel (1992), 'Norge som mål for arabisk terrorisme', *NUPI-rapport,* **158,** 1–147.

Herman, Edward S. and Gerry O'Sullivan (1989), *The 'Terrorism' Industry: The Experts and Institutions That Shape Our View of Terror*, New York, NY: Pantheon Books.

Herman, Edward S. and Gerry O'Sullivan (1991), '"Terrorism" as ideology and cultural industry', in Alexander George (ed.), *Western State Terrorism*, Cambridge: Polity Press, pp. 39–75.

Herman, Valentine and Rob van der Laan Bouma (1981), 'Nationalists without a nation: South Moluccan terrorism in the Netherlands', in Juliet Lodge (ed.) (1981), *Terrorism: A Challenge to the State*, Oxford: Martin Robertson, pp. 119–45.

Herz, John H. (1982), 'Denazification and related policies', in John H. Herz (ed.), *From Dictatorship to Democracy: Coping with the Legacies of Authoritarianism and Totalitarianism*, (Contributions in Political Science No. 92: Global Perspectives in History and Politics), Westport, CT: Greenwood Press, pp. 15–38.

Hoffman, Bruce and Donna Kim Hoffman (1996), 'The Rand–St Andrews Chronology of International Terrorist Incidents, 1995', *Terrorism and Political Violence*, **8** (3), 87–127.

Hoffman, Robert Paul (1984), *Terrorism: A Universal Definition*, PhD dissertation, Claremont Graduate School

Högman, Gyrid (1986), 'Ålänningarna och Ålandsfrågan', in Sune Jungar and Nils Erik Villstrand (eds), *Väster om skiftet: Uppsatser ur Ålands historia*, (Åbo Akademi, Historiska Institutionen, Meddelanden, No. 8), Åbo: Åbo Akademi, Historiska Institutionen, pp. 117–37.

Holden, Robert T. (1986), 'The contagiousness of aircraft hijacking', *American journal of sociology*, **91** (4), 874–904.

Horne, Alistair (1984), *The French Army and Politics, 1870–1970*, London: Macmillan.

Humana, Charles (1992), *World Human Rights Guide*, 3rd edn, New York, NY: Oxford University Press.

Hutchinson, Martha Crenshaw (1978), *Revolutionary Terrorism: The FLN in Algeria, 1954–1962*, Stanford, CA: Hoover Institution Press.

Ionescu, Ghita (1976), 'Raymond Aron: a modern classicist', in Anthony de Crespigny and Kenneth Minogue (eds), *Contemporary Political Philosophers*, London: Methuen, pp. 191–208.

Jackman, Robert W. and William A. Boyd (1979), 'Multiple sources in the collection of data on political conflict', *American Journal of Political Science*, **23** (2), 434–58.

Jacob, James E. (1994), *Hills of Conflict: Basque Nationalism in France*, Reno, NV: University of Nevada Press.

Jamieson, Alison (1989), *The Heart Attacked: Terrorism and Conflict in the Italian State*, London: Marion Boyars.

Janke, Peter (1983), *Guerilla and Terrorist Organizations*, Brighton: Harvester Press.

Jenkins, John R.G. (1986), *Jura Separatism in Switzerland*, Oxford: Clarendon Press.

Jenkins, Philip (1990), 'Strategy of Tension: the Belgian terrorist crisis 1982–1986', *Terrorism: An International Journal*, **13**, 299–309.

Kaase, Max (1990), 'Political violence and the democratic state', *Scandinavian Political Studies*, **13** (1), 1–19.

Karber, Phillip A. (1971), 'Urban terrorism: baseline data and a conceptual framework', *Social Science Quarterly*, **52**, 521–33.

Keesing's Contemporary Records/Keesing's Record of World Events, London: Keesing's/Longman.

Kolinsky, Eva (1984), *Parties, Opposition and Society in West Germany*, London: Croom

Helm.

Kourvetaris, Yorgos A. and Betty A. Dobratz (1987), *A Profile of Modern Greece in Search of Identity*, Oxford: Clarendon Press.

Kuter, Lois (1985), 'Labeling People: who are the Bretons?', *Anthropological Quarterly*, **58** (1), 13–29.

Lane, Jan-Erik, David McKay and Kenneth Newton (1997), *Political Data Handbook OECD Countries*, (Comparative European Politics), 2nd edn, Oxford: Oxford University Press.

Laqueur, Walter (1987), *The Age of Terrorism*, Boston, MA: Little, Brown & Company.

Laufer, David (1988), 'The Evolution of Belgian terrorism', in Juliet Lodge (ed.), *The Threat of Terrorism*, Brighton: Wheatsheaf Books, pp. 179–211.

Lewis, J.R. and A.M. Williams (1984), 'Social Cleavages and electoral performance: the social basis of Portugese political parties, 1976–83 ', *West European Politics*, **7** (2), 119–37.

Lodenius, Anna-Lena and Stieg Larsson (1994), *Extremhögern*, 2nd edn, Stockholm: Tiden.

Maxwell, Kenneth (1982), 'The emergence of Portugese democracy', in John H. Herz (ed.), *From Dictatorship to Democracy: Coping with the Legacies of Authoritarianism and Totalitarianism*, (Contributions in Political Science No. 92: Global Perspectives in History and Politics), Westport, CT: Greenwood Press, pp. 231–50.

McClelland, Charles A. and Gary D. Hoggard (1969), 'Conflict patterns in the interactions among nations', in James N. Rosenau (ed.), *International Politics and Foreign Policy: A Reader in Research and Theory*, New York, NY: Free Press, pp. 711–24.

Manuel, Paul Christopher (1996), *The Challenges of Democratic Consolidation in Portugal: Political, Economic, and Military Issues, 1976–1991*, Westport, CT: Praeger.

Merkl, Peter H. (1986), 'Approaches to the study of political violence', in Peter H. Merkl (ed.), *Political Violence and Terror: Motifs and Motivations*, Berkeley, CA: University of California Press, pp. 19–59.

Merritt, Richard L., Robert G. Muncaster and Dina A. Zinnes (1993), 'Event data and DDIR', in Richard L. Merritt, Robert G. Muncaster and Dina A. Zinnes (eds), *International Event-Data Developments: DDIR Phase II*, Ann Arbor, MI: University of Michigan Press, pp. 1–18.

Mickolus, Edward F. (1991), *International Terrorism: Attributes of Terrorist Events, 1968–1977*, ICPSR 7947, Code book to data set, n.p.

Mickolus, Edward and Edward Heyman (1981), 'Iterate: monitoring transnational terrorism', in Yonah Alexander and John M. Gleason (eds), *Behavioral and Quantitative Perspectives On Terrorism*, New York, NY: Pergamon Press, pp. 153–74.

Middelthon, Carsten (1975), *Terror i Italia*, Oslo: Gyldendal.

Mommesen-Reindl, Margareta (1980), 'Austria', in Peter H. Merkl (ed.), *Western European Party Systems: Trends and Prospects*, New York, NY: Free Press, pp. 278–97.

Moxon-Browne, Edward (1981), 'Terrorism in Northern Ireland: the case of the Provisional IRA', in Juliet Lodge (ed.), *Terrorism: A Challenge to the State,* Oxford: Martin Robertson, pp. 146–63.

Moxon-Browne, Edward (1983), 'Terrorism in France', *Conflict Studies*, **144**, 1–26.

Moxon-Browne, Edward (1988), 'Terrorism in France', in Juliet Lodge (ed.) (1988), *The Threat of Terrorism*, Brighton: Wheatsheaf Books, pp. 213–28.

Niclauss, Karlheinz (1982), 'Political reconstruction at Bonn', in John H. Herz (ed.), *From Dictatorship to Democracy: Coping with the Legacies of Authoritarianism and Totalitarianism*, (Contributions in Political Science No. 92: Global Perspectives in History and Politics), Westport, CT: Greenwood Press, pp. 39–56.

Norman, Torbjörn (1986), 'Slutakt med efterspel. Ålandsuppgörelsen, Sverige og NF', in Sune Jungar and Nils Erik Villstrand (eds), *Väster om skiftet: Uppsatser ur Ålands historia*, (Åbo Akademi, Historiska Institutionen, Meddelanden, No. 8), Åbo: Åbo Akademi, Historiska Institutionen, pp. 177–213.

O'Leary, Brendan (1989), 'The limits to coercive consociationalism in Northern Ireland', *Political Studies*, **37**, 562–88.

Opello Jr., Walter C. (1985), *Portugal's Political Development: A Comparative Approach*, (Westview Special Studies in West European Politics and Society), Boulder, CO: Westview Press.

Perdue, William D. (1989), *Terrorism and the State: A Critique of Domination Through Fear*, New York, NY: Praeger.

Peterson, Sophia (1972), 'Research on research: events data studies, 1961–1972', in Patrick McGowan (ed.), *Sage International Book of Foreign Policy Studies*, Vol. 3, Beverly Hills, CA: Sage, pp. 263–309.

Picard, Robert G. (1986), 'News Coverage as the contagion of terrorism: dangerous charges backed by dubious science', *Political Communication and Persuasion*, **3** (4), 385–400.

Picard, Robert G. (1989), 'Press relations of terrorist organizations', *Public Relations Review*, **15** (4), 12–23.

Picard, Robert G. (1991a), 'The journalist's role in coverage of terrorist events', in, A. Odasuo Alali and Kenoye Kelvin Eke (eds), *Media Coverage of Terrorism: Methods of Diffusion*, Newbury Park, CA: Sage, pp. 40–48.

Picard, Robert G. (1991b), 'News Coverage as the contagion of terrorism: dangerous charges backed by dubious science', in Alali, A. Odasuo and Eke, Kenoye Kelvin (eds), *Media Coverage of Terrorism: Methods of Diffusion*, Newbury Park, CA: Sage, pp. 49–62.

Pickles, Dorothy (1973), *The Government and Politics of France, Volume II: Politics*, London: Methuen.

Pollack, Benny and Hunter, Graham (1988), 'Dictatorship, democracy and terrorism in Spain', in Juliet Lodge (ed.), *The Threat of Terrorism*, Brighton: Wheatsheaf, pp. 119–44.

Post, Jerrold M. (1987), 'Group and organisational dynamics of political terrorism: implications for counterterrorist policy', in Paul Wilkinson and Alasdair M. Stewart (eds), *Contemporary Research on Terrorism*, Aberdeen: Aberdeen University Press, pp. 307–17.

Psomaides, Harry J. (1982), 'Greece: from the Colonels' rule to democracy', in John H. Herz (ed.), *From Dictatorship to Democracy: Coping with the Legacies of Authoritarianism and Totalitarianism*, (Contributions in Political Science No. 92, Global Perspectives in History and Politics), Westport, CT: Greenwood Press, pp. 251–73.

Reinares, Fernando (1987), 'The dynamics of terrorism during the transition to democracy in Spain', in Paul Wilkinson and Alasdair M. Stewart (eds), *Contemporary Research on Terrorism*, Aberdeen: Aberdeen University Press, pp. 121–9.

Riker, William H. (1957), 'Events and situations', *Journal of Philosophy*, **54** (3), 57–70.

Rogers, Vaughan (1990), 'Brittany', in Michael Watson (ed.), *Contemporary Minority Nationalism*, London: Routledge, pp. 67–85.

Rokkan, Stein (1987), *Stat, nasjon, klasse*, Oslo: Universitetsforlaget.

Rousso, Henry (1991), *The Vichy Syndrome: History and Memory in France Since 1944*, Cambridge, MA: Harvard University Press.

Rummel, Rudolph J. (1971), 'Dimensions of conflict behavior within and between nations', in John V. Gillespie and Betty A. Nesvold (eds), *Macro-Quantitative Analysis: Conflict, Development, and Democratization*, Beverly Hills, CA: Sage, pp. 49–84.

Russett, Bruce M., Hayward A. Alker, Karl W. Deutsch and Harold D. Lasswell (1964), *World Handbook of Political and Social Indicators*, New Haven, CT: Yale University Press.

Savigear, Peter (1983), 'Corsica: regional autonomy or violence?', *Conflict Studies*, **149**, 1–16.

Schlesinger, Philip (1991), *Media, State, and Nation: Political Violence and Collective Identities*, (Media, Culture and Society Series), London: Sage Publications.

Schmid, Alex P. (1984), *Political Terrorism: A Research Guide to Concepts, Theories, Data Bases and Literature*, Amsterdam: North-Holland Publishing Company.

Schmid, Alex P. (1988), 'Politically-motivated violent activists in the Netherlands in the 1980s', in Juliet Lodge (ed.), *The Threat of Terrorism*, Sussex: Wheatsheaf Books, pp. 145–78.

Schmid, Alex P. Janny and de Graaf (1982), *Violence as Communication: Insurgent Terrorism and the Western News Media*, London: Sage.

Schmid, Alex P., Albert J. Jongman, Michael Stohl, Jan Brand, Peter A. Flemming, Angela van der Poel and Rob Thijsse (1988), *Political Terrorism: A New Guide to Actors, Authors, Concepts, Data Bases, Theories and Literature*, Amsterdam: North-Holland Publishing Company.

Schrodt, Philip A. (1993), 'Machine coding of event data', in Richard L. Merritt, Robert G. Muncaster and Dina A. Zinnes (eds), *International Event-Data Developments: DDIR Phase II*, Ann Arbor, MI: University of Michigan Press, pp. 125–48.

Sederberg, Peter C. (1989), *Terrorist Myths: Illusion, Rhetoric, and Reality*, Englewood Cliffs, NJ: Prentice Hall.

Seton-Watson, Christopher (1988), 'Terrorism in Italy', in Juliet Lodge (ed.), *The Threat of Terrorism*, Brighton: Wheatsheaf, pp. 89–118.

Shubert, Adrian (1990), *A Social History of Spain*, London: Unwin Hyman.

Silke, Andrew (1996), 'Terrorism and the blind men's elephant', *Terrorism and Political Violence*, **8** (3), 12–28.

Smith, T. Alexander (1965), 'Algeria and the French *Modérés*: the politics of immoderation?', *Western Political Quarterly*, **18** (1), 116–34.

Stöss, Richard (1991), *Politics Against Democracy: Right-Wing Extremism in West-Germany*, (German Studies Series), Oxford: Berg.

Targ, Harry R. (1988), 'Societal structure and revolutionary terrorism: a preliminary investigation', in Michael Stohl (ed.), *The Politics of Terrorism*, 3rd edn, New York,

NY: Marcel Dekker, pp. 127–51.

Taylor, Charles Lewis and David A. Jodice (1983), *World Handbook of Political and Social Indicators. Volume 2: Political Protest and Government Change*, 3rd edn, New Haven, CT: Yale University Press.

Thackrah, Richard (1987), 'Terrorism: a definitional problem', in Paul Wilkinson and Alasdair M. Stewart (eds), *Contemporary Research on Terrorism*, Aberdeen: Aberdeen University Press, pp. 24–41.

Thompson, Robert J. (1989), 'Referendums and ethnoterritorial movements: the policy consequences and political ramifications', in Joseph R. Rudolph Jr. and Robert J. Thompson (eds), *Ethnoterritorial Politics, Policy, and the Western World*, Boulder, CO: Lynne Rienner Publishers, pp. 181–220.

Thornton, Thomas P. (1964), 'Terror as a weapon of political agitation', in Harry Eckstein (ed.), *Internal War*, New York, NY: Free Press, pp. 71–99.

Tilly, Charles (1985), 'War making and state making as organized crime', in Peter B. Evans, Dietrich Rueschemeyer and Theda Skocpol (eds), *Bringing the State Back In*, Cambridge: Cambridge University Press, pp. 169–91.

Waller, Michael and Meindert Fennema (eds) (1988), *Communist Parties in Western Europe: Decline or Adaption?*, Oxford: Basil Blackwell.

Weber, Max (1994), *Political Writings*, (ed. by Peter Lassman and Ronald Speirs), Cambridge: Cambridge University Press.

Wilkinson, Paul (1986), *Terrorism and the Liberal State*, 2nd edn, London: Macmillan.

Wilkinson, Paul (1987), 'Foreword. Terrorism: An international research agenda?', in Paul Wilkinson and Alasdair M. Stewart (eds), *Contemporary Research on Terrorism*, Aberdeen: Aberdeen University Press, pp. xi–xx.

Wright, Vincent (1983), *The Government and Politics of France*, 2nd edn, London: Hutchinson.

Zimmermann, Ekkart (1989), 'Political unrest in Western Europe: trends and prospects', *West European Politics*, 12 (3), 179–96.

Index